Conor Cruise O'Brien introduces Ireland

Edited by
Owen Dudley Edwards

ANDRE DEUTSCH

FIRST PUBLISHED 1969 BY
ANDRE DEUTSCH LIMITED
105 GREAT RUSSELL STREET
LONDON WC1
COPYRIGHT © 1969 BY ANDRE DEUTSCH LIMITED
ALL RIGHTS RESERVED
PRINTED IN THE REPUBLIC OF IRELAND BY
HELY THOM LIMITED
LONDON AND DUBLIN
233 95990 4

Preface

I, as editor, am responsible for the choice of all the essayists in this book, and in all but a few cases, for the nature of the subjects covered. The publishers retained the right of final editorial decision, and have exercised it most notably in two areas: the inclusion of certain subjects for which they envisaged a particular need, and the exclusion of a few essays initially allowed for, but for which space was not finally available. I assented readily to the inclusions, but less readily to the exclusions, and wish to express my gratitude to the authors of these essays for their cooperation and courtesy, and my regret at their non-appearance.

I must also thank the many friends and colleagues whose help has made my task more pleasant and its results more satisfactory. These include Máire Cruise O'Brien; Ailfrid MacLochlainn; Aindreas O Gallchoir; the Director of the National Library of Ireland, Mr Patrick Henchy, and his staff; Miss S. F. P. Massey; Mr Douglas Riach; Mr Conal R. C. Smith; Dr Paul Dukes; Professor R. Dudley Edwards; Professor Owen Lattimore; Dr George Mollans; Dr Isobel Murray; Dr Colm O'Boyle; Elaine Greene; Diana Athill; Ilsa Yardley; Mr John Horgan; Senator Owen Sheehy-Skeffington; Mr Maurice Fridberg; Captain Basil Peterson, Miss Flavia Wade; Miss Margaret Jamieson; and Mrs Leslie Campbell.

Special thanks are due to the Irish Tourist Board (Bord Fáilte Éireann) and Aer Lingus for their assistance in providing the illustrations, and to Mr Douglas Gageby and the staff of the *Irish Times* for many helpful answers to problems. My mother, Mrs R. Dudley Edwards, knows how much I appreciate her help on points of difficulty in textual matters, and my wife has been the equal of any wife ever thanked in a book.

I have also had the constant advice and encouragement of Professor Patrick Lynch, who has been a tower of strength. And the whole enterprise has been transformed for me by the privilege and pleasure of working with the introducer who has been a well-spring of ideas and of laughter; the reader will have the benefit of the first, and the second will be available to research students after the lapse of five hundred years.

Imperfections of taste and of fact are chargeable to me as well as to the authors, but none of us should be blamed for the opinions of any of the rest of us.

December 1968   OWEN DUDLEY EDWARDS

Notes on Contributors

CONOR CRUISE O'BRIEN. For many years in the Irish diplomatic service, and was seconded to the United Nations Secretariat for which he took charge of the Katanga mission in 1961. Resigned and published an account of his experience in *To Katanga and Back.* Historian, critic and commentator on European, African and American current affairs. His *Parnell and his Party 1880–90* is a work of scientific historical scholarship on a phase of modern Irish and British politics. Has also published *Maria Cross,* a study of aspects of twentieth century Catholic writing; *Writers and Politics,* a collection of his essays on history, literature and politics: *Murderous Angels,* a play confronting the interaction and deaths of Lumumba and Hammarskjold in the Congo crisis; *The United Nations: Sacred Drama,* a study of the ritualistic significance of the U.N., its value and the forces which weaken it; and many articles as yet uncollected. Currently writes for *The Listener,* the New York *Review of Books,* and publishes less frequently in a wide variety of journals including the *Observer,* the *New Left Review,* and *Irish Historical Studies.* Vice-Chancellor of the University of Ghana, 1962-65. Albert Schweitzer Professor of Humanities in New York University since that date. Lives in Ireland when not engaged in his academic duties.

OWEN DUDLEY EDWARDS. Irish historian and journalist. Graduate student and university lecturer in the USA, 1959–65. American correspondent for the *Irish Times* during that period. Assistant Lecturer in History, University of Aberdeen, 1966–68. Lecturer in History, University of Edinburgh, since 1968. Has published *Celtic Nationalism* (with Gwynfor Evans and others), and *James Connolly* (1868–1916). Co-editor with Fergus Pyle of *1916: the Easter Rising.* Currently writes for the *Irish Times* and *Tribune,* and occasionally elsewhere.

LIAM DE PAOR. Irish archaeologist, historian and former curator of ancient monuments. Numerous publications, including *Pre-Christian Ireland* (with Máire de Paor). Lecturer in history, University College, Dublin.

MÁIRE CRUISE O'BRIEN. Scholar in early Irish literature, linguistics and civilisation. Served in the Irish diplomatic service, resigning at the same time as Conor Cruise O'Brien, whom she later married. Publications include studies in early Irish culture, and many remarkable poems in Irish.

SEAN MAC RÉAMOINN. In the Irish diplomatic service for some years, and later in Radio-Telefís Éireann. One of the most influential figures in the Irish religious reappraisals of today, who writes extensively in English and Irish, and who covered the Second Vatican Council.

PATRICK LYNCH. Associate Professor of Political Economy, University College, Dublin. Author (with John Vaizey) of *Guinness's Brewery in the Irish Economy.* Director of O.E.C.D. surveys *Investment in Education* and *Science and Irish Economic Development.* Socio-economic researcher. Author of and contributor to significant studies of Irish economic history and economic policies.

MICHAEL VINEY. English-born journalist now an Irish citizen. Author of many studies of sociological phenomena in Irish life, initially written for the *Irish Times*. Has made valuable enquiries into various forms of economic deprivation in Ireland.

KEVIN SULLIVAN. Associate Dean, Graduate Faculties, Columbia University. Author of *Joyce among the Jesuits* and other studies in twentieth-century Irish literature. Has visited Ireland many times and is prominent in Irish studies in the United States.

BENEDICT KIELY. Irish novelist, literary critic, journalist and lecturer in creative writing. Author of *The Captain with Whiskers* and other portrayals of Irish life in fictional form. His critical work includes a study of the early nineteenth-century Irish novelist Carleton, and his latest novel is *Dogs enjoy the Morning*.

SEAMUS KELLY. Drama Critic, *Irish Times*, since 1945. Chairman Dublin Drama Critics' Circle. Quidnunc of 'An Irishman's *Diary*' (*Irish Times* daily column) since 1949. Founder Council Member Dublin James Joyce Society. Contributor to *Guardian*, *Times*, *Observer*, *Spectator*, *The Bell*, etc and to *Holiday*, *Cosmopolitan* (USA) and *Enciclopedia della Spettacola* (Italy) Publications: *1916 Illustrated* (1946), *The Celts and Their Capital* (1965).

VALENTINE RICE. Professor of Education at Trinity College and head of the School of Education of the University of Dublin. Previously taught and studied at Cork, Galway, Maynooth and Harvard, and worked for a time in the state Department of Finance.

DOUGLAS GAGEBY. Editor of the *Irish Times*. Previously held various appointments in journalism, including the first editorship of the Dublin *Evening Press*.

BASIL PETERSON. Irish journalist, air pilot, shark-fisher and writer on military history and military affairs, author of a maritime history of Ireland. Models physical maps of many Irish localities which have met with considerable success in Ireland and Europe.

MAURICE CRAIG. Author of an architectural study of Dublin before the twentieth century, and of many other publications.

NIALL SHERIDAN. Writer, doctor and *éminence grise* in the Irish television world, an important figure in the literary scene. 'Brinsley' in Flann O'Brien's *At Swim-Two-Birds*.

MONICA SHERIDAN. Wife to Niall Sheridan. Well-known on Irish television, and has published various works on the Irish tradition in cookery, including a recent volume of Irish recipes.

GARRY CULHANE. Irish businessman and controversialist. A ferocious enthusiast for fishing, in which he is believed to engage from a time machine.

JAMES PLUNKETT. Irish author playwright and television director.

CLAUD COCKBURN. If you don't know who he is, read his *I, Claud* – immediately.

A. R. FOSTER. For many years a schoolmaster in Foyle College, Derry, and Belfast Royal Academy.

FRED HOYLE. Plumian Professor of Theoretical Astronomy and Experimental Philosophy, University of Cambridge. FRS. Author of *The Nature of the Universe*, *Frontiers of Astronomy* and various works of science fiction.

SIR COMPTON MACKENZIE. Author of over a hundred books including his autobiography, *My Life and Times*.

JOHN MONTAGUE (b. 1929). One of the finest Irish poets, his most recent volume being *A Chosen Light* (MacGibbon and Kee, 1967).

Contents

List of Illustrations

Introducing Ireland

Conor Cruise O'Brien

At a conference on higher education in Africa, held in 1962 at Tanan-arive, Madagascar, I made the acquaintance of the Minister for Education of a West African country, which I shall call Nimbia. The Minister had spent many years in Dublin, studying, or being deemed to be studying, medicine at University College. In this process, or stasis, he had acquired several characteristics of the Dublin 'chronic medical': a leisurely and speculative affability, a pertinacious thirst and a tendency to rely on a single adjective. He had also a strong Dublin accent, and radical views on Irish politics – although, in relation to his own country, he made no secret of the satisfaction and advantages which he derived from belonging to the Fulani aristocracy. It was not however about his own country that he most liked to speak. We found one another's company congenial, and we dined together. One evening as we did so we were joined by a friend of mine who was representing an American foundation, and was exceedingly knowledgeable about African affairs. The conversation of the Nimbian Minister, which was then in full spate, continued to roll in its accustomed channel. It was, he said, the —— ing bishops who had destroyed the Mother and Child Health Scheme of Dr Noel Browne.

We both silently registered the respect implied by the omission of the customary adjective before the name of Dr Browne.

I suggested that it was not so much the bishops as conservative lay interests, who had used the bishops for their own purposes. Mr Costello . . .

The Minister bestowed his adjective on Mr Costello but thought that Mr MacBride, similarly qualified, had been even more to blame.

My American friend avowed himself at a loss. He had thought he was familiar with the principal issues and personalities of Nimbian politics, but he could not follow what we were talking about. He had not previously heard of any controversy about a health scheme in Nimbia and he was hearing for the first time the names of the Nimbian politicians, Browne, Costello and MacBride.

The Minister resolved his difficulty. 'We're not talking about ——ing Nimbia,' he said. 'We're talking about ——ing Ireland.'

He went on to discuss the internal divisions in the Clann na Poblachta

Party, as these had affected the policies of the Inter-Party Government in 1949–51.

Now, if the Nimbian Minister had been asked to describe Ireland to someone who did not know that country, the lineaments which he would have traced – following the critique of his left-wing Irish friends – would have been quite repulsive. Yet in practice he found the country so attractive that its affairs took complete possession of his mind: my American friend told me he had never seen – not even among the French-speaking African élite – such a complete case of 'intellectual colonization'.

The Nimbian had in fact become an Irishman, and the nature of his obsession – combining theoretical disapproval with emotional attraction – was thoroughly Irish. The Irish intellectuals are naturally most conscious of this: 'Talking about ——ing Ireland' is their job, their trouble and their delight. Yeats said he had been tempted, 'from this craft of verse' by:

The seeming needs of my fool-driven land . . .

Yet the seeming needs also, throughout his long life, tempted him again and again into using his craft of verse. And James Joyce went into exile in order to be fully free to 'talk about ——ing Ireland'.

An Irishman invited to 'introduce' Ireland is faced with an odd kind of challenge. The lady is of venerable age and already of wide, though mixed, reputation. To the introducer she 'means' as they say 'a lot'; though what exactly she does mean he cannot be quite sure. To those to whom she is introduced she means, perhaps, a holiday, a retreat from modernity, a reservation, a version of pastoral, an empty road, a laugh. Such an introduction necessarily feels like introducing one's mother descriptively, to a roomful of strangers. Its wording might, in 1968, run like this:

'I should like you to meet Mother. She is quite an ignorant woman, I'm afraid, and very superstitious – in fact that has been her most marked characteristic, apart from the bottle to which she is also, as you can see for yourselves, much given. Her slatternly appearance is in no way misleading; she does hardly any work and her housekeeping is both incompetent and extravagant. It is true that she has had a hard life. It seems she had some kind of affair with her nextdoor neighbour. The facts are hard to make out. He seems to have acted rather possessively and – according to her – he used to beat her and often let her go hungry. She says this went on for seven hundred years but of course this is just her exaggerated way of talking – another of her characteristics. I took the trouble to check with this neighbour, as a matter of fact, without saying who I was. He's a big fellow, getting on in years now, a bit pompous perhaps. He says he hardly knows the woman, but that she has a bad reputation in the neighbourhood for brawling and untruthfulness.

14

He denies that he used to beat her, but adds that if he did, it was for her own good. If she went hungry it was her own fault, for not eating. He also denies her story that he still has some property of hers. My own opinion is that neither of them is telling the whole truth, but I cannot see that it matters very much now. As a matter of fact, since she got the TV, Mother herself doesn't go on nearly so much about the whole business. She's changed a lot these last few years. Mellowed, you might say, I suppose. Makes life a bit easier on the younger kids – though a lot of them still run away from home as soon as they can. She used to go round burning our books you know, but she doesn't do that any more – not that it makes any difference because we don't read the books anyway. Everyone's too busy watching TV. She hardly ever talks any more about that property she used to say she had in the North and that's a relief too. The other day one of us said something about Cathleen ni Houlihan's Four Beautiful Green Fields – you know, Yeats – and she said she supposed so, but she couldn't get colour on her set. Quite a change, that. Then there was that language that she'd forgotten herself, but insisted on teaching to all of us. We don't hear so much about that any more, either. Luckily she still goes to Mass in the morning, and the pub in the evening: if she didn't we'd hardly know it was still Mother. Oh, there's been an improvement, I agree. And yet, somehow, it worries us all. We all believe in what Mother calls the echo-mechanical movement and so on. But sometimes, you know, we miss the old days of ranting and roaring and Up the Republic. It wasn't very reasonable and it didn't, as you say, get us anywhere, except, of course, where we are, however you interpret that. But it seemed to suit Mother; it gave her a good colour, kept her spirits up, brought her out in the open air and provided her with plenty of exercise. Now she's much more gentle and sensible of course but, with being indoors all the time watching TV, she seems to have faded somehow. And we can't help worrying about that because, you see, she is our Mother, and we love her very much.'

The element of truth in this metaphor is large enough to shock Irish people. Yet the attempt to extricate this truth makes a distortion. This is a difficulty of a general kind, yet it is felt in particular force by those who, like Irish writers, are writing about their own country for a public mainly composed of foreigners, and about a mainly Catholic community for a public mainly composed of ex-Protestant agnostics. In these conditions, writer and reader are unwittingly drawn into a kind of collusion in the invention of a special country; the Ireland of literature. This is a distilled essence of Irish peculiarity; it leaves out of account the considerable extent to which Ireland is like other places, and Irishmen like other people. Now in literature – as distinct from the sub-literature of popular songs, musicals and novels written for an Irish-American public – Ireland's peculiarity emerges as an oppressive quality. All the greatest Irish writers have helped to establish this. Shaw's Ireland is a place of

15

futility, failure and endless, pointless talk. Yeats contrasts a heroic Ireland of the imagination (and of a few rare epiphanies) with the reality of Biddy and Paudeen and

The daily spite of this unmannerly town . . .

Joyce, above all, created a Dublin, which compelled assent by the intensity of its realism, and which was a diagnosis of paralysis. This diagnosis was amply confirmed by reports from the provinces. The small-town Ireland of Brinsley MacNamara's *Valley of the Squinting Windows* (1918); the Cork of Sean O'Faolain's *Bird Alone* (1936); the rural Ireland of Patrick Kavanagh's *The Great Hunger* (1942), are places without hope, even through emigration.[1]

These statements about the human condition, as experienced in Ireland, have rather naturally created the impression that Ireland is a place in which the human condition is considerably worse than it is elsewhere. This impression is reinforced by the tendency of readers of Protestant tradition to regard Catholic forms of turpitude as more heinous than other forms. When a young Oxford historian referred recently to Ireland as 'an unhappy bigot-ridden nation', he could certainly have introduced a formidable body of literature in evidence in support of this opinion. Yet to me, who lives most of the year in New York and each summer in Ireland, it seemed strange to have to think of *Ireland* as either especially unhappy or especially bigot-ridden. It seemed rather that the forms of its unhappiness and of its bigotries – and also of its happiness and of its charity – were archaic and rural, instead of being modern and urban. I do not know whether it can be shown that the modern and urban forms are necessarily more agreeable. The Catholic Archbishop of Dublin is rather widely deemed to be a bigot – and I agreed with what my Nimbian friend had to say about him – yet his pedantic and morose jurisdiction seems to me much less to be feared or reprobated than the sophisticated and modern bigotry of an Enoch Powell. Not that Irish people are immune to racial bigotry: Gaelic poetry, since the Tudor Conquest reflects the conviction that the Irish are whiter than the English, frequently referred to as 'swarthy' (*crón*) or 'yellow' (*búi*); the Irish for John Bull is a racist term, *Seán Búi* ('Yellow John').[2] Yet on the whole the Irish character, as it has been formed both by religious influences and by Wolfe Tone republicanism, is rather resistant to racism; had it not been, my Nimbian friend could not have

[1]See also the present writer's essay 'The Embers of Easter 1916–1966' in *1916: The Easter Rising* (edited by O. Dudley Edwards and Fergus Pyle: London, 1968). I have not wished, here, to go over much of the ground covered in that essay.

[2]Some recent work by physical anthropologists suggests that the Irish are in fact the whitest people in Europe. On the other hand the leading racial theorist, Gobineau, believed that the shortcomings of the Irish – incompatible, in his opinion, with Aryan status – were due to their having been *mélangés avec la race jaune.*

16

become as Irish as he did. I once overheard a conversation, in Stephen's Green park in Dublin, between two girls, workers from Jacob's biscuit factory. The elder was saying, 'All the same, Mary, when you get right down to it, the nicest race of all is the white race.' And the younger, dreamily, 'Jaysus, Margaret, I doan't know.'

A 'backward' situation can be, as Sartre has said, also a point of vantage, especially in a time when people are increasingly questioning the results of a forward movement – as they must, granted the condition of the great American cities, often seen as the furthest forward edge. It is true, of course, that backward peoples are subject to the delusion that they have peculiar virtues which are about to redeem neighbours, who are endowed with more obvious advantages. What Dostoevsky's Holy Russia was supposed to be on the point of doing for Europe was much the same as what the Irish Literary Revival supposed, in the 'nineties, it might do for the English-speaking world. (No salvation in fact ensued, but in both cases human culture was enriched, out of sources which themselves appeared especially impoverished.)

'Where today,' a Swedish student asked me, 'are your Yeatses and your Yoyces?' Alas we have none, and neither has anyone else. In literature, as in other ways, Ireland seems something of a 'burnt-out case'. We have no longer any Messianic hopes or pretensions. Yet the strange and intensely felt history of the country has marked the people and has produced a recognizable 'Irish mind'. Berkeley who liked the phrase 'we Irish men,' reminded himself to curb his own 'satyrical nature'. Yeats thought that the mark of the Irish mind was 'a cold, hard, detonating impartiality'. Few would agree, yet it is true that Irishmen do sometimes – almost, it seems, absent-mindedly – achieve this condition. Even when they do not, they may appear to, since certain prejudices which are natural to Englishmen and Americans, and are not perceived by them, are not the Irishman's particular prejudices. This may be among the reasons why Irish writers – even in our own Yeatsless and Yoyceless days – still win the attention of an English-speaking world to which many of their forefathers were unwilling recruits.

About Ireland, however, it is peculiarly difficult for Irishmen to be impartial; as we have seen, the honest effort to be so has created an Ireland of literature, narrower, colder and more oppressive than the reality. Another Ireland – that of the increasingly active and efficient Irish tourist services – is kinder, more joyous and more welcoming than the Ireland of reality or any other territory populated by humans.[1] Here and there in the present collection of essays the reader will en-

[1]The intelligent exploitation by the tourist services, for prestige reasons, of the corpus of literature produced by Irishmen creates a paradox, since the literature in question presents an 'image' of Ireland very different from the one presented by the tourist services. I expect one day to find County Wexford, finally becoming Brinsley-MacNamara-conscious, hanging out great signs: *Welcome to the Valley of the Squinting Windows*.

17

counter traces of both these phantom Irelands – and indeed he may encounter both of them in Ireland itself. But generally the editor, Owen Dudley Edwards, and the contributors have tried, it seems to me, to avoid both the deforming rigour which follows from the effort to achieve an inhuman degree of detachment, and also the soft blurring which is caused by the effort to give offence to none. They write about the Irish situation, or predicament, as about something in which they are themselves involved, and from which they cannot easily or for long step back, either to hiss or to cheer. There is a strong undercurrent in most of the essays, of a traditional Irish patriotism: now chastened and rather baffled, but neither soured nor extinct. This is not precisely 'cold, hard, detonating impartiality' – a quality normally available only for non-Irish subjects – but the facts are respected and, for this reason, a certain number of detonations inevitably ensue.

The picture of Ireland which the essays make is not absolutely consistent, nor could it be so: each contributor's experience shapes for him an Ireland which differs at least slightly in its contours from anyone else's Ireland. In some cases the differences are highly significant. The reader will notice that Douglas Gageby's fine essay on Northern Ireland flatly rejects the view that the island of Ireland contains two nations, while my own essay – on Ireland in International Affairs – implies the acceptance of some kind of 'two nations' view (see pp 179 and 104). The difference is important, but should not be overstated. Douglas Gageby would, I am sure, agree that his 'one nation' is in fact divided, not just by an 'artificial border', or by foreign troops, but by two separate religious-political traditions, of great strength and marked stability. I agree that my 'two nations' – basically the Protestant descendants of the seventeenth-century settlers and the Catholic descendants of the autochthonous Gaelic-speaking inhabitants[1] – have much more in common than some of their spokesmen allow; that they overlap to a small but significant degree; that some kind of fusion between them seemed possible at the time of Wolfe Tone's United Irishmen; and that such a fusion may take place in the future.

In Ireland it is the spokesmen of the autochthonous majority who are in the habit of affirming 'one nation', while the spokesmen of the settlers affirm 'two nations', through their slogan 'Ulster is British'. In this book these positions are reversed: it is the 'autochthone' who says 'two nations' while the 'settler' replies 'one'. Underneath the contradiction there is an agreement, which is a repudiation of the way the two elements in the population – 'nations' or not – have in fact under their

---

[1]Or rather, in both cases, persons who deem themselves to be so descended. In fact, of course, many of today's Protestants are descended from soup-eating Papists, while many Catholics are descended from the assimilated sons of Cromwellian troopers or from promiscuous Protestant squireens. Whatever about 'two nations' there are certainly not 'two races'.

respective leaders behaved towards one another. In each case repudiation begins at home. I have had to repudiate the tendency, long prevalent in Dublin though now weakening, to pretend – in public but not always in private – that the differences between the two kinds of Irishmen are trivial and that the border could be peacefully removed by agreement between London and Dublin. Douglas Gageby, a Belfastman, rightly finds it more urgent to repudiate Belfast's efforts to emphasize division, through the deliberate inculcation of religious bigotry – which also may now be weakening – and by the commemorative stimulation of 'racial' pride based on conquest. Thus, our apparent difference masks a common aspiration: the hope that, after a reduction of the propaganda level on both sides, the people who inhabit Ireland may wish to become one, and that, whatever other problems and conflicts may remain or arise, the quarrels of the seventeenth century may at least be laid to rest.

The edges, in any case, tend to become blurred, not only between the 'two nations' but between Ireland generally and the rest of the English-speaking Atlantic society. Television speeds up – relatively speaking – a process begun by conquest, helped on by famine, emigration, the National School system and later the cinema and radio. Yet the historic residues, which form and hold national character, remain extremely potent. This month (July, 1968) the Orange North celebrated the Protestant Conquest with all the accustomed pomp of processions, drums and triumphal arches. In the same month the medieval world, whose ruin is therein commemorated, continued quietly to show its strength elsewhere in Ireland. The age-old pilgrimage to the top of the holy mountain of Croaghpatrick, in County Mayo, is reported to have drawn this year the largest number of pilgrims in living memory. It is not a soft pilgrimage: before me as I write is a photograph, on the front page of this morning's paper (29th July), of a barefoot pilgrim kneeling among and on the sharp rocks which cover the upper part of the mountain. He had, literally, walked in the footsteps of some two hundred generations of pilgrims, and walked their painful way in the same spirit with them.

Crowds gather, too, for the ballad singing in the Abbey Tavern, at Howth, near Dublin. The crowds are partly foreign; the ballads are, as they say, a tourist attraction. For the Irish – present also in considerable numbers – the ballads are also something else: a stirring of their history in themselves. It is their history, because they think and feel it to be theirs. It is the history of the Irish rebels: the United Irishmen, Robert Emmet, the Fenians, the Invincibles, the men of 1916, of the war against the Black and Tans, and of the Irish Civil War. And the tradition does not stop, for the ballad singers, where it officially – and reasonably – should. One of the most popular ballads commemorates Sean South of Garryowen, County Limerick, who died in 1957 from gun-shot wounds received in the course of an IRA raid on a police barracks in

19

Northern Ireland. South was an outlaw, not merely from the point of view of the Belfast Government, but from that of 'his own' Government in Dublin, and of the whole of the democratically elected Parliament there. Objectively, his act was not merely useless but harmful, in relation to what he himself desired: it strengthened, instead of weakening, the main line of division between Irishmen. A cynic could say that his only real service to his country has been the posthumous one of contributing to Ireland's external assets by adding local colour to places of entertainment: his bones have become bait in a tourist trap. Yet it is not really quite like that; it would be safer if it were. Watching the passionate face of one of the young ballad singers, and hearing the response she evoked, I thought of something entirely unconnected with tourism – of Stephen Gwynn's comment after seeing Maud Gonne in Yeats's *Cathleen ni Houlihan* (1902): '. . . I went home asking myself if such plays should be produced unless one was prepared for people to go out to shoot and be shot . . .'

By far the best remembered part of *Cathleen ni Houlihan* is its curtain, where the Poor Old Woman is transfigured:

PETER (to Patrick, laying a hand on his arm): Did you see an old woman going down the path?

PATRICK: I did not, but I saw a young girl, and she had the walk of a queen.

A quarter of a century later, after many of her sons had gone out to shoot and be shot, Cathleen had turned back into an old woman. In Denis Johnston's *The Old Lady Says 'No!'* (1926) she has become 'an old tattered Flower Woman in a black straw hat', crooning about her 'four beeuutiful gre'in fields', and cracking dirty jokes with a wheezy cough. In an earlier part of this introduction I have sketched a possible 1968 reincarnation, much closer to Johnston than to Yeats, but milder, more middle-class and vaguely 'modern' (for her). To portray her romantically – even with Johnston's romantic irony – would now be impossible. Yet, as the ballad singers know, there remains on the imaginative retina of all who would own to being Irish, that faint and dangerous shadow: 'a young girl, and she had the walk of a queen.'

The Burden of Irish History

Owen Dudley Edwards

> *Pride in your history is pride*
> *In living what your fathers died*
> *Is pride in taking your own pulse*
> *And counting in you someone else.*
>
> Louis MacNeice 'Suite for Recorders'
>
> *The fathers have eaten sour grapes,*
> *and the children's teeth are*
> *set on edge.*
>
> Ezekiel, XVIII. 2

You may remember how, in one of the early scenes in John Le Carré's *The Spy Who Came In From The Cold,* Alec Leamas and Liz, the doomed central characters, have a conversation at an initial stage of their relationship about her beliefs. He makes an incorrect guess, and then –

"Then what do you believe in?"
"History."
He looked at her in astonishment for a moment, then laughed.
"Oh, Liz . . . oh *no.* You're not a bloody Communist?" She nodded, blushing like a small girl at his laughter, angry and relieved that he didn't care.

There is a hint in the book that Leamas is Irish, and had his thoughts been more on his ancestry than his occupation, Liz's belief in history might have suggested to him he was conversing with a fellow-country-man. History, or a form of it, is in the marrow of the Irish people.

But it is not in any sense of conviction of its proof of their triumph's inevitability, that the Irish believe in history. The Irish, as Conor Cruise O'Brien has remarked, are brooders where the English, and others of similar confidence, are gloaters. History may have proved to the Irish that they were right, but not that they would win or that they have or had won. It told them a story of what they had lost, offering pitifully little hope of regaining it. And it was with them eternally. In the aftermath of the 1916 Rising, an American consul in Cork, seeking to explain the event to his government, observed that the Act of Union of 1800, the great famine of the late 1840s, the struggle of the Catholics in the 1830s

21

against paying tithes to the established Protestant episcopalian church – all were current political issues. If history is, in the words of E. H. Carr, 'an unending dialogue between the present and the past', it has for long been in Ireland a dialogue in which the present had been reduced to making simple affirmative statements, in support of the past's assertions.

There have been many Irelands. And virtually all of them have been prisoners of history. 'To hell with the future, we'll live in the past' was how a bitter commentator on Ulster Protestant bigotry saw its mentality, and the unceasing slogans on Ulster walls, 'REMEMBER 1690', testify to his veracity. Like all forms of history which buttress political, religious or social credos this type is of course selective: the Orangemen who so vociferously recall and luxuriate in the Boyne victory of that year by the Protestant William III over the Catholic James II, are forever oblivious of the delight William's victory brought to Pope Innocent XI. It is a perpetual justification: the Victorian historian James Anthony Froude, whose *The English in Ireland* captured so much of the attitudes of the Protestant ascendancy in Ireland (and was captured by them), protested that no further concessions should be granted to Ireland until the Catholics acknowledged their guilt for having massacred thousands of innocent Protestants during the rebellion of 1641. Two can play that game. During his negotiations with De Valera at the height of the Anglo-Irish war, Lloyd George, at an interval in the talks, was asked how far they had got. 'To the Confederation of Kilkenny', he answered bitterly. Nor has independence wrought much change. At the present day the two leading Irish political parties are formed and hold their loyalties on the basis of agreement with or opposition to the Anglo-Irish treaty of 1921. At the height of the Cold War, the Irish-language pantomime in the Abbey Theatre presented Stalin as the villain one year, Cromwell the next. To the audience, both were equally real, Cromwell probably the more so.

Why has this consciousness of the past pervaded so many sectors of Irish society in the last hundred years, regardless of the barriers of religion, class and ethnic affiliation? For one thing almost all sections of Ireland share in common a sense of defeat. Ulster, the most industrialised part of Ireland, was robbed of her chance to assume economic leadership of the island by political events, and has instead been forced to maintain herself as a poor relation of the larger island. Nor did Ulster Unionists obtain their true desires in the peace settlements of the early 1920s which partitioned Ireland into the Twenty-six counties and the Six. They had seen themselves as fighters to preserve the unity of Great Britain and Ireland, not to settle for a truncated island and the abandonment of their southern Unionist and Protestant brethren. The holy ground of the Boyne itself lies totally within the Twenty-six counties. Proud Derry, Protestant bastion in the same much-venerated war, is cut off from the Donegal hinterland which in strict economic terms should be at its disposal. Ulster Unionists may speak in terms of 'preserving' the achievement of William III; in fact their slogans serve to palliate the smart sustained by the withering of his legacy.

The peculiar circumstances of Ireland invite a comparison with other societies of similar characteristics, such as the southern portion of the USA. The American South, as its foremost historian, C. Vann Woodward, has pointed out, possesses a history of 'military defeat, occupation, and reconstruction. Nothing about this history was conducive to the theory that the South was the darling of divine providence.' The Irish experience parallels that of all Southerners. The remnant of the Protestant ascendancy, like that of the Southern aristocrats, can lean on former days of power; the Ulster Unionists, children of a recent industrial revolution, like the Southern urban bourgeoisie and *nouveaux riches,* can flatter their own vanity by identification with a colourful past which, in the main, is unconnected with their lineal ancestors. Memories and myths of that past make it easy for them to shrink from the apparently inexorable trends of the present – in the white Southerners' case, racial integration, in the case of Ulster Unionists, fusion with the Republic whether in a free trade area or possibly even a European super-state. The same memories and myths enable the most deluded in either group to charge bull-headed against the inevitable, with results that hasten the destruction of their cause where passive resistance might defer it.

The Southern parallel is total, for the Irish Catholic experience over centuries has approximated closely to that of the American Negro. In both instances a long history of utterly indefensible repression was followed by a strange middle period of awakened consciences and broken promises by the rulers, of Utopian expectations and bitter awakening by the ruled. In both cases, after much dependence on presumed friends in the rulers' camp, the ruled were forced to rely on themselves to seize what freedom they could and were then blamed for not being grateful for its concession. In both cases preliminary success was won by mastery and wide usage of the tactics of non-violence, by the Irish during the land war of the 1880s, by the Negroes in the civil rights struggle of recent years. In neither case was the previous history a non-violent one: the Negro had his slave revolts and his occasional private recourse to extreme ends in disposing of a tyrannical master; the Irish peasant had a past of secret agrarian societies which wreaked an occasional vengeance, and from time to time private assassinations of rack-rent landlords and their agents. It was Charles Stewart Parnell and Michael Davitt who popularised and preached non-violent agrarian warfare, much as Martin Luther King was to do later in the civil rights context. In the end, the Irish, come to full political consciousness within the British Empire, were to become imbued with the gospel of violence which permeated the world of their rulers. Many a guerrilla leader of the

Anglo-Irish war of independence had received his indoctrination in the martial spirit (plus valuable lessons on how *not* to fight battles) in the trenches of World War I. And if, as at the present time seems possible, the American Negro also turns to violent methods, the society against which he struggles will have its own martial spirit to thank.

Professor Woodward quotes Arnold Toynbee to advantage in the Southern context:

> I remember watching the Diamond Jubilee procession myself as a small boy. I remember the atmosphere: It was: well, here we are at the top of the world, and we have arrived at this peak to stay there forever! There is, of course, a thing called history, but history is something unpleasant that happens to other people. We are comfortably outside all that. I am sure, if I had been a small boy in New York in 1897 I should have felt the same. Of course, if I had been a small boy in 1897 in the Southern part of the United States, I should not have felt the same; I should then have known from my parents that history had happened to my people in my part of the world.

And had he grown up in Ireland a similar knowledge, with all that it entailed, would have been his portion. He would also have learned that his people lived two lives, one for purposes of communications to the rulers, one among themselves. In this context, Michael Innes's fantasy, *The Journeying Boy,* is highly plausible in portraying an Irish landowner who insists on his servants employing the dialect immortalized by Synge – which in this case isn't their dialect. Irish servants, tenant-farmers and labourers were accustomed if not to alter their dialect, at least to ornament it with flowers of rhetoric and flattery which were notably absent when they conversed among themselves. So effective had been the tradition of servility that the ruling class sustained a brutal psychological shock when the peasantry turned on them in force in the last quarter of the nineteenth century. Their indignation, like that of the paternalistic white Southerner, imperfectly concealed a chagrin occasioned by their having come to believe their own idyllic pictures of landlordism, a belief sustained by the smiling countenances of their inferiors. Like the Bourbons, the Irish landlords learned nothing; unlike them, they forgot much, including the fact that in the earlier part of the century a tiny segment of the peasantry, risen to bourgeois status, had despoiled several of them and were even enabled, notably after the Encumbered Estates Act of 1849, to obtain the lands of a few of them. Maria Edgeworth chronicles an eighteenth-century instance of this in *Castle Rackrent.*

The fruits of this double life for the peasantry have been manifold. It has left ingrained in the Irish, not so much a capacity for double-dealing – although that was and is present in large measure – but a belief that in social matters one should follow the dictates of one's 'desire to please', in Harold Nicolson's phrase. What this often means in practice is that the interlocutor is to be charmed, even to the point of one's making promises while knowing full well they will not, and probably cannot, be fulfilled. It is a quality which dictates that a good story must be told to entertain the audience, without regard to any possible breaches of confidence or injury to the reputation of the subject. And a natural corollary is to breed a secretive approach towards anything that might be interpreted as a 'scandal' of one's own. The Irishman and, still more, the Irishwoman, when confronted by 'company', assumes an entirely different manner and voice to those exhibited to the nearest and dearest. And of course a further consequence of the double life which masked a burning land-hunger is an almost unfathomable pride in the ownership of land today, plus a rabid conservatism about its use, for fear that an innovation would place this hard-won prize in danger of being lost. The tenant-farmer's land-hunger gave an edge to this duality of manner, and the edge was sharpened by the consciousness that his ancestors had once owned the land of which they had been dispossessed by reason of religious adhesion, or unhappy politics, or an arbitrary confiscation by English rulers. Margaret Mitchell popularised a version of the American South which bore no relation to reality in her *Gone With the Wind,* but there was much historical truth in the intoxication with land which she ascribed to her Irish-American family, the O'Haras. Perhaps that grain of truth may account for the fact that her two bushels of chaff were enthusiastically devoured by the Irish reading public; or maybe it had something to do with the fact that the ensuing film was denounced as being beautiful and immoral by an eminent and scholarly Jesuit, who had never been at a film previously so far as I know. (Irish legend credits the film company with having offered the holy man an enormous fee to condemn their next spectacular.)

Mention of the above Jesuit, however irrelevant, brings us to another major strand in our analysis of the permanence of the past in Ireland. Again it is one which underlines the similarity between the Irish Catholic and the Negro of the American South – religion. Somebody once wanted to bring out a book on Ireland in which religion would not be mentioned: a touchingly optimistic dream, since to write of Ireland without discussing religion would be to write *Hamlet* without Horatio, Polonius and the Ghost. In the ensuing pages Sean Mac Réamoinn gives it a full discussion, but the number of other essayists into whose discourse it shows a tendency to creep may amuse you, and the present writer is no more immune than any other.

In brief, then, Catholicism over the years sustained the Irish peasantry as did no other force. It was a religion whose profession had played its part in reducing the Irish peasantry to helplessness and poverty, a condition of affairs sanctified by the majesty of penal laws passed despite the objections of Orange William by a Protestant Irish Parliament in the 1690s, and extended by its successors in the early eighteenth century. And in their condition of utter gloom, without hope or prospect of alleviation save vague dreams of Stuart reconquest growing increasingly faint as the eighteenth century advanced, the Irish peasantry took comfort from the assurance and promise given them by their faith. In one respect they were less fortunate than the Negro in the South: the Negroes became fixed and devoted adherents of a Bible-based fundamentalism, and in the accounts of Daniel or Esther or Nehemiah derived the conviction that however harsh the Babylonian or Persian rule under which they groaned, their day would come, and God would not forget His people. Irish religion offered less basis for material optimism. The Irish peasant rested his faith much more strongly in tradition, for his culture and his faith were as one in being based on folklore rather than on the printed word. Hence he stressed the foundations of faith both most available to him and most significant for him. It was to stories based on Christ's passion, and not to the Israelites by the waters of Babylon, that he turned for reassurance, and it was a precedent he could understand, couched as it was in terms of seemingly hopeless defeat of righteousness with all the forces of alien state and established church arrayed to destroy Him. It was also of great psychological value that Catholicism, as the Irish knew it, laid such stress on the rôle of the Virgin Mary, for in Ireland, even when things were worst, man found solace in other men's company or sometimes in illegally distilled spirits, while to woman was left the terrible task of planning for the present and future both for herself and for her household. It was a task of peculiar difficulty, since it demanded both foresight and knowledge of the right decision, combined with a diplomacy which would lead the man to accept and implement it without having to admit to himself that his wife ran the house. Small wonder that she turned to the example of a woman whose trials were manifestly more terrible than her own, and whose suffering during her Son's passion could all too easily be conjured up in the imagination.

This is a very moving heritage, and one which accounts for the strength and conservatism of Irish Catholicism. It is by no means clear that the Irish clergy appreciate the nature of the adhesion of their flocks to the faith. There is an easy and understandable, but nonetheless foolish, tendency on the part of the clergy to confuse devotion to the religion with devotion to the priests. The priests hold a prominent position, to be sure, a position enhanced by a humble snobbery on the part of their parishioners. But the faith held firm in days when priests were few and far between, (and, incidentally, lost its hold in a few instances when legal barriers were removed and Catholics began to acquire economic, but not social status). From time to time in Irish history, priests have overstrained the loyalty of their flocks, and either met with a rebellion as startling to them as its counterpart was to the landlords, or won grudging agreement which imperceptibly lessened their hold on their following. The literary *locus classicus* of such an excessive strain on parishioners' loyalty is of course James Joyce's account of his family's reaction to the priests' onslaught on Parnell after his divorce and party split in 1890–91. *A Portrait of the Artist as a Young Man* is unforgettable in its description of the impact of clerical over-strain on congregations as revealed in Joyce senior – but has even greater force as the reader examines the more subtle and much more radical effects on Joyce junior.

Macaulay observed of the late seventeenth-century Highlands that their religion was 'a rude mixture of Popery and paganism'. The diagnosis is superficial, but in looking at the history of another Celtic people we may give it a moment's reflection. Christianity, after all, has been rooted in Ireland for a mere 1,500 years and in a country where the past has shown so durable a character, 1,500 years is not a particularly long time. Formal paganism may be no more (although it certainly held out for many generations after St Patrick), but paganism has left its heritage, conscious and otherwise. Insofar as the Irish have a folklore awareness of a golden age, it is in the first millennium AD, and to at least some leading figures in recent Irish history, the first millennium was as close as the events of the previous century. Patrick Pearse, leader of the 1916 Rising, made so much of the ethics of the fabled hero Cú Chulainn and his legendary companions, the Red Branch Knights, that his pupils were expected to model their code of behaviour on those pagan heroes. The Fenians, who threatened insurrection in 1867 and, in Ireland and in the USA, provided the springboard and wellsprings for devolutionary and revolutionary Irish movements for the next fifty years, chose their name from another legendary pre-Christian militia. (Admittedly, monastic scribes made haste after the conversion of Ireland to pop a few orthodox glosses into the pagan legends such as causing two of the Fianna to survive by magic for three hundred years to be converted to Christianity, or having the king of the Red Branch Knights expire with rage on being told by a seer of the Crucifixion, but the poverty of the attempt was laid bare by the shameless usage of pagan devices to accomplish these Christian ends. The conversion of Ireland to Christianity does not seem to have been along a purely one-way street from paganism. The poetic versions of dialogue between the surviving Fianna and St Patrick are certainly far more sympathetic to paganism than would be warranted by a climate where conversion had been absolute.)

Certain of the pagan legends, preserved in folklore and retold down the centuries, have a chilling relevance for Irish history as a whole. Thus we are told how the Tuatha Dé Danaan who inhabited Ireland during the Bronze Age were defeated by the Milesians, who had escalated themselves into the Iron Age. The Tuatha Dé Danaan thereupon became

27

gods, and so has any other Irish hero of stature who has been defeated ever since. It was as if the Irish realized that defeat gives a psychological (or, as the word is used in Ireland, a spiritual) advantage to those who sustain it. There is a widespread delusion that the Irish are anti-English. It is a very absurd one. The English have to exist in order to listen to the Irish, by way of a start, for the Irish certainly won't listen to each other. It is true that a great deal of feeling existed at one time, much more notably among the exiles who departed from Ireland and fed their hatred of England without the questioning of one's emotions which contact with reality must bring. But, now that the whole business is over (or nearly) I would say that the chief Irish reaction is one of pity. Many Irish were, for instance, indignant at English treatment of Cyprus, but the dominant emotion was one of sympathetic reflection that the poor conquerors can never learn from previous mistakes with others whom they have conquered. If the above implies that the Irish see themselves as gods by virtue of their defeat, their opinion of themselves does little to falsify the assumption.

Christianity or no, the pagan gods certainly lasted for indecently long life-spans. An eighteenth-century poet, writing in the Irish language, could compare Bonnie Prince Charlie, whose prospects he was extolling, to Aonghus Óg (the pagan deity whose rôle at many points paralleled that of Apollo), with the certainty that everyone would know what he was talking about. Other pagan figures were equally persistent, and even odder in the way they jostled Christian symbols. In that beautiful Irish lullaby 'The Castle of Dromore' the second verse calls for protection from pernicious pagan forces such as 'Dread Spirit of the Blackwater Clan Eoghain's wild *bean sídhe'* or, as it is commonly anglicized, Banshee, that lachrymose and ethereal female without whom no death-bed of persons with social pretensions can be said to be complete. But the next line reads: 'And holy Mary pitying us, in Heaven for Grace doth sue' which is, of course, excellent Roman Catholic theology, paying devotion to the Virgin but making it clear that her place in the Heavenly hierarchy, as far as human souls are concerned, is that of a supplicant. So powerful a sense of survival of the pagan does Ireland still evoke, indeed, that we are in some danger of becoming a horror-story writer's paradise. In some cases the influence is implicit, as with Irish writers who have absorbed the prevailing atmosphere and then go on to bring their special insights to bear on other locales in which they pitch their narratives. Lord Dunsany, Sheridan Le Fanu, C. R. Maturin and Bram Stoker are probably our leading domestic practitioners in this regard – if Oscar Wilde is to be omitted. But even more impressive are the out-siders whose creative art has received stimulation from this Irish atmosphere. William Hope Hodgson, if his execution did not reach the ambition of his conception, nonetheless deserves pride of place for what he made of the survival of Irish paganism. M. R. James, with all of his masterly capacity for the employment of antiquarianism in the service of the ghost story, throws a chilling half-light on the potentialities of the Irish pagan legacy for the export market in 'the Residence at Whitminster'. And it has been left to the greatest of modern horror-story writers, H. P. Lovecraft, to give us a short story, 'The Moon-Bog' whose historical matter relates to the Parthalonians, or earliest of Irish legendary invaders, his interpretation being based on the oldest source-material relating to them. If Lovecraft be correct, the insidious influence of the Parthalonians is with us to the present day, a circumstance which would make teenagers of the Tuatha Dé Danaan, as far as influence goes, and leave St Patrick a veritable babe in arms.

I am not making a plea for the existence of ghosts and extra-human influences. I would be more inclined to argue that in the context of Ireland the traveller would be well advised to suspend both belief and disbelief in this connection. That the past survives to play an utterly disproportionate rôle in Irish life is, I think, undeniable. Where scientific analysis seems to me to break down is in the determination of whether this phenomenon can be accounted for in purely human terms, or if some more intangible factor has to be allowed for. Were the minds of men swayed by the past purely through environmental circumstances, or is something present which our inadequate vocabulary describes as 'possession'? And, if so, is the extraneous influence willed by those whom it comes to dominate, or else who – or *what* – has called it up? We find ourselves perpetually surrounded by imponderables which mock at our investigation, from the early monks who knew too much to reject coexistence with pagan survivals, to Yeats, who in poetry strove with success to catch a glimpse of these intangibles, and in prose and conversation often stumbled into the banal on the same theme.

To return to the purely human sphere, with an uneasy backward glance, there is enough cause for alarm even there. Folk poetry only serves to remind us of further consequences of the peasantry's double life. Satire in English is usually uneasy, and feels forced to give itself away at times, lest some dull-witted auditor miss the point it intends to make. Satire in Irish makes no such concession – a truly Irish satire reads like a paean of praise in honour of the main theme. But the use of this technique is not limited to the Irish language. Swift, whose sources included material available only in the peasants' tongue, at his zenith demonstrated more enthusiasm for the Irish satiric model than the English. He also followed Irish tradition in his use of the allied art, the lampoon which, though as clearly and ferociously malevolent as the satire pretends to be flattering, is commonly grouped with it in the Irish word *aor*. The *aor,* whether satiric or denunciatory, is extremely ancient both in its virulence and in the near-preternatural power assigned to it. Professor Arthur F. Beringause, in his article 'The Presentness of the Past in Ireland' (*Journal of the History of Ideas* April, 1955), has noted

29

the fear with which the lampooner was regarded in the early Irish sagas. It is a fear not unlike the hostility evinced in Ireland today towards realistic writers, whereof Benedict Kiely speaks later in this volume. The anger which these writers have engendered is often hard to comprehend, but if we appreciate an ancient tradition that a satire or lampoon can bring actual harm to its victim, we may conclude that the attitude has antiquity, if not logic, on its side.

Professor Beringause is, it seems to me, on less sure ground in stressing the permanence of the ancient Celtic tradition that 'their men of learning [were] nearly the equivalent of gods'. In malevolent literature there is something in this, if we remind ourselves how closely linked gods may be to devils. But on a more general level it seems to me that the bard and his descendant held a high social position because they offered reassurance, being a part of the establishment and glorifying the foundation-stones of the social order which maintained them. The official bard is still present in Ireland, and is still honoured, and a crashing bore he is into the bargain. Hand in glove with Irish denunciations of their first-class writers' *aors* and disgraces go even more maddening eulogies of orthodox tenth-raters. It is a repulsive phenomenon which requires more detailed analysis than it has received, other than in such works as the Belfast novels of Brian Moore and in Harry Sylvester's *Moon Gaffney*. Moore and Sylvester have captured this and other deformed growths among Irish Catholics with a heritage of many hundred years' persecution, and their delineation is all the more stark in that both of them are dealing with Irish Catholicism in the ghetto – whether Belfast, or, as in Sylvester's case, New York. The continued injustice of the ghetto gives an additional immediateness to the past, sharpens the more introverted and almost incestuous facets of a culture which easily falls into imitation of the bigotry of its oppressors, and brings to light features which in the parent society may be dormant or extinct. On the latter point, it was not until Robert Briscoe, Dublin's first Jewish Lord Mayor, travelled to the USA that many American Jews learned that the anti-Semitism of the Irish-American ghetto had no indigenous parallel in Ireland.

Other pre-Christian traditions hold sway to the present time. Hospitality is often stressed in this connection, and any glance at oral tradition or mythological compilations relating to ancient Ireland will confirm the degree to which it was enjoined as an obligation to welcome the stranger and feed him to the point of bodily discomfort. The sense of obligation persists, but the tradition has not come down to us without qualification. Harsh fate curtailed the implementation of Irish wishes in this connection, and a far more recent event, the great famine of 1845–50, forced its survivors to exhibit a thrift hitherto alien to them. It is for this reason that Irish hospitality, notably in urban Ireland, takes the form of being unstinted when offered, but of being offered seldom. Tradition dictates that the host offer the guest everything but his womenfolk – restraint in this connection being equally founded in antiquity. Therefore, since the amount of trouble involved in such a proceeding is enormous, and since capital is in short supply, folk-memories of the destruction of an all too hospitable society prompt restraint in any invitation beyond the self-exculpatory 'you must come round to the house sometime.' Curiously enough the less wealth an Irishman has, the more ready he is with an invitation. If the all one has to offer is little, its dispensation will not deprive one of much. This may appear paradoxical until it is realized that most present-day Irish city-dwellers had peasant ancestors who directly felt the weight of the great famine. It is they who learned its lesson, became more ambitious and conscious of the need to protect their security. Their brothers who stayed on the land in small holdings drew less radical morals from it.

The only other point which I have time to make now is the antiquity of the hero, and of the anti-hero, in Irish history. Both cults account for part of the Irish predilection for mixing intense enthusiasm with intense irony, cynicism and self-mockery. The hero and anti-hero votaries are often to be distinguished, but many Irishmen are both. The greatest zealots for a cause can be its most sardonic commentators. Theobald Wolfe Tone, father of Irish republican nationalism and of the United Irishmen who rebelled (as usual, unsuccessfully) in 1798, is a splendid example. No patriot was more committed, no social critic more searing, and no diarist more self-deflatory. Parnell barnstormed the United States in early 1880 to raise funds against a threatened famine, and for the financing of an agitation to destroy landlordism – hitherto the permanent root-cause of famine; and his subsequent comment on his method was: 'When Dillon and I had sufficiently depressed the public we went around with our hats.'

An Irish patriotic leader who lacks this readiness to be anti-hero as well as hero can weaken his *rapport* with his countrymen by failing to perceive, and allow for, the existence of the dual tradition. When Patrick Pearse made himself high priest of the Cú Chulainn cult, no doubt he did not realize he was rejecting a vital part of the saga's legacy. Pearse put forward his gospel in idealistic terms. But the ancient legends and subsequent folklore also told of a somewhat different figure, of a Cú Chulainn who bordered on the buffoonish. Yeats, for all of his unreality, caught this strand of the tradition in 'The Only Jealousy of Emer'. Pearse missed it, as he seems also to have missed the implications of a cult glorifying a legendary hero whose major achievement was to save Ulster from conquest by the rest of Ireland. 'Through the mouths of Carson and of Pearse all Ireland heard ancestral voices prophesying war', observed Conor Cruise O'Brien. 'Different ancestors and a different war.' *Different* ancestors? I rather think Cú Chulainn made cousins of them, much though they might both have denied it.

31

The anti-hero is even more noticeable in the other great mythological cycle. In the *Fianna* stories the great hero sometimes appears as contemptible as does the god-like Odysseus in the anti-Homeric tradition from which Sophocles drew, in his *Philoctetes*. Thus in the famous Diarmuid and Gráinne story, Fionn Mac Cumhaill, the heroic warrior, bard, strategist, leader and codifier of ethics, becomes an absurd, malignant, treacherous old man, lusting after a girl young enough to be his granddaughter, and falling somewhere between the ludicrous and the despicable.

It is possible that heroic and anti-heroic traditions were once as distinct as the professions of bard and satirist. But so dreadfully have they become fused, that abuse has become a form of affection in Ireland, and savage verbal duel a sign of *camaraderie*. Beware of a faintly derogatory reference to a person, an idea, or a movement: it usually betokens admiration. Of course there are, as I have said, panegyrists, and there are even more debunkers. But these are the defectives in Irish life. It was not wholly a joke (it never is, in Ireland) that James Joyce was portrayed in Flann O'Brien's *The Dalkey Archive* as a zealous Catholic. His mockery of Catholicism held much of affection and sprang from an initial devotion. To contrast his view of the Church with that of his truly anti-Catholic brother Stanislaus is to perceive something of this. He simply took his heroic and anti-heroic legacies into areas which for many Irishmen are off-limits.

In Ireland, therefore, the intending traveller needs maps with dimensions not merely of space but of time. At any stage he may find himself engaged in an experience which throws him against a past still as active as ever whether prehistorical, historical or unhistorical. Formal emphasis on the past may be disappearing, and indeed was often a somewhat mannered and artificial business. The Irish patriot of the 1914–22 vintage often suffered from the fact that his impassioned account of Irish historical wrongs was not so far removed from Goldsmith's wish among the swains to show his book-learnt skill. But the informal, often unacknowledged, and even unrecognized leaning on the past is a different matter. The growing urbanization of Ireland will bring novel twists to this activity. It is unlikely to end it.

'*En avant,* then', remarked Hercule Poirot at the commencement of yet another investigation, but added, on reflection: '*Non.* To the contrary. *En arrière.'*

Portrait of Christ – a page from the Book of Kells which the visitor can see at Trinity College, Dublin (photo, Tom Hayde)

Antiquities
Liam de Paor

In a way history has not been kind to antiquities in Ireland. Elsewhere there are cathedrals, churches or mansions which have been in continuous use since they were first built in the Middle Ages, and one may still watch a bull-fight in a Roman amphitheatre. In Ireland, however, wars, rebellions and religious conflict have rendered such material continuity extremely rare: everywhere ruin has supervened. And yet, although the country is full of ruins, total destruction is less common than elsewhere. Gutted buildings have been abandoned, but not pulled down as they would have been in thriftier, tidier places. The mill which has ground no corn for almost a century, the railway station with no railway, the police barrack burnt out by the IRA in 1920 – they all remain, draughty and roofless, choked with nettles and overgrown with ivy. And until very recent times the farmer has ploughed around the rath, the ancient mound or the ruined megalith, not grudging the piece of his field which they have rendered unusable. As a result Ireland is, comparatively speaking, extraordinarily rich in 'field-monuments' of the past.

Such monuments often have local names, and sometimes legends to amplify the names. In many parts of the country if you enquire for 'the giant's grave', the people will point out a structure of great grey weathered stones rising from the bracken of a hill-slope. In one of Ireland's earliest written documents, an account of St Patrick's journeys written in the seventh century by a man called Tirechan, there is a story about such a tomb. It was discovered somewhere near the river Moy in Co Mayo by disciples of Patrick who came to the saint and said they found it difficult to believe that so huge a man had ever lived. Patrick offered to prove to them that he had. He performed a miracle, opening the tomb and resurrecting the giant, who told them his name – and that he had been murdered a hundred years before. Declining his offer to accompany them – on the grounds that he would strike terror into all who saw him – Patrick's company baptized the giant and sent him back to his grave.

The interesting point about this fantastic story is that the author, who is here writing about his own part of the country, includes in it a brief but accurate description of a tomb, one hundred and twenty feet long

33

A Donegal cottage with its peat stack

and built of great stones, such as may still be seen today in a number of examples in the same neighbourhood, as well as elsewhere. These were already three thousand years old when Tirechan wrote, and are among the oldest of Ireland's monumental antiquities.

The earliest inhabitants of the country, who arrived some thousands of years earlier still, were shore-dwelling fishers and hunters who left no enduring structures and who yield evidence of their occupation only to the archaeologist's spade. But some time about 3,000 BC groups of farmers began to arrive, travelling by sea from the continental mainland, and they brought with them ideas and rituals, ultimately of Mediterranean origin, which demanded the construction of huge and elaborate structures for the disposal of the dead. Such megalithic chambered tombs, known from various parts of Mediterranean and Atlantic Europe, are unusually numerous in Ireland, where they represent several different traditions. The tomb in Tirechan's story would seem, from his description, to belong to the class nowadays called court cairns. These tombs, possibly embodying the earliest megalithic tradition in Ireland, were built throughout the northern half of the country, but are especially numerous around Kilalla Bay, near Carlingford Lough, in Co Donegal, and across south Ulster. The builders laid out a long straight-sided mound, usually in the form of a trapeze, with a revetment or retaining wall to hold back the mound material. In this they incorporated an open court, sometimes in the centre but much more commonly at one end. The curving wall of the court was faced with great upright stones and gave access to megalithic galleries which ran into the body of the mound. Burials, sometimes cremated, sometimes inhumed, were placed in the galleries and the court no doubt served as the setting for such ceremonies as were associated with them. The tombs were collective, not individual, and the numbers still remaining suggest that enough may have been built to accommodate the whole neolithic population of the region over a period of some hundreds of years.

The mounds or cairns of stones which covered these tombs are usually found to be more or less denuded, and the megalithic structures themselves have often been damaged or partly demolished in the course of time, with the result that the scale of these monuments often fails to impress, especially on first sight and at a distance. Nonetheless, a visit to the excavated and well conserved tomb of Creevykeel, conveniently adjacent to the main road from Sligo to Bundoran, or to the great ruined galleries of Carnanmore, set in the wild scenery of Glencolumbkille in Co Donegal, cannot fail to strike even the most casual visitor with their ancient grandeur.

Megalithic tombs of other traditions are often more immediately impressive. Among these the passage graves are outstanding. These are covered with round cairns, built usually on hilltop sites, and commonly grouped in cemeteries. They vary considerably in size. There is as a rule a megalithic kerb to retain the mound, and the burial chamber, under the cairn, is approached by a megalithic roofed passage. The most important cemetery is situated in the bend of the river Boyne, a few miles upstream from Drogheda, and comprises three large cairns – at Newgrange, Knowth and Dowth, each covering almost an acre of ground – and many smaller tombs. Newgrange has long been recognized as one of the most spectacular prehistoric structures in western Europe, partly because of the great size of the artificial mound and the massive construction of the passage and the high domed burial chamber which (like many Irish passage graves) has three subsidiary chambers opening off it; partly too because of the wealth of engraved ornament – spirals, zigzags, meanders and other devices – on the mighty stones of the kerb and tomb structure. Indeed the Boyne cemetery and the large concentration of tombs on the bare hills of Lough Crew in north-west Co Meath form two richly furnished galleries of neolithic art. The art, which was no doubt ritual in purpose, has many parallels outside Ireland – as has the design of the tombs themselves – in Britanny, the Iberian peninsula and further afield, and the whole character of the passage-grave culture conveys the impression of a rural society founded by sea-borne immigrants who still preserved some traditions of a nascent urban civilization in the distant Mediterranean.

From the streets of Dublin one may glimpse the hills to the south of the city, where there is a somewhat scattered group of tombs. A large cemetery (without art) at Carrowkeel on Bricklieve mountain commands a wide view over that most beautiful of Irish counties, Sligo, and just to the south of Sligo town there is a large group of denuded tombs in the passage-grave tradition. This cemetery, at Carrowmore, is overlooked by the noble mountain of Knocknarea, breasting the Atlantic storms, on whose summit a tremendous unopened cairn, probably covering a passage grave, forms the centre of a small group of tombs. Yet another important group of passage graves may be seen on the hills of south and north-east Ulster.

Most of the chambered tombs of the type which Irish archaeologists call 'dolmens' (although the term has different meanings elsewhere) are thought to derive from the court cairns. These are usually totally denuded of the small mounds which would originally have covered them, so that the megalithic structure is fully exposed. A capstone, often extraordinarily massive, rests on a small arrangement of large uprights to form a relatively simple burial chamber. These simple but most striking monuments may be seen in many parts of Ireland. They are ⸻merous in the eastern counties and there is a complementary ⸻ss the Irish Sea in Wales.

A qui⸻nt megalithic funerary tradition, and, broadly speaking, a somewhat la⸻ne, is represented by another very numerous class of tombs found in ma⸻y parts of the island in areas especially of good pasture land. These are straight-sided galleries with double megalithic walls, shaped like a broad wedge on plan. Many have been excavated, and it seems that they represent a late megalithic funerary tradition, of Bronze Age rather than neolithic date. Usually little remains of the cairn, so that the main structure is exposed. A good example may be seen quite near Dublin, at Ballyedmonduff, and a number of examples of an interesting variant, conditioned by the locally available building material, may be seen in the Burren district of Co Clare. In the course of the long Bronze Age period burial customs changed: collective tombs were replaced by single graves. These were often inserted in mounds – sometimes natural mounds or ridges, sometimes the cairns of older megalithic tombs, sometimes earthen barrows specially built for the purpose. The graves were usually lined with fairly small stones to form a kind of box into which the body was inserted, in crouched position or reduced by cremation to a couple of pints of calcined bone. Pots and sometimes ornaments or other equipment accompany the burials. Towards the close of the prehistoric period burials, in general appear to have become simpler still and often there is no surface indication of their presence.

Tombs are not the only prehistoric megalithic structures to be seen in Ireland. Isolated standing stones are quite numerous, as are circles of such stones. The stone circles, related to similar monuments in France and Britain, have a wide range of date but belong predominantly to the Bronze Age. They were essentially ritual sites, or open-air temples. While there are no sites in Ireland that can be compared in elaboration with Stonehenge, in England, there are a number that are fully monumental in scale. The larger circle at Grange, near Lough Gur, Co Limerick, has a massive outer bank supporting a ring of immense stones enclosing a space 150 feet in diameter. This is but one of a number of circles concentrated in this area, and such concentrations occur in other regions: on peat-covered hilltops in Co Tyrone, on the western slope of the Wicklow hills, in the west Cork area and elsewhere. They vary considerably in size and character. The west Cork circles, as exemplified by the excavated site of Drombeg, have one horizontal or recumbent stone diametrically opposed by a pair of standing stones taller than the others. Sometimes, as at Athgreany, Co Wicklow, there is an outlying stone apart from the main circle. There are some apparently ritual enclosures which are marked not by a stone circle but by an earthen bank: outstanding among these is the Giant's Ring in Co Down, which has a megalithic tomb at its centre. Isolated standing stones probably varied in purpose as well as in their date of erection. In north Co Kildare two exceptionally tall monuments of this kind appear to have marked Bronze Age graves. The custom of erecting such stones was being practised at the beginning of Christian times as we know from the 'conversion' of some of them by the addition of an engraved cross, or from the series of stones with *ogham* inscriptions. *Ogham* is a form of writing, based on the alphabet, in which the letters are represented by strokes, up to five in number, cut across or on either side of a stem line. The inscriptions, in an early form of Irish, give the name of a person followed by the name of an ancestor. These are very numerous in the counties of the southern seaboard, but are much rarer elsewhere in the country. They are found also in areas of Irish overseas colonization in the early historic period, especially in Wales.

While the populations of Ireland in neolithic times and during the Bronze Age constructed elaborate and enduring tombs and ritual centres, they built far less permanent dwellings for themselves, usually of wood and other perishable materials, and even when a house stood in an enclosed site few traces as a rule remain on the surface: these dwellings can be revealed and studied only through excavation. Lake-dwellings, however, some of which date from the close of the Bronze Age, can often be detected by superficial observation. An artificial island was constructed in or on the margins of the waters of a lake, with layers of stones and brushwood forming a platform for the wooden buildings. The tradition of building in lakes continued, or was renewed, in the early historic period, when the structures were known by the Irish word *crannog* (from *crann*, a tree or pole). Crannogs may be seen in many lakes. A remarkable concentration of them was revealed in Lough Gara, on the borders of counties Roscommon and Sligo, when the lake was partly drained a number of years ago. It is often impossible to tell, without excavation, to which period a crannog belongs: some were built and rebuilt at widely separated dates.

At the time when our written records begin, in the fifth century AD, it is clear that the population of Ireland spoke Irish. This is one of the Celtic group of languages, related to British and Gaulish, and its existence as a vernacular must be the result of a sizeable immigration from some part of Celtic Europe. But when we turn to the material evidence at present available we find it very difficult to pinpoint this immigration. Some specimens of recognizably 'Celtic' metalwork have been found, often of high quality, but in limited areas of the country – in Ulster and in the Shannon region. Celt monuments in stone are found in the same two areas. At Turoe, Co Galway, and Castlestrange, Co Roscommon, there are carved monumental stones of a somewhat phallic appearance, covered with engraved abstract curvilinear designs in a variant La Tène style. In the neighbourhood of Armagh were a number of barbaric-looking figures of gods, some of which have been gathered into Armagh cathedral, and similar figures may be seen on Boa Island in Lough Erne, Co Fermanagh.

The great field monuments of Celtic societies in Britain and on the Continent are the tribal centres – *oppida* or hill-forts. There are equivalent monuments in Ireland, but they are relatively few and they exhibit, in comparison with the British and continental examples, some interesting peculiarities, often having the appearance of ritual rather than defensive structures. They often occupy sites known from historic documents or sagas to have been royal centres: Ailech, Co Donegal, Tara, Co Meath, Knockaulin, Co Kildare, Navan, Co Meath. Promontory forts on the other hand, formed by constructing defensive earthworks or stone walls across the neck of a small peninsula, are numerous all around the coasts and are usually thought to be of the Iron Age. Fine examples may be seen on the Antrim coast, and again on the Dingle Peninsula in Co Kerry. Some promontory forts were constructed inland. For the able-bodied it is well worth the strenuous scramble up to the summit of Caherconree, near the butt of the Dingle Peninsula, to see the stone-walled promontory fort built on a narrow ridge which commands a tremendous view of north Kerry from the lakes of Killarney to the Blasket Islands and the distant hills of Clare.

St Patrick and other missionaries arrived in Ireland from the Roman Empire in the fifth century, converting the people to Christianity and bringing with them many elements of Roman culture including the Latin alphabet and language, but Roman armies never attempted the conquest of Ireland. Prehistoric traditions and culture lived on, modified but not radically altered by Roman Christianity. The characteristic, and extremely numerous, antiquity of this period is the rath, or ring-fort, an enclosure, roughly circular, often with a raised interior, surrounded by a bank and an external ditch. Occasionally the bank-and-ditch defences are multiplied, and the evidence of early texts suggests that these were the raths of kings or chiefs. The rath is simply the enclosed homestead of a farmer of the early historic period or perhaps somewhat earlier. In many parts of the country, in later times, they became associated in the popular imagination with supernatural beings – some are still locally referred to as 'fairy forts' – and partly because of this there was until very recently a strong prejudice against interfering with them. As a result, many thousands still remain, and they may be seen in almost any part of Ireland. Enclosed dwelling sites were constructed in quite early prehistoric times and it is not always easy to distinguish these from the raths of the first millennium AD, but the earlier structures have usually left much slighter surface indications. Less numerous but broadly contemporary enclosures defended by massive unmortared stone walls also occur, especially in western areas where stone was readily available, while wood and even earth were relatively scarce. The fort of Ailech, Co Donegal, seat of northern kings, is well preserved on its hilltop overlooking Lough Foyle and Lough Swilly. A well defended gateway tunnels through the broad base of the wall, there are mural chambers, and flights of steps on the interior lead up to the broad rampart walk. The very similar structure of Staigue, Co Kerry, has a feature unusual in the stone forts – an outer ditch around the stone wall. Stone forts are numerous in Co Clare and on the Aran Islands. The Aran forts, especially Dun Aonghusa, are peculiarly impressive largely because of their setting on magnificent cliffs rising from the Atlantic. Some of the Clare and Aran forts have an additional defence in the form of *chevaux de frise,* a kind of broad thicket of upright stones closely set before the wall. The date of these structures is uncertain. One of the Clare forts which has been excavated, Cahercommaun, was found to be relatively late – well into the Christian period – but monuments like Dun Aonghusa have features which suggest comparison especially with Iberian forts of the Early Iron Age.

We have almost no material evidence for the churches and other buildings erected by the first Christian missionaries, but in the course of the sixth century the Irish Church assumed a monastic character, and we can see that the early monasteries had much in common with secular structures. Here again we must reckon with the different survival rates of timber and stone. Of some of the great and populous monasteries, such as Clonard, Co Meath, virtually nothing can be seen on the ground, although air photographs often reveal traces of the ancient complex of buildings. But some of the smaller establishments on the western seaboard, where stone was the building material, survive sufficiently intact to form some of the most remarkable monuments in existence from the formative period of mediaeval European civilization. It is a boat journey of some twelve miles over the open Atlantic swell from Valentia in Co Kerry to the Great Skellig, a pyramid-shaped rock where tens of thousands of sea birds have made their habitation. Here too, some thirteen hundred years ago, Irish monks built a small monastery, perched like a precarious nest six hundred feet above the waves, and they carved flights of steps from the rock to give access from the skin coracles tossing on the broken water below. The steps may still be climbed: beyond the gateway that cuts through the dry-built enclosure wall the monastery still stands, as if the monks had just left it for a few hours to go fishing on the sea which formed the background to their lives. Half a dozen large stone huts huddle together in the inner enclosure, domed like beehives with corbel vaults constructed without mortar. Their doorways face two small oratories of similar construction; a large rough-hewn cross, almost like a prehistoric standing stone, rises in the middle of the enclosure, and a small graveyard bristles with stone slabs incised with simple crosses.

All along the west coast similar island monasteries may be seen, in less perfect states of preservation. On Illauntannig, off Tralee Bay, a monastery very like Skellig is surrounded by a circular stone wall. This is a flat grassy island and the enclosure is much more spacious than that of Skellig. Inishmurray, off the Sligo coast, has a similar circular stone enclosure. While the buildings are less well preserved here, the monastery is remarkable for the variety of incised slabs and small boulders that are to be seen. Most have crosses of diverse forms engraved on them. A few have Irish inscriptions asking prayers for the dead. In such sites, where most of a small monastic complex survives, and in isolated buildings and monuments elsewhere we can trace the emergence from the prehistoric past of a new and lively culture, in which ancient traditions are blended with Christian and other foreign influences. At Gallarus, Co Kerry, there is an oratory corbel-built like those on Skellig, but using mortar, and refined in structure and finish. At St MacDara's Island, off the Connemara coast, a further stage of development may be seen in a little church which draws on native traditions of building in both stone and wood. It is a simple gabled building, with mortared joints, copying the appearance of wooden churches in the *antae,* or projections of the side walls at the end, which are carried up the gable as a projecting barge, and in the treatment of the roof to give the appearance of a covering of shingles. The roof in fact is of stone and of corbel construction. Such mortared stone churches were probably first built in the eighth and ninth centuries, but the style continued for hundreds of years. The simple slab-cross of Skellig, too, provided the basis for elaboration and refinement. At Fahan, Co Donegal, a great dressed stone slab is richly carved in low relief with crosses and figures and ornamented with a variety of seventh century motifs, including interlacing. Some miles to the north the tall slab-cross of Carndonagh, reminiscent in its shape of the simple monument at Skellig, is similarly finished and ornamented. It is flanked by curious low pillars with incised figure drawings, secular, ecclesiastical and apparently mythological.

Putting together the evidence of various sites and written sources, we can see that the monastery in early historic Ireland was, depending on size, a village or a city, enclosed by some kind of wall and containing dwellings, small churches (which were increased not in size but in number as the community grew large), workshops, forges, mills and other offices, a graveyard with inscribed slabs, and carved crosses standing in the open. In a community which was otherwise wholly rural, these were the towns. They were not in general withdrawn from the world, since they served the religious needs of the country around; nor were they purely ecclesiastical, since they housed pilgrims, students, and tenants and workers of various kinds. They were the centres which produced the elaborate and meticulous manuscript painting and ornmental metalwork of the seventh, eighth and ninth centuries.

It was probably the monasteries which served as the main means of change in the period which saw not only Viking raids and invasions but also the Carolingian renascence on the Continent. At any rate it is by visiting the great monastic sites that we can best see how prehistoric traditions gradually faded out of Irish culture to be replaced by traditions which had much more in common with early mediaeval Europe as a whole. The process can be traced in various ways. At Clonmacnoise,

Co Offaly, a magnificent series of inscribed grave-slabs (which is without parallel elsewhere) spans the period from the seventh to the twelfth century and forms, in itself, a compendium of stylistic change. But in stone the free-standing cross probably best registers the change. In the Suir valley, at Athenny, Co Tipperary, and Killamery, Co Kilkenny, beautiful eighth-century crosses may be seen, no longer slab-like but carved fully in the round. There is some figure carving, chiefly on the cross-base, but the main ornament is abstract and decorative – clearly modelled on the styles and forms evolved by the metalworkers. Soon however, as may be seen at Kells, Co Meath, or Castledermot and Moone, Co Kildare, the carvers were employing more strictly sculptural models and a Carolingian iconography in figure-carving. The noble early tenth-century monuments at Monasterboice and Clonmacnoise anticipate full Romanesque schemes of religious figure-sculpture while retaining as subsidiary ornament many Irish motifs. At about the same time architectural ideas were being imported and put into practice in a distinctive way. The round towers, most Irish of monuments, to be seen at numerous monastic sites, are in fact but slightly modified versions of the free-standing belfries of early mediaeval Europe.

A period of reform and innovation in the eleventh and twelfth centuries formed the basis for the large-scale introduction of continental styles and ideas on the eve of the twelfth-century Anglo-Norman invasion of Ireland. An elaborate small Romanesque church was built in 1134 by Cormac Mac Carthaigh, King of Desmond, on the Rock of Cashel, where it forms part of the most spectacular group of mediaeval buildings in Ireland. Its example was widely followed, but Irish Romanesque churches remained small and structurally simple. They are distinguished by great enrichment and elaboration of ornamental carving on doorways and chancel arches, among the finest examples of which are the doorways of Clonfert, Co Galway, and Killeshin, Co Laois, and the doorway and chancel arch of the Nuns' Church at Clonmacnoise. In this period too the first monasteries of the continental type were built. The foundation of Mellifont, Co Louth, in 1142, marked the introduction to Ireland of the foreign order of monks which was to take root most successfully, the Cistercians. Little more than the foundations, which have been excavated, remain here, although the site is of great historical interest, but much more extensive ruins of Cistercian buildings of the later twelfth century may be seen at Jerpoint, Co Kilkenny, Boyle, Co Roscommon, and Abbeyknockmoy, Co Galway. The Irish tradition in stone-carving, exemplified in these buildings, continued to flourish and to develop in the west while much of the country was being over-run by the Anglo-Norman invaders. The work of the western school of sculpture, which came to an end about 1230, can best be viewed in the varied work on the doorways and cloister arcade of Cong Abbey, Co Mayo.

41

The invaders, as in England a century earlier, constructed as their first works flat-topped mounds crowned by timber fortifications, with adjoining palisaded enclosures, and these motte-and-bailey defences, less the wooden buildings, are still numerous. About the year 1200 they began to build large castles of stone. Two of the earliest and largest remain as impressive ruins at Trim, Co Meath, and Carrickfergus, Co Antrim. They built cathedrals and churches too, in Early English style, often importing stone or carved work from Wales or England. Many of the mediaeval cathedrals have been partly rebuilt in modern times after a period of decay or ruin, but there is usually interesting thirteenth-century work to be seen in them. The fourteenth century was a period of famine, war and plague, in which little building was done. The Anglo-Norman attempt at conquest had failed and over much of the country dispossessed Irish families began to return to their lands. A lively and original Hiberno-Norman culture came into being to flourish over a large part of Ireland throughout the fifteenth and part of the sixteenth centuries. It has endowed the Irish landscape with two very character-istic features: tower houses, which are numerous in most parts of the country, and late mediaeval friaries, which are to be seen mostly in the west. The tower house is a stone building of four or more storeys, lightly fortified and crowned with stepped battlements, and usually with an attached walled courtyard or bawn. This type of building is particularly common in the area around the lower Shannon, although examples which are really well preserved, complete with the bawn, are comparatively rare. Two of the best preserved are in south Co Galway, at Pallas and at Dungory. The Franciscan friary of the fifteenth century is the triumph of the Irish feeling for architectural design manifest in late Gothic, intimate in scale and character, original in detail, especially sculptured detail, and elegant in its setting in the landscape, with, as main accent, the slender tapering tower which reflects ancient traditions. At Quin, Co Clare and at Ross Errilly, Co Galway, ruined but almost intact friaries may be seen.

The middle ages in Ireland came to an end in a further period of bitter warfare and destruction, as the country was conquered for the English crown. This time a major cultural break occurred: the language of the country changed, and with it one social system was replaced by another. But the process of fusion of old traditions with new continued, as it still continues. Reminders of the past are perhaps more numerous in Ireland than in most places, and perhaps partly because of this the attention of the Irish has often seemed to be too much directed to the past. This may be less true nowadays, but the monuments remain, and there is no town or village in the country from which a wide range of antiquities may not be seen in an hour's drive.

The Two Languages

Máire Cruise O'Brien

> 1. *The Irish language as the national language is the first official language.*
>
> 2. *The English language is recognised as a second official language.*
>
> CONSTITUTION OF IRELAND, *Article* 8.

i. Origins

Old Irish is the earliest Celtic language that can be reconstructed from written sources. From the eighth and ninth centuries onwards, when the scholarship of Irish monks preserved the oldest surviving material, an unbroken literary tradition connects it with the present day. Through its initial contact with Christianity the language when we first meet it is already to some degree Latinized, but many distinctive features foreign to the English – and indeed the non-Celtic – European speech-sense have continued on into Irish today producing a sense of the exotic which is readily confused with the archaic. This, of course, where modern Irish is concerned is entirely subjective. Irish in so far as it survives at all is just as much a contemporary language as any other now spoken. It is true that writers in Irish in their time have often been conscious archaisers, but this, as appears to be the rule in analogous conditions, is offset by unconscious innovation. It is worth noting in this context that Ireland does not represent the first point of contact of English with the Celtic languages. The Angles, Saxons and Jutes had already lived out their own languages-in-contact situation with the original Celtic-speaking inhabitants of Britain centuries before the Norman invasion of Ireland.

The substance of the tradition involved, on the other hand, does justify a sense of the antique. Transmitted by Christian hands, it is often pre-Christian in origin, older therefore at least than the fifth century of our era, and, if we take into account the time-lag inherent in the expansion of cultures from the centre to the borders, it leads back with startling immediacy to the Celtic world that preceded the Roman conquest of Western Europe, the world of the waggon-burials of Halstatt and the chariot-chieftains of La Tène. To this antique tradition there clings

43

nevertheless an extraordinary freshness, as from the morning of time, a vividness and spontaneity which have captivated generations of half-incredulous scholars drawn to its study by many motives other than the pursuit of literary enchantment. You will find the equivalent of this judgment, indeed almost the identical phrases, in practically every account of Celtic literature you take up. One notable exception is recorded: 'All Celtic literature is folklore and all folklore is at bottom obscene.'

Ancient Ireland, perhaps, could not be described as a nation; it was rather, like Homer's Achaia or the complex of the Akan peoples of West Africa, the centre of a universe, an organic if loosely-knit cultural and linguistic system within which a man's sense of identity comprised the cosmos. To our view of the course of history this little world is peripheral; to its inhabitants it was central, indeed unique, and events outside its compass were vague and irrelevant. For example, the immediate effects of the Roman conquest of Britain in terms of movements of peoples, at a time when the Celtic dialects of the two islands are believed to have been mutually intelligible, can be deduced with some degree of probable correspondence to fact from Irish sources, but there appears to have been no recognition of the implications of the Empire's existence nor later of its decay which left the island of Britain open to, among other invaders, the Irish. A group of peoples, whose conception of life for centuries had included mass migration, cattle herding and local conquest, was still on the move, resettling and readjusting within the territory available. The circumstances which halted the spread of conquest where it did halt, and the consequences of this for the survival of their way of life, do not seem to have preoccupied them at the time, or indeed much at all ever since! When the mediaeval passion for schematization reached Ireland the gentlemen whom we somewhat unkindly call 'the synthetic historians' calmly dovetailed as much as they felt to be acceptable of the Judaeo-Christian-Classical background with which they had become familiar into their Hiberno-centred chronologies and topographies, without in any way upsetting the primacy of local notions as to relative importance.

The earliest Irish society which we can envisage from the myth and hero-tales which survive was aristocratic, pagan and tribal. We associate it with a material culture of an early Iron-age type and with chariot-fighting kings and warriors like those of the Celtic tombs and sculpture of Gaul and of Britain. Its virtues were the stereotyped heroic virtues: personal courage, honour, of which perhaps the term 'face' gives a more accurate concept, and generosity; its concomitant savagery and cruelty appear to have been early offset by an intense sense of beauty and by the status consequently accorded to artists, artisans and artificers, among whom pride of place went to the learned caste. Wealthy, privileged, feared and respected, they are in essence Caesar's druids and the source of their power is supernatural. They are poets, historians, jurists and physicians, but they are also priests and thaumaturges, and to a great extent already, in the form in which the records reach us – one of the many qualifications which must be understood to accompany all general statements in an attempt of this type to convey simply and clearly what is actually complex and incomplete – the function of the poet subsumes the rest. The very name of poet in Irish is etymologically the equivalent of the English 'seer'. In classical accounts of British and continental druids we sense already that pragmatism allied to conservatism which, when we study Irish history, emerges as the distinguishing characteristic of a culture showing, in the face of peculiarly unpropitious circumstances, a remarkably high propensity to survive.

The first real test it must have stood, after the respite from Latin dominance, would be the introduction of Christianity. Traditionally there is an almost bloodless and deeply moving acceptance by the Gael of the new faith. There is no reason to doubt the main substance of this belief, but the records do indicate, though usually only implicitly, controversy and compromise between the old and the new. If the tribal fabric had to make adjustments, the territorial basis of Roman Church government on its side became also so relaxed as almost to be abandoned and the poets kept their privileges, though it was a close-run thing. Many of them adopted the new discipline and became clerics and there seems to have been a general convention that the supernatural part of their powers could be legitimately exercised only within Christian orders, although still dormant and to be feared in the lay practitioner of their art. The happy synthesis arrived at is epitomised in the figure of Colmcille (Columba, the founder of Iona) as he is revealed to us in history and in legend, certainly the most attractive of the Irish saints. A prince and a scholar and subject in his youth to the temptations of both these arrogant classes, the name bestowed on him in his pious childhood, 'Dove of the Church', came to reflect the essential, but by no means insipid, gentleness of his mature years. He united in his person the old learning and the new, and established that polarity between asceticism and humanism which is such a disarming feature of the Celtic Church. His Latin verse is historically attested; in the vernacular as many as two hundred poems are ascribed to him and, while all of these must be taken to be dramatic lyrics put into his mouth by later poets, it is inconceivable that they should not reflect a reality where the permanent respect and affection in which he is held by the literary caste stem in no small part from his personal competence in their specialty. The Convention of Drumceat in 597 sees the poetic order threatened with suppression by the Christian establishment. The role of mediator and defender of the poets falls to Colmcille, and a *modus vivendi* is achieved for them within society. It is a clear manifestation of the spirit informing the early Irish Christian schools which feared neither 'the lure of Apollo

45

nor the temptations of grammar'. The same beneficent spirit continuing to radiate from Colmcille's Iona through Northumbria seems also to have fostered the growth of the first English vernacular literature over a hundred years later.

So in due course, with such reserves, excisions and euhemerizations as are only reasonable, the pagan myth and saga, still primarily an oral canon, work their way into the repertory of the monasteries and are ultimately committed to writing in the monastic scriptoria. Meanwhile, a lovely personal lyric note, deeply at one with the natural world, is born of the Latin hymn metres and the old tongue, and for both king and cleric, sophisticated romances interspersed with lyric interludes embroider the early themes or embody fresh ones. Other crises loom and are surmounted. The terror and destruction of the period of Viking raid and settlement produce a conscious, if not always well-judged, renaissance. The partial conquest by the Normans seems, in spite of the efforts of the central power from London, rather to favour than otherwise poetry in the Irish mode: the great Earls' tenure of their 'swordland' is legitimized in praise-poems by professional Irish court poets and the foreigners in return introduce the troubadour love-song from the continent. The dignified style of Irish classical verse is perfected and maintained in Ireland and in the Highlands of Scotland for more than three centuries. Tudor and Elizabethan politicians recognize the role of the bard as a trouble-maker, and the overt attack on the Gaelic way of life is intensified and systematized. It is time to take serious stock of the second language in Ireland.

ii. Co-existence

The history of the English language in Ireland begins with the colonists who followed the first Norman-French- and Welsh-speaking invaders. These established themselves in the towns and by the thirteenth century there was a distinct Anglo-Irish dialect, now known as Mediaeval Anglo-Irish, which survives in some manuscript material. It did not thrive, but became rapidly extinct in the countryside and fought a losing battle even in the towns. When Henry VIII was proclaimed King in Dublin the proclamation was read in Irish to the Irish Lords by the Duke of Ormond in his own translation, he being the leader of the 'English Party' in the Parliament of Ireland and the only member of the House to speak both languages. The state papers abound in ordnances directing the King's subjects to avoid such practices as speaking Irish and to adhere to such others as shaving the upper lip! Ironically, if this Anglo-Irish survives at all today it is only in the speech of the impoverished and uneducated descendants of the original burghers, a very small proportion of the present urban population. The new middle class is rarely more than a generation or two established in the towns, comes of country stock and speaks what has been christened by a leading authority in the field Common Anglo-Irish, based largely on the rural dialects of recent growth and much influenced by Standard English. The point has been made that this is a class rather than a regional dialect: its distinctive features represent a common denominator of all Irish dialects of English.

The Cromwellian plantation in the seventeenth century saw the establishment of a new English stock with a very high survival value. Irish which, even after the collapse of the old social order with the Flight of the Earls (1603) at the time of the 'Old Queen's' death, had remained the language of the overwhelming majority of the people, began to retreat significantly. On the eve of the Great Famine (1845–50) it was still spoken as their first language by between half and two-thirds of the population; estimates vary. Within the next hundred years it had dropped vertiginously to the present approximate 30,000 or 1 per cent of the population. Accordingly, the first post-famine generation remaining in Ireland, as distinct from those forced to emigrate, are the first bilinguals on any considerable scale (Irish lords under Elizabeth, as present-day romantics love to remember, could be bi-lingual in Gaelic and Latin!). The English they learnt would be that of their neighbours of Cromwellian planter stock. They adapted the seventeenth century English to their native sound-systems and in-built feeling for syntactical effectiveness; the speech of their children is the direct ancestor, the author would hazard, of as high as 90 per cent of the English spoken today in Ireland outside those parts of Ulster where, for a different set of historical reasons, the regional variety of English presents distinct and independent features. The Irish sound-system, which is at the base of all Irish dialect speech today, acted as a type of selection grid for the realization of English phonemes producing those features most commonly sought to be reproduced in English fiction: lightly voiced consonants, frequent devoicing even of vowels and the distinctive Gaelic symmetrical opposition of palatal to velar quality. Shakespeare's Celtic fringe-characters speak this way. Unfamiliar sounds were equated to native ones, but where seventeenth century English provided sounds which coincided with the Irish system these were adopted and tenaciously preserved. Hence, for example, the classical Anglo-Irish 'tay', 'say', 'lafe' for 'tea', 'sea', 'leaf'.

iii. The submerged centuries

Before however the linguistic retreat began in earnest, in that baleful, apocalyptic time for Ireland that followed the Flight of the Earls, the impulse of the counter-reformation in Europe, allied with an extraordinarily clear and tragic sense of the end of an era in Ireland, produced the great scholarly flowering of the Irish Franciscan order in Donegal

47

and in Louvain. Of this the principal monuments are Colgan's *Lives of the Irish Saints* (in Latin) and the *Annals of the Four Masters*.

They are called four and perhaps they would not like to be sundered. Their names were Michael O Clery, Peregrine O Clery, Cogitosus O Mulconry and Peregrine O Duigenan – the two Peregrines have a mournful ring of exile to them – but the greatest of the four was Michael O Clery, 'the poor brother' as he styled himself and as he has been known affectionately to generations of Irishmen since. For fifteen years he tramped Ireland searching, copying, collating, gathering together, with a clear-sighted courage born of despair, all that store of learning that in his view 'future generations would not willingly let die'. The quotation, lest the context should lead to misunderstanding, is from Milton. He founded a tradition, the end of which he could not foresee, but which, patient and enduring, survived the centuries underground and almost miraculously, it now seems, brought safe its precious burden to the light of day. There is often an almost unbearable pathos about the later manuscripts in the Irish collections; again and again in the colophons as recently as the 1840s the scribe, perhaps a hedge-school-master, perhaps a small-tradesman or farmer, even an itinerant labourer, records his conscious intention of preserving the learning of Ireland and – in the light of that noble aim – solicits the reader to forgive his errors. Even at that late date many such conservationists must have died without knowing that they had not worked in vain and their predecessors can have seen the future only with the eye of faith. That their hopes were fulfilled beyond all reasonable expectation is certain; it is equally certain that they would have found the manner of their fulfilment very strange.

The debt that Irish studies owe to the great European philologists, French and German, is generally acknowledged; a corollary to their major achievements was undoubtedly that of rendering the Celtic languages, divorced from their subversive presents, suitable subjects for study by gentlemen in our insular universities – in both islands. It is not so widely realized that in the first half of the nineteenth century, before Catholic Emancipation, the native tradition itself, unaided, produced two formidable scholars whose immense industry and mastery of the Irish language, their mother tongue, can be said, without exaggeration, to have laid the foundations for all work in that field since their day. Yet both John O Donovan and Eugene O Curry – they were close friends and brothers-in-law – could in their youth, have served as the prototype for Carleton's poor scholar. Neither had any formation beyond what the country school and – in the home – the traditional local poet, story-teller and scribe could offer; O Curry's brother was himself a recognized local poet. Then fortune, in the shape of the British Ordnance Survey, intervened and placed at their disposal the equivalent of a University education, access to all the Irish manuscript resources of Great Britain

48

and Ireland. Both died in the early 1860s, so that once again, as with the Four Masters, when disaster – in this case the Famine – threatened the whole basis of the national consciousness, the extraordinary caste of the traditional learned men of Ireland, whose origins, as we saw, go back in time beyond Caesar's druids, had taken steps again to ensure the survival of its heritage. Before, however, the fruits of their devotion could reach their own people – some enabling catalyst was needed.

Young Ireland and the Fenian Movement drew a certain inspiration from the vanished glories of Erin as brought to light by the O Curry-O Donovan circle – indeed the Fenian name testifies to this – but it was in no way central to their purposes; there were other and more immediate issues. After the Fenian Rising, the excitement and rigour of the Land War, the triumph and tragedy of Parnell fill the scene, but meanwhile the seed of the old learning has quickened in an extraordinary way and as in the mediaeval story the barren staff breaks in blossom.

iv. Anglo-Ireland as an agent of Revival

The Protestant community in Ireland had no other home. Settled for centuries in most cases, augmented by native stock, they were bound to the Irish scene by all the normal human pieties as well as by the interests of a dominant caste. Generosity among them could not but turn to Irish patriotism – as the roll of those names that kept the spirit of Irish separatism alive testifies. Consistently the pressure to identify with Ireland seems to have been intensified by the fact that they were never entirely accepted in English society. They had grown into a provincial class to which, in England, it was not wholly advantageous to belong; in Ireland they could lead. Rejected as being Irish by the English, the more passionate and stormy spirits among them tended to become even more strongly what they were in fact already in all but formal loyalties, Irish. Among the vehicles adopted to effect the final transition, the closest identification, was the Irish language. The children of the minor Protestant ascendancy, in particular, growing up in the country which was still in many parts Irish-speaking, in parsonages or isolated demesnes, benefitting often from a benevolent neglect due to genteel penury or family difficulties, unhappy at their English schools, these were often Gaelic in speech from their earliest years, or at least in their alienation and loneliness felt that they ought to be and strove to become so. Charles Lever has left us a moving portrait of such a youngster in 'Tom Burke of Ours' and there are glimpses of him in Thackeray and in George Borrow, and of course in Somerville and Ross. The description is almost tailored to fit the superb picaresque figure of Standish Hayes O Grady, but it will suit, or partially suit, others of the group: the small unhappy Yeats running, illiterate, wild through Sligo with his two dogs; or Hyde the clergyman's gentle and retiring son; or the young

49

Parading for the Curragh Derby

Lady Gregory, 'an unpaid social worker on her father's estate', as her biographer has put it. There is the tormented little Synge afraid of the dark and of hell; or, oddest of all, the infant James Stephens, a Protestant pauper and juvenile delinquent at the age of six. In all cases the circumstantial compulsions towards a foster-identification are very clear.

Standish Hayes O Grady was born in 1832, of an old native princely stock long gone over to the Establishment, and the son of a British Admiral. He was educated at Rugby and at Trinity College, Dublin and was bi-lingual in English and Irish. Irish was a recognized subject in Trinity practically since Elizabeth's time, primarily because of its utility in converting the heathen, but also, one must believe, a little bit for its own sake and a love, however suppressed, of things Irish generally. To this strange underworld of antiquaries, apprentice proselytizers and the broken remnants of an old culture, O Grady was drawn immediately, and from the first he seems to have suffused it with his own flaming energy. He took no degree, but while his name was still on the books of the College he was already a recognized authority in Irish manuscript studies. Characteristically, his first publication was an edition of the picaresque autobiographical verse romance *The Adventure of the Unfortunate Fellow* by an eighteenth century poet Donncha Rua MacConmara (Red Dennis MacNamara), whose name is a by-word in folk memory for wildness and general unreliability, cut from one cloth with the *Ciarraíoch Mallaithe,* the fierce Munsterman and the *Spailpín Fánach,* itinerant hired-hands and poets, reflected later in Colum and in Synge. Meanwhile, the editor grows restless in his turn, becomes a civil engineer, goes to America, mines for gold and runs a coasting schooner. He learns Arabic and works his passage to Australia. He stands for the chair of Celtic in Edinburgh which, perhaps not altogether surprisingly, he doesn't get. His application, presented with a directness faintly, but probably unintentionally, offensive to the University authorities, might still stand as a blue-print for the ideal School of Celtic Studies. In 1886 we find him working on the Catalogue of Irish Manuscripts in the British Museum. The first volume, for which he is responsible, is one of the most rewarding and entertaining commonplace books in the world. It abounds in witty and erudite comment, in illuminating full-length translations and in brilliant historical perspectives. Unfortunately, it proceeded slowly and was not, in the minds of the Trustees, a substitute for a good, anonymous anodyne working catalogue. They remonstrated with their employee. The legend goes that he put down his pen in the middle of a word and walked out, never to come back. It was his habit to spend his holidays with the North Sea fishing fleet! His publications and translations are the main conduit by which, directly, the saga literature and the mediaeval Irish world reached the Anglo-Irish movement.

O Grady was a translator of genius, entirely free of the element of condescension which it is difficult not to sense in some of his successors. His English is the English of the Irish gentleman, at once classical and idiosyncratic, with just that touch of the arrogant provincial which, paradoxically, is a common feature crystallizing the values of all independent Irish writing in English. It is the English of the later Yeats. It says unmistakeably, 'You be damned!' A typical annotation from his Catalogue of the Mss. in the British Museum is on an entry for the early fourteenth century in the Four Masters, an entry to the effect that a 'chief captain of the O Connells' had been burnt by one Rolfe MacMahon. O Grady writes, 'Such burning of individuals (by no means rare) was not carried out deliberately at the stake, but was simply incidental to legitimate arson, perpetrated in feud or in warfare'. To the same school, as it were, with similar antiquarian tastes, but with a milder and more governable personality, belongs Sir Samuel Ferguson. Ferguson's superb narrative verse retellings, in the same idiom as O Grady's, of the ancient stories, have been much undervalued as a factor in forming the style of Yeats. Yeats loved and admired Ferguson and never reneged on him, though one senses he became unsure and a little ashamed of the attachment later – a not uncommon fate for his enthusiasms. The cadences and alliterations of Ferguson and O Grady and a touch of the consciously antique in the diction, marvellously echo their originals. Nor is it fanciful to perceive here the 'tremulous Anglo-Irish note' attributed to Edmund Burke. Burke himself in his very early youth attended a hedge-school with his Papist cousins and must have spoken Irish. Epithets like Yeats's 'mackerel-crowded seas' abound in this material in descriptions of the Land of the Young (the Celtic other-world) and of kingdoms ruled by virtuous kings. His 'I came on a great house in the middle of the night' is only a late-comer in a long series of 'ruin' poems: metrically it is an Irish eighteenth century treatment; the theme, which is still productive in verse in Irish today, finds parallels, of course, in the earliest Anglo-Saxon poetry.

It has been fashionable to commiserate with the enthusiastic Irish youth endeavouring to learn his ancestral tongue, at the turn of the century, with only archaic legends and antiquarian treatises for texts – no Maupassant, no Ibsen. In fact, in the works of O Grady alone, as that acute and generous critic, Thomas MacDonagh (executed for his part in the 1916 Rising) has pointed out, the enthusiasts were introduced at once to much of what was most evocative in the corpus of traditional literature, superbly presented in a medium which they may have undervalued insofar as it was native to them. We now know how this inspiration was immediately and lastingly productive. The great symbolic figure of Cuchulain in Yeats' verse is still recognizably the old countryman's 'hero of the misty ages'. The Deirdre of the Abbey Theatre released from Synge's 'wormy parchment', is now for millions the type of tragic love. James Stephens was to continue uncannily the dialogue and humour, conscious and unconscious, of the anecdotes that enliven the great compendia of history and epic: '"One could not call them beautiful," said Fionn. "One could," said Conan, "but it would not be true."' A whole school of Irish comic writing down to Flann O Brien and Mervyn Wall was born with him.

A very important effect of the Celtic strain in the Anglo-Irish culture emerges, I think, at this point. The Gaelic supernatural, at least in the form in which it reaches us, is rich in mystery, but it is amystical. To the fashionable esotericism of Madame Blavatsky and the Golden Dawn, to the exalted and introverted symbolism of Blake, it opposed what Yeats has described, with a typical interaction of flux and reflux, as a mythology that was 'objective . . . well-born and independent'. Its topography was geographically established, its gods and heroes inhabited not only the borders of history, but tangibly identifiable mounds, rivers and trees. Their recorded characteristics were disconcertingly corporeal, their speech was racy and epigrammatic, their sartorial arrangements and physical appearance minutely catalogued. Long association with the Irish other-world could only serve to establish the feet more firmly in this. And so in the *Land of Heart's Desire* the butter is real; on *Baile's Strand* the Fool and the Blind Man steal not only the bread but the play from the pagan fates. No one now reads James Stephens' *Crock of Gold* for its painstaking Blakean system of symbols but for the exquisite picture of the children, the evocation of the Irish countryside, and the warm human comedy of the philosopher – the philosopher who is the portrait of the great arch-mystic himself, George Russell, Æ. Interrogating the Celtic Twilight for the secret that would make life meaningful, the seekers, as in some Voyage-Tale from the Bardic inventory, are drawn towards a country whose circumambient element is not twilight, but the endless everchanging light and colour of the terrestrial Irish scene. In any event with the coming of the folk-lorists, Douglas Hyde and Lady Gregory, the balance, in so far as it had favoured the heroic, was shortly to be redressed – so that when Lennox Robinson was later questioned as to whether he knew Gaelic, he was able to reply, 'Yes, if you will confine your conversation to kings and charioteers and the distance to Macroom.' He expresses the polarity very nicely.

An ironic enigma is the strangely impervious response of the young Synge to his first contacts with the world of Standish O Grady. That he should study Irish as a University subject at all may seem strange at first sight – until we remember the place of the language in the armoury of just such zealous evangelical low-churchmen as his mother's people had been. We learn from T. R. Henn that an uncle of Synge's had once thought of organizing a mission to the Aran Islands. Did he, one wonders, the Uncle, contemplate acquiring the Gaelic? At all events, Synge at Trinity took a prize in Irish, one of the specific endowments intended to encourage his clergyman-grandfather's 'war against popery in its thousand forms of wickedness'. He studied under a Parson Goodman, an ardent collector of folk-music and college friend of O Grady, who was later to become a legendary figure on the still Irish-speaking Dingle peninsula for his refusal to permit in his parish that form of proselytism, the exploitation of destitution for the greater glory of God, which was one of the uglier features of respectable Protestant reaction to the Irish Famine, and which, with typical rural distrust of the abstract, is known in our folk-speech generically to this day as 'The Soup'. But no charisma seems to have reached Synge. He speaks of 'an amiable old clergyman' who made him 'read a crabbed version of the New Testament and seemed to know nothing, or at least care nothing about the old literature of Ireland, or the fine folk-tales and folk-poetry of Munster and Connaught': a negative and nameless elder person and a boy almost entirely withdrawn from the adult world and above all from the world of the clergy, Catholic or Protestant. Even when years later Synge visits West Kerry he does not advert to Goodman's existence. Music, which might have proved a common interest, could only, in all probability, have driven them farther apart, for Synge's formal musical education seems to have closed his mind to the Irish mode. He speaks of the Aran islanders being unable to appreciate anything in his own playing on the fiddle other than the rhythm. Had he lived, such an acute and sympathetic intelligence as his must have realized in time the basis for the cross purposes: the non-correspondence of intervals. As it is, it seems as if Synge were perversely determined to come on the hidden Ireland by his own unaided instincts only, ignoring such bonds as already existed between it and his own class, and despising the advantages he might have enjoyed. Of how this course led him ultimately to Aran and the achievement that ensued, it would be superfluous to write. Synge did not think that Irish could survive, but he saw it as the express vocation of the revival to transfuse all that was good and native to the language into the English speech of Irishmen, both in substance and in expression, so as to feed the literature of the new nation. In the meantime he judged the Gaelic League to be useful for keeping the patient alive till the specialists were ready!

The coincidence in character between the two practical idealists of the movement, Dr Douglas Hyde and Lady Gregory, is interesting. It was from their labours, most of all, that the revival drew its 'Antaeus-like' quality – that contact with the life and language of the Irish country-side, which Abbey actors were later, irreverently, to call PQ, short for 'peasant quality'. In its degenerate forms it became a commodity not very clearly distinguishable from that stage-Irishness which the Abbey had been founded to counteract, but at its best it did embody, often instinctively, some important psychological truths bearing on the connection between culture and self-respect. Both Hyde and Lady Gregory

53

were people in whom considerable intellectual power and much talent were allied with principle, idealism and a capacity for conscientious hard work, the self-abnegating industry that makes the great folk-lorist and linguist. Both were consummate diplomats, endowed with genuine kindness and consideration for others, the basis of all effective diplomacy – endowed also with that strength of character which saves a man from being carried away by his own diplomacy. They were unfailingly generous, not only materially, but in sympathy and appreciation and, though both were genuinely creative personalities, they were singularly without that defensive instinct which gives rise to the aphorism: *'toute conscience veut lo mort de toute autre'*.

The magnitude of Dr Hyde's achievement hardly needs to be stressed – the whole structure of the preservation and revival of Irish is more his doing than any one other man's. That side of the Irish character that Yeats crystallized in the words 'great hatred, little room' often chooses to ignore the grandeur of his vision and see only the inadequacies of its execution. Much that in his youth must have seemed utopian impossibility he lived, as first President of Ireland, to see accomplished fact. The publications of his early days, the *Religious Songs of Connaught* and the *Love-songs of Connaught,* with their sensitive and accurate translations, completed the heroic picture with a human pathos, humour and beauty. It was as if the little figures going about their daily avocations in the background of some aristocratic mediaeval painting had suddenly begun to move and sing. This is that Irish folk-poetry which has been so brilliantly served by its translators from Ferguson to Frank O Connor. It is again Thomas MacDonagh who observes how the traditional Gaelic speech is often revivified in translation. Essentially, what had happened was that in the Irish folk way of life the refinement and expertise of the old noble castes, driven underground by historical reverses, had combined with peasant directness and passion to produce a poetry of the human condition. Victorian English-speaking Ireland, dehumanized and provincialized, devoured this mode with the appetite of famine. In the resultant abundance of productive energy the importance of Lady Gregory's enthusiasm not only for Irish itself, but for the English speech of the West of Ireland, has perhaps been overlooked. It was for a long time customary to regard her scrupulous reproduction of the dialect spoken around Coole Park as artificial. 'Kiltartanese' became a contemptuous term for the stylized rural speech of the Abbey Stage. Recent research, however, has attested the essential genuineness of Lady Gregory's instinct and inspiration in spite of a certain rigidity in their realization, so that Synge's vision of a new medium combining the strengths of both languages is a great deal less fantastic than it has been fashionable to suppose. Linguists and sociologists are just beginning to realize how important it is for the development of the individual that the mother-dialect, the first language, should not be regarded with contempt. The native Irish subconscious has probably more reason to be grateful to Lady Gregory and to Synge than it generally chooses to recognize.

In the majority of Irish writers of English in our own day the debt to Irish language and literature is acknowledged and obvious. Occasionally, as with Brendan Behan, who – it is not generally known outside Ireland – wrote in both languages, it is copiously acknowledged and not obvious. Austin Clarke is explicit and tells us how 'that wonderful trio of scholars, Douglas Hyde, Sigerson and Stephen MacKenna, incarnated the Gaelic tradition' for him when he was still a student at University College, Dublin. A contemporary critic holds that 'Austin Clarke is the fulfilment of MacDonagh's dream of a separate Irish mode; the first completely Irish poet to write in English'. In effect his novel, *The Singing Men at Cashel* actually fills a lacuna in our repertory of mediaeval romances. It is the lost tale of Queen Gormley of Cashel – wife in turn to three kings and left at last destitute – of which only the lyric interludes survive to us from the Irish original. The two great exceptions are undoubtedly of significant stature: Joyce and Beckett. Joyce's attitude to Irish is part of the *odi et amo* complex of his entire attitude to Ireland; a Sheehy family tradition goes that he owned an Irish dictionary heavily annotated in his own hand. His actual use of Irish is superficial; the irreducible minimum of native culture from which not even a Dublin-man is safe. As for Beckett, it can justly be said of him that if he has rejected Irish he has also rejected English.

v. Living Speech

The existence as a literary medium, with a distinctive place in the English canon, of a regional variety of English which it is convenient to call Anglo-Irish has long been recognized. The sense of strangeness which Anglo-Irish literature conveys to many non-Irish readers is to a considerable extent linguistic in origin. Until recently, however, existing studies of the language were based entirely on literary sources and added very little to an intelligent layman's catalogue of the obvious points of difference from standard. Now Irish scholarship is aware of this field perhaps among the results will be the rehabilitation socially of the Irish way of speech.

The circumstances of the language situation in Ireland comprise a series of coherent dialects of English, showing marked individual and un-English characteristics. Most of the rural areas concerned were, we have seen, Irish-speaking little more than a hundred years ago. The urban areas also have an Irish-speaking history, but more remote.

In the field of syntax in particular, the debt of Anglo-Irish to native Irish is most pronounced. Irish syntax concentrates on the expression of states rather than actions; its verbal system is highly aspective, with the subject of the sentence as the focus of the utterance and all occurrences relating back thereto. It shows a marked predilection for the substantival cast of sentence, i.e., a sentence where the noun carries the main burden of content. It has a peculiarly highly developed prepositional system widely employed; prepositions in Irish supply many of the functions of the verb in English. In the speech of the first bi-linguals, insofar as it has been recorded, and in that of present-day native speakers of Irish the expedient of superimposing the vocabulary of English on the Irish syntax is often resorted to, and sentences like, *If it is a thing that he do come:* 'If he should come', and, *I was working at him with a week:* 'I worked for him for a week', are surprisingly frequent even today. As, however, English establishes itself as the dominant of the two languages, it seems that these extremes are rejected, and only Gaelicisms inherently amenable to the recipient structure are retained in mono-lingual Anglo-Irish. Sometimes there is quasi-independent development as in periphrastic sentences of the type, *It's a man he is* corresponding to the simple statement, 'He is a man'. So characteristic of Anglo-Irish and so obviously un-standard in English is this usage that it is felt to be a direct translation from Irish while in fact it is rather a creation of the Anglo-Irish speech-sense, a resuscitation of the Irish tendency to periphrastic constructions in a context where in the original language the element of periphrases has disappeared semantically.

From the predispositions just touched on there results in Anglo-Irish a preponderance of constructions with the verb 'to be' and its supplements, e.g., verbs like 'put', 'leave', 'have' etc. in conjunction with nouns and noun equivalents and/or with prepositions giving sentences like these, immediately recognizable as Hibernian:

Are you for going?: 'Do you intend to go?'
Have it off him: 'Take it from him.'
She has him crying: 'She has made him cry.'
Leave west your tay: 'Drink up your tea.'
I put the fear of God on him: 'I frightened him severely.'

Against this background a sentence form like the well-known *I am after going,* a literal translation of an Irish construction, links with a standard English usage, extends its scope semantically and is a natural to run riot in Anglo-Irish. It is a difficult construction for a non-dialect-speaker to handle. Its statal or aspective character is absolute. It may be compounded with most tenses of the verb 'to be', but it must always communicate a state ensuing on the completion of an action. This rules out the imperative mood. In the writer's experience *Be after getting along with you* is only possible as a parody of stage Irish. Similarly the construction is never the equivalent of a simple future; such a usage might be described as void of uncertainty. *I'll be after going* for 'I will go' is a common error in Anglo-Irish pastiche, but the sentence has no such meaning in genuine dialect. It corresponds quite simply to the English future perfect and is of its nature of relatively limited occurrence, except with a subjunctive extension of the future; *Will he be after seeing the priest?* means 'I wonder whether he has seen the priest?' *A fortiori,* the construction can have no volitional significance. *What will you be after having?* in the sense of 'What will you have to drink?' has become current in Common Anglo-Irish as a take-off of the visiting foreigner, but the elements of choice and the non-finite implications of the action envisaged nullify the concept of a definite state subsequent to a completed action, and that concept is the essence of the construction. The only meaning which the sentence might be capable of carrying in dialect usage would be the rather far-fetched 'What disease can you have succeeded in contracting?' Another marked feature of this construction – certainly in Common Anglo-Irish thought not perhaps to the same degree in the rural dialects – is the element of subjective qualification it very often implies. The commoner general usage suggests reproach, disbelief, disapproval, perhaps because it enters most middle-class vocabularies in childhood through the speech of servants and elderly relatives. The preposition conveys the notion of an irreparable consequence, viz:

What are you after doing?
Look what he's after doing!
He's not after going, surely!
He's after pinching the baby.

Also standard in Common Anglo-Irish are *He's after going* for 'He has just gone' and more recently the Anglicized compromise *He's just after going.* That constructions of this type are not mere barbarisms, but have a validity and force of their own corresponding to an essential element in the Irish way of thought, was a discovery of the Revival which we have not as yet faced in all its implications.

vi. Apologia and Polemic

The most disturbing aspect of the revival movement in our own day, or the most heartening perhaps, is its emotive power. Why should such a very fringe minority language exercise such an intense influence over a people for 99 per cent of whom it is an acquired tongue? What produces such fanatical partisanship in its adherents and such counter-fanaticism in its opponents? The founders of the Gaelic League endeavoured for honourable motives to keep the language movement out of politics. With what startling lack of success is well-known. 'When Pearse summoned Cuchulain to his side! What stalked through the Post Office?' The place accorded to Irish under the Constitution, its compulsory status as a school subject, mistaken as they may be in many rational

57

eyes, do represent the spirit of the 1916 Rising, and, in the opinion of this writer, do correspond to some imperfectly realized but genuine aspiration on the part of the people as a whole. And, most importantly, the language has not died, neither repression nor solicitude has succeeded in stifling it. It remains a literary vehicle of great force and beauty employed by people for whom there is no valid alternative, for the Irish-speaking districts of the Western sea-board continue to produce creative writing of a kind peculiarly important in the contemporary world where it seems increasingly that only the minority group, Burke's 'little platoon', can save us from the threat of monolithic conformity.

It is a fallacy only too widespread that opinions held with passion must of their nature be illogical or ill-informed, and the first premise that I would like to postulate is that all thinking about language is emotional. The linguistic faculty is such an integral and mysterious part of the personality that it could not be otherwise. Nor must we fall into the error of thinking that only the language learnt at the mother's knee can evoke intense feeling. The world would be a simpler place to live in if this were so. But it is not. We have seen governments prepared to take life rather than abandon the imposition of a largely artificial dialect on their people and people prepared to die rather than accept it. There are many further intermediate stages between this and the American linguistic experience, say, where any evidence of cultural or racial identity distinct from the white Anglo-Saxon Protestant concept of American nationality is to be deprecated. None of this is admirable, but it seems an inherent potential of the human condition. Irish people need to guard against being made to feel inferior because they are capable of being moved and excited by a question which seems to superficial observers remote from contemporary realities. It may well be that we are fortunate to have this catalyst to precipitate our sense of identity.

Another mistake would be to assume that the monopoly of emotion is on one side. The rational arguments in favour of the abandonment of the Irish language are easily stated. Their very simplicity is a danger signal. The public, however, is entirely within their rights, indeed they may be fulfilling an obligation implied by the Constitution, in speculating whether there are not deeper currents beneath the surface, the middle-class fear and hatred of poverty and all its associations for example, which so easily become fear and hatred of the poor. The onus is on those who hold certain stereotyped views on the non-utility of Irish in education to show by their actions in other spheres that this association is groundless.

A similar onus, of course, falls on a person like the writer to show what positive utility the study of Irish can have in the education of our people. I would maintain that it is primarily psychological. A nation has a personality, even as an individual, and self-knowledge and self-respect are as essential to its collective health as to that of each member.

For better or worse the Gaelic element in our culture is a part of the Irish personality. I have tried here, sketchily enough I fear, to demonstrate how this has come to be so. When it is suppressed we are maimed. It is not only that we lose our identity in the English-speaking community. It is that we enter it as inconsiderable elements, as second-class citizens inhibited by an inferiority complex from making any serious contribution. Our speech habits, so intrinsic a part of ourselves, are at best a source of amusement; at worst, productive of ill-feeling and scorn. A whole historical and social environment is disrupted and the individual is left defenceless and at a loss. The education that will fit an Irishman to take his place as a fully-equipped human being either within or outside his own country must begin by giving him a pride in himself, not as he might be, but as he is, and a knowledge and love of Irish seem to me an essential part of this education. The Irishman must realize his English speech not as a regrettable sub-standard variety but as a rich and beautiful hybrid before he can, first, make the necessary concessions to Standard English to be understood without humiliation and psychological damage, and, second, acquire a genuine competence in that tongue. This process is impossible without key personnel who know and appreciate Irish, who realize from actual knowledge the quite extraordinary lack of coincidence between Standard English and the native Irish thought-processes and who can see the strength and beauty of the bridge Anglo-Irish provides between the two modes. The attraction of Anglo-Irish literature to non-Irish people is its foreignness; it must be normal and native to us.

This kind of appreciation and its consequent joy can be dismissed as a luxury. I consider it a vital factor in the country's mental health. However, even if it were a luxury, it is one to which the people of Ireland have access by constitutional right. They should not be tricked into abandoning it without being made clearly aware of what they are losing: something – again to fall back on Milton and adapt him – which future generations may not willingly learn to have been let die. Lest this might seem fanciful there are some readily ascertainable facts we might consider. All over the world where educational authorities are coping with regional varieties of English and their social implications, the importance for the self-respect of the learner of his recognizing the validity of his dialect and of the non-English substratum where it exists, is realized to be of paramount importance. Fringe people, if they are to thrive, need massive reassurance as to the dignity and worth of their own culture. It can be argued that this is work for specialists. Where in our supposedly democratic society are we to get specialists if the brains and talents of those most apt instinctively to grasp Irish modes of expression are not put under contribution, the brains and talents of the Irish rural working-class? These people have an asset in their habits of speech and thought without which we would all rapidly become rather boring and provincial. I am disconcerted at this point to find myself in close agreement with no less a person than T. S. Eliot who, further, thought similarly about the Welsh! Could there be in the opposition to the compulsory teaching of Irish a concealed resentment of an avenue of social mobility? For, no mistake about it, the culture to which Irish is a key is, in our time, a revolutionary culture. It is a culture of the oppressed, the almost legendary dispossessed. It is impossible to know it without becoming caught up in the great wave of historical indignation which informs the world-wide social revolution of today. No man reared in this tradition can feel any confidence in great-power virtue, or in the benevolence of the Right. No adult in the Irish-speaking districts, has any doubt who killed President Kennedy. '*Na* bosses – *cad eile?*' *Il eterno presente nemico dell Umanita.* No realist need be astonished at the politics of Peadar O Donnell or for that matter of Kickham or of Davitt. Irish set Synge free from the crippling hypocrisy and sadism of the Victorian backwater in Ireland – 'God blast this English tongue in which a man can't swear without being vulgar!' – Irish might well save us from the complacency and selfishness of Christian Democrat Europe. But it cannot save us if we do not know it. Translation is good – indeed in our peculiar linguistic circumstances, translations from the Irish are often uncannily good. But that fount will dry up if the number of those who hanker after the original is not renewed.

Official measures to preserve and propagate the Irish language are in clear fulfilment of the responsibility implied by the Constitution to provide all children with the honest opportunity to acquire a basic competence in the language. I would regard such measures not as an imposition, but as prudent and legitimate means towards preserving their heritage for the people of Ireland and ensuring for them an informed acquaintance with the language and culture which, whether they will or not, have shaped and will continue for some time to shape much of the national character. Of course the young must exercise their judgment independently about their cultural adherence, but they must exercise it on a basis of knowledge and assurance and not of confusion, exploitation and deprivation, nor must it be forgotten that all cultures involve conscious acceptance and rejection as well as historical and environmental conditioning. It should be part of the function of our generation to transmit our traditions and pieties. If I am correct in the contention that an affinity exists even today between this surprisingly tenacious language and the Irish psyche, further development, once a carefully calculated minimum of husbandry and priming had been guaranteed, might be left largely to voluntary pressures and preferences.

The Religious Position

Sean Mac Réamoinn

Catholic Ireland . . . . priest-ridden country . . . . island of saints and scholars . . . . clerical obscurantists . . . . spiritual values . . . . censorship . . . . clean-living . . . . mediaeval . . . . worst slums in Europe . . . . loyalty to the Church's teaching . . . . half-educated . . . . pseudo-intellectuals . . . . FASCISTS . . . .

Well then: a few facts and figures. Three out of four Irishmen (and/or Irishwomen) are Catholics: or, if you prefer, every fourth Irishman (-woman) is a Protestant. That's putting it very roughly of course. Closer statistics would slightly favour the Catholic majority and would also provide a tiny pocket for Jews and 'others'. By 'Catholics' I mean members of the Roman Catholic Church, and I think it's fair enough to say that while other Christians here rightly resent being described by the negative term 'non-Catholics', very few indeed of them would object to being called Protestants. So I propose to stick to the ordinary names 'Catholic' and 'Protestant' in these pages, using them in the sense I have indicated.

Now, while it is obvious that the phrase 'Catholic Ireland' is an inadequate description for a country one quarter of whose population are Protestants, the actual demographic distribution of the minority does support the use of two other descriptions: 'the Catholic South' and 'the Protestant North'. In the Republic the twenty-five per cent shrinks to a mere five per cent: in Northern Ireland Protestants form the majority. Nevertheless it cannot be too strongly emphasized that the political border has no institutional equivalent in any of the Irish Churches; they are all organized on an all-Ireland basis. In fact, for reasons which have nothing to do with modern politics (even stretching 'modern' to take in the Williamite settlement!) both the Roman Catholic Church and the Church of Ireland – which is part of the Anglican communion – have two primates apiece: their sees are in Dublin and in Armagh. But in both cases the Archbishop of Armagh, which is a town in Northern Ireland, holds the title 'Primate of All-Ireland', and has a seniority of honour among his fellow bishops.

The other two most important Christian bodies in Ireland are the Presbyterian and Methodist Churches. Their greatest numerical strength is in the north-east, yet they also regard the whole of Ireland as their area of responsibility: the General Assembly and the Methodist Conference meet more often in Belfast than in Dublin, but this has no institutional significance. It would be beyond the scope of this chapter to enter into a detailed description of the organization of the other Christian churches and communions – Baptists, Non-Subscribing Presbyterians, Congregationalists and so on – but again the general picture is much the same: numerical strength in the north-east, closely linked with small groups in the Republic, chiefly in Dublin. However, as one moves further away from the traditional theological and institutional 'centre', one finds that the small independent groups – may one call them 'sects'? – exist almost exclusively in the North: their exuberant multiplicity can be glimpsed by reading the advertisement columns of the *Belfast News-Letter* on any Saturday in the year.

This plurality of witness, coupled with the maintenance of certain Sabbatarian austerities, help to support the idea of Belfast as a 'Protestant city' – especially on a Sunday. The corresponding idea, indeed the more-or-less proud claim of Dublin to be a Catholic city – if not *the* Catholic city – cannot fail to make sense to even the most superficially observant Sunday visitor to the capital: the sight and sound of half a million people going to mass takes some explaining away. In fact church-going figures in Dublin among all denominations are very high (among Catholics something well over ninety per cent), and while the type of congregation varies from district to district, and again as between early and late, morning and evening masses, the over-all heterogeneity of mass-goers is, to the visitor from, say, France or Italy, as startling as their numbers: the pious old women are jostled by far from pious-looking young men, the bourgeois share pews with the beatniks – there are as many beards and mini-skirts as there are sober serge suits and demure mantillas, or bonnets and shawls.

By and large, the pattern repeats itself in the smaller cities and towns, and, of course, all over the countryside. And, again, this is as true of the Catholic parishes in the North as it is in the Republic. Naturally enough, the smaller and more tightly-knit the social community, the more can mass-going be regarded as a social function: it would, however, be unwise to generalize from this. Traditional rural, or even modern suburban, social pressures are undoubtedly factors to be taken into account in any attempt to evaluate the conformist element in Irish attendance at mass, but once again 'Catholic Dublin' would seem to provide evidence that this element is not as important as one might imagine. 'Being seen at mass' becomes less and less significant where a wide choice of churches and mass hours caters for a population whose non-religious Sunday activities are of considerable diversity and, indeed, 'worldliness'. Sabbatarianism of even the mildest kind is regarded as a distinctively Protestant phenomenon: in the Republic and among the

62

Catholics in the North, Sunday is, for example, the great day for sport. Of the three football codes, which to their supporters are almost para-religious ideologies, only rugby tends to favour Saturday as the day for 'big' games. Soccer matches are held on Sunday afternoons in Dublin and other centres: only fixtures with Northern Irish teams must, out of respect for religious conviction, be played on a weekday. Gaelic football and hurling, the two 'national' games, are completely free from Sabbatarian inhibitions – to a very large number of Irishmen Sunday means three things: mass, a football or hurling match, and a post-mortem on the match, usually held in the pub. Indeed it would not be unfair to say that pub-opening hours on Sundays are geared to mass and match-going, with a decent gesture to family life in the shape of an interval for dinner, and 'early' closing at 10 p.m. The Catholic clergy are as enthusiastic in their match-going as the laity are constant in their mass-going, and indeed the bigger games are – or were until very recently – often begun by a bishop throwing in the ball!

This portrait of the Irish Catholic Sunday, idyllic or revolting according to taste, does not of course tell the whole story, but I think it is fair enough as a majority report. If the emphasis on sport and sporting pubs seems to exclude an important section of the community, who are in fact slightly in the majority, let me say that girl friends and even un-attached young women are by no means rare attendants at hurling, and football games: even wives are not unknown, though admittedly less numerous. And in recent years the Irish pub has become something quite different from the all-male sanctuary of a previous generation. As well as all that, there are the cinemas and the dance-halls, institutions which, in spite of television, attract on Sunday evenings congregations comparable in size and variety to those who earlier crowded into the churches. Indeed, and this is the important point, the church-goers, the pub-goers, the cinema audiences and the late-night dancers are all the same *kind* of people and see little or no conflict in these various activities.

Undoubtedly there are many Catholics, as well as Protestants, who disapprove of alcohol, or, at least, of what they would regard as excessive drinking. Many of them are total abstainers. But the temperance and total abstinence movements have never pressed for prohibition: they confine their public activities generally to problems of excess, teenage drinking and the like. In private life they are usually tolerant and their own abstinence is rather an act of personal religious commitment than of rejection. Traditionally, dancing, as an 'occasion of sin', was, until fairly recently, a regular object of clerical denunciation, and, even still, there are occasional rumbles from one or two of the older bishops: now, however, the emphasis is usually laid on the undesirability, for health reasons, of dances which continue until the early morning. And the attitude which regarded all forms of dancing and dance music of later origin than the waltz as indecent, if not positively

63

orgiastic, has faded: Irish pop musicians tend to be pillars of the church.

The compass then might appear to be set fair for the foreseeable future: a swinging religion in a swinging society. From ballads to bingo, from 'planned giving' to bigger and better car-parks, the Roman Catholic Church in Ireland could well be regarded as, if not quite *with it,* at least well on the road to that desirable state. In the affluent Ireland that is to be, there will always be an honoured place for the affluent Church.

Fortunately for those who care about Christianity, or about Ireland, things are not really quite like that. Among Roman Catholics the ideas of renewal and reform which became crystallized in the acts of the Second Vatican Council are beginning to exercise a disturbing influence. Inevitably there has been a considerable effort made to contain this influence, to minimize the disturbance, to tame the ideas themselves or at least to present them in comfortable words so that, to quote one Archiepiscopal statement which has become something of a byword, the faithful could be assured that the 'tranquillity of their Christian lives' would not be broken.

Let it be said at once that the author of this statement was speaking out of deep conviction and care for his flock. His Grace the Most Reverend John Charles McQuaid, Archbishop of Dublin, is a man whose public *persona,* rigid utterances and often inscrutable actions are subject to constant criticism from many quarters. None of his critics, however, would doubt his immense integrity and genuine pastoral concern. If he is sometimes compared to prelates of renaissance or even mediaeval times, it is for what appears to be an excessively authoritarian cast of mind and action: his sense of commitment is unquestioned. What is in doubt is his position in a changing Church and a changing Ireland, or more specifically, his awareness of and attitude to change.

And, indeed, one might say the same thing about the majority of the other Irish Catholic bishops, his colleagues if not his confidants. A few, a very few, of the dioceses of Ireland are 'ruled' by men whose virtues of heart and head make them seem to be what their office supposes them to be – fathers, and, at the same time, servants of their people. The rest, however devoted and honest – and I believe they all are that – or however learned – and some of them can make claims to a scholarship superior to that of most of their critics – the rest are, it must be admitted, sadly but truly, men whose relevance to the hard facts of Christian life in Ireland today is scarcely visible to the naked and, at times, cold eye of their flocks.

The sport of bishop-baiting is as old as heresy itself, but it needs to be sharply distinguished from it. Many a man who regards his bishop with impatience still acknowledges him as his father in God: in fact if he didn't he wouldn't be impatient. Loyalty is a word which tends to be bandied about with some looseness in the Church as in every institution, but the taking of a good hard look at the meaning of loyalty is one of the most significant, and surely one of the most healthy of current Irish Catholic activities.

Two matters have brought the whole thing to a head just recently: one of purely domestic, the other of world importance. The domestic matter is one of higher education.

For some time past, a realization of certain inadequacies in the Irish university set-up had been producing a growing ferment, making inevitably for institutional change. A government commission, a ministerial *ukase,* a great popular debate, another ministerial *ukase* – these have been the main ingredients of what might to the detached observer appear to be a reasonably important academic development but hardly a traumatic socio-religious crisis. But the detached observer would be wrong, through a pardonable lack of appreciation of the curious position of Trinity College, Dublin.

Trinity College or Dublin University (the distinction need not concern us here) was set up in the reign of Elizabeth I and however academically admirable has, for historical and religious reasons, been regarded by the vast majority of Irish Catholics down to our own time as an 'alien institution'. For a very long time religious tests made it difficult or impossible to enter it in good conscience, and even with the removal of these tests, and certain forms of discrimination, it continued to be regarded as a 'Protestant' university – a description, incidentally, regarded with some irony by non-Anglican Protestants who in the past suffered, in this as in other matters, the same disabilities as did Catholics.

As late as 1956 the Plenary Council of Maynooth, which is the chief legislative body of the Irish Catholic Church, restated a number of previous pronouncements and enacted as follows:

We forbid under pain of mortal sin:
1 Catholic youths to frequent that College.
2 Catholic parents or guardians to send to that College Catholic youths committed to their care.
3 Clerics and religious to recommend in any manner parents or guardians to send Catholic youths to that College or to lend counsel or help to such youths to frequent that College.

Only the Archbishop of Dublin is competent to decide, in accordance with the norms of the instructions of the Holy See, in what circumstances and with what guarantees against the danger of perversion, attendance at that College may be tolerated.

The central position of the Archbishop of Dublin in this matter is obvious. What is more to the point, however, is this: that an apparently inevitable integration of Trinity College into a wider university framework, although taken as one of the fundamental facts of life by all the 'secular' parties involved (though with great and deep reservations as

65

An eighteenth century interior, Dublin

to scope and form) has not yet led either the Archbishop, or any of his colleagues, much less the Episcopal Conference as a body, to make even a minimal statement suggesting that 'mortal sin' is no longer a real issue in the affair. By the time they get around to doing so, even the most 'loyal' Catholics will, one fears, greet their Lordships' statement with a polite yawn.

The tragedy of such an attitude (and to a committed Catholic it must be a real tragedy) shows itself far more forcefully in the not so domestic matter of the Papal Encyclical *Humanae Vitae*. Without entering into a discussion of the ethics of contraception, which does not immediately concern us here, one must place on record the fact that the crisis of authority in the Church, which of course exists everywhere, has been so far (at the time of writing) greeted in Ireland with a frightening silence by the heads of our church. And this cannot be excused by a similar silence on the part of the laity. In this as in the university affair, people – especially young people – have become splendidly articulate, even if at times a trifle intemperate.

Is there then a new spirit abroad among your Irish Catholics? And, if so, where does it come from? Does it imply a long-delayed open rejection not only of authoritarianism but of authority, and indeed of religion itself? How far is it all confined to intellectuals? Is there a genuine crisis of faith among this new generation, these youngest sons and daughters of one of the strongest Christian communities of Europe? And does this bring with it a crisis of morality?

These are questions of considerable pertinence and urgency and, so far, there is little evidence that Irish church institutions are even beginning to tackle them in any effective way. Sociological enquiry is not our strongest suit, although in fairness it must be said that in what little is being done, Catholic priests are among the pioneers.

But, rushing in where rarer spirits may fear to intrude, I might suggest that the last question might be the most rewarding to tackle first. In fact I would suggest that there *is* among young people in Ireland today a crisis, not so much of morality, as *in* morality. There is, I think, the beginning of a confused but genuinely new understanding of what morality *is,* what it's all about, what it's *for.*

To say that, in Ireland, 'morality' has tended to mean sexual morality only, is an ancient platitude. But like all such platitudes, there is a great deal of truth in it. The equation has never been quite absolute but, by and large, if Mr A or Mrs B were described as living immoral lives one didn't think of them as possibly profiteers, crooked politicians, sadistic schoolteachers, dishonest tradesmen or even malicious gossips. Similarly an immoral society elsewhere was more likely to be one that countenanced free love than one where the poor or the sick or the lonely were left to fend for themselves.

A fuller understanding then of the meaning of morality is something new in Ireland. By that I don't mean that the Irish have been singularly lacking in a wider moral sense, but that Irish society as a whole has not been very quick to see certain social issues at home or abroad as being essentially moral issues. The emphasis has been on the individual, on private behaviour, and it has to be freely admitted that among Catholics at least, although, I suspect, not among them alone, this has been to a great extent due to an over-emphasis on the individual in Christian teaching and formation. 'Am I my brother's keeper?' has been a popular biblical phrase, but we tended to forget who asked the question.

This imbalance in Christian, and more particularly Catholic doctrine and life, is by no means exclusively Irish. Nor is the current reaction to it: indeed the moral preoccupation of many young Irish people today with questions of racialism, world hunger, nuclear warfare and so on is obviously a reflection of a world trend. Horizons have been widened with the coming of television, increased foreign travel and other barrier-breaking factors, and much good has come of it. And it has not been without an effect on attitudes to domestic issues. Politics is at long last, beginning to be regarded as something more than at best a career, at worst a dirty word.

If I am right in thinking that there is an awakening of moral passion among the younger generation I still have to show that this has anything to do with religion. I believe that it has – at least *negatively*. After all this new moral concern is, at root, an old-fashioned youthful idealism with, and this is crucial, a new dimension of honesty, of criticism. Formerly a lot of this idealism was channelled into purely 'spiritual' or devotional activity, into para-missionary organizations like the Legion of Mary (often criticized, but with concrete social achievements to their credit), or into the priesthood and religious life.

Now whatever may be the case about a crisis of faith there is un-doubtedly a crisis in 'vocations'. In Ireland, as elsewhere, fewer young people are offering themselves as candidates for the ministry or as novices in religious orders. This does not *necessarily* mean that belief in God or Christ or the institutional Church is on the decline, although it may mean just that. It most certainly does mean that there is a growing impatience with the modes and forms in which the Christian faith is presented and put into action, a growing scepticism about the relevance of these modes and forms – from devotions to dogmas, from church-building to church-going.

Nor, and this is important, is this impatience confined to the young 'secular' intellectuals. The minority who are engaged in the specifically 'religious' life are equally disturbed; within the seminaries there is as much of a ferment as in any other of the centres of higher education. And from this perhaps one might, optimistically, draw the conclusion that the crisis is not of faith but of communication, of language, of a conflict between immediate relevance and traditional values. Faith can

67

in fact be seen to co-exist with criticism of the most fundamental kind, and Christian commitment to provide for, even to imply, secular commitment.

Those ideas of course represent the most urgent thinking of the Vatican Council and radically-minded seminarians can appeal to Conciliar documents as warrant for their questioning of, and reluctance to conform to, hitherto sacrosanct attitudes. And indeed very many of those responsible for their direction and teaching encourage this new approach, so it looks as if the Irish priesthood of tomorrow is going to be very different indeed from the old image of more or less benevolent despotism. How far this image has already failed to represent reality – if it ever did – is a separate question: tyranny, if it ever existed, is long a thing of the past, if only because the Irish capacity for docility has always been shot through with a strong sprinkling of rebelliousness, but *paternalism* has, on varying levels of activity and influence, continued to be one of the hallmarks of the Irish clergy. Bishops and priests have tended to lay down decisions, rather than enter into dialogue with the laity, and this has been at least as much the fault of the laity as of themselves. Many a 'progressive' cleric has desperately tried to share responsibility with his people, only to be met with a firm refusal to participate in what was 'the priest's job'.

Fixed ideas on what was the priest's or the church's job have been one of the contributory factors to the maintenance of clerical near-monopolies in a number of important fields, not the least being that of education. The clerical management of primary schools (in theory, on behalf of the parish) and the clerical control, ownership and part-staffing of the great majority of Catholic secondary schools is a case in point. However the teachers may grumble, most parents and indeed the Department of State responsible for education, have been only too willing to leave it to the clergy and to the religious communities who, as the phrase goes, 'have served them so well in the past'. It's not an empty phrase either: the Irish people are deeply indebted to communities like the Irish Christian Brothers and certain congregations of nuns, who tackled the educational problem in the nineteenth century, when there were few others able or willing to compete with them. Their dedication has been total, but, unfortunately, today this dedication has acquired the encumbrance of something of a vested interest. And among the 'new stirrings' in Ireland is a growing dissatisfaction with the educational *status quo* and a realization of the inadequacy of existing facilities. This is acknowledged by all the political parties, indeed educational reform is taking a central place in the policies of both the government and the opposition groups.

That this must involve tensions with the clerical establishment was only to be expected, the real wonder is that an open conflict has been so long delayed. There have been already one or two preliminary skirmishes, sharp enough to promote peace moves even before war is declared. Perhaps there won't be a war: there are certainly many men of ability and goodwill among all the interests involved who could provide a blueprint for a new educational deal.

In all this I have of course been dealing almost exclusively with the situation in the Republic, although among Catholics in the North much of what has been said is equally applicable. The most significant new stirring among Protestants is probably the growth, slow but steady, of the spirit of ecumenism, both between the Protestant Churches themselves and towards Catholics. A reciprocal attitude is developing among Catholics, not so much on the official level – although with a certain guarded official blessing – but rather among unofficial groups of priests and laymen. This infant movement towards common understanding and common action among Christians, with the ultimate aim of full unity which has shown itself most articulately in a series of inter-denominational conferences, suffered a severe blow late in 1966 with the tragic death of the young Benedictine Abbot of Glenstal, Joseph Dowdall, a man of charismatic zeal, intelligence and humanity.

But the ecumenical movement will continue to flourish in Ireland for the simple reason that it must. The appalling legacy of inter-religious and communal bitterness and strife, which is the central factor in the frustrating situation in the North, must be destroyed. It can only be destroyed through the building of a new kind of Christian ethos, not for fear of, or in opposition to, the advance of secular ideas and institutions but rather working through and in these for the building of a new society.

In the Republic the need for inter-Church fellowship may not appear to be so urgent but it is nevertheless of vital importance for the future. Again the Vatican Council has provided the inspiration and the norms for ecumenical development, and any lack of enthusiasm cannot be justified by appeals to orthodoxy. A common Christian witness, north and south, is emerging: there are and will continue to be growing pains, but these must be lived through and overcome if Irish Christianity is to maintain itself as a vital force in the future.

I have already used the word 'secular'. It is perhaps the key-word in our Christian future. This may seem a paradox to some, to others a form of capitulation, to a few, perhaps, a suggestion that the gospel should be reduced to a mere ethic for an age in which the death of God is finally acknowledged.

On the contrary, if this were a theological essay, I should argue that it is in the full recognition of the secular, in an age when secular society has reached maturity, that Christianity can best realize its mission. The world is potentially on the threshold of such an age and Ireland is, though we sometimes try to forget it, part of the world. The dominance of secular structures is something that Christians should welcome: their

69

task is not to dominate but to serve. Now this service has in the past, necessarily entailed the formation of para-structures, of specifically Christian (or Catholic, or Protestant) institutions to deal with urgent human needs. Ireland is a classic example of this process: history, that robbed us of our natural secular social dynamic, forced us to recover it through religious leadership and institutions before we could re-build for ourselves. It is no betrayal of our past, no ungrateful rejection of tradition to recognize that this was a passing if prolonged phase in our development. (Something of the kind could, of course, be necessary again, although hardly in recognizably the same terms.) Nor is the acknowledgement of a secular dynamic a denial of the transcendant: Christians believe that God works in history not alone through His Church but also, and normally, through His world.

But can, say, the Roman Catholic Church come to terms with living in a secular Ireland? Despite what cynics might say, there are already heartening signs that it can and will. Liturgical renewal, which is the very core of the post-Conciliar movement, is already getting well under way, and it is from this, and from the associated renewal in catechetics, that a new or rather a rediscovered understanding of the real nature of the Church's mission must surely come. It may be difficult for even the most sympathetic outsider to understand how what may superficially appear to be a mere reformed methodology, in worship and doctrine, can have such a profound effect. But it has always been a maxim of the Church that the *lex orandi* and the *lex credendi* are inseparable: the teaching power of the liturgy is in fact the central Christian social dynamic.

The relationship between this dynamic and that of secular society has in the past been too often a troubled one, in Ireland as elsewhere. It can never be a completely comfortable one – indeed, whenever it appears to be, then is the time for protest and prophecy. But there are some indications – in a Donegal co-operative, in a Kilkenny social service centre, and in a few places in Africa, that the Irish can make it work.

The Economic Scene

Patrick Lynch

The first British Empire fell when the United States of America achieved independence. For nearly a century afterwards, many Englishmen expected other parts of their surviving empire – the 'colonies' as they were then called – to become separate self-governing states without, of course, the need, in each case, for a 'war of independence'. Some even hoped that Britain might become a Little England, shorn of its overseas territorial responsibilities. This was not to be. The vision of Disraeli and the chauvinism of Joseph Chamberlain combined to defeat the hopes of the Little Englanders and Britain began to annexe new territories extending to the ends of the earth until a great Empire emerged with the Union Jack arrogantly, if not firmly, planted in every outpost of it. The flag followed trade and, according as the electorate at home was enlarged by successive reform acts, the new imperialism earned the enthusiastic support of the English masses just as Mr Enoch Powell was able to whip up some gullible, popular support for white racialism a century later. Nearest, geographically, Ireland remained Britain's oldest and most reluctant imperial asset until 1921 when Ireland became the first country to be released from the second British Empire, and so to set an example that other subject countries were to follow.

From the first British conquest of Ireland over seven hundred years ago, until Irish political freedom was partially secured in 1921, the relationship between Britain and Ireland had been an uneasy one. Ireland's many attempts at separation culminated in the Rising of 1916 and in the guerrilla war that followed. In 1922, with a treaty with Britain, the new Irish Free State came into existence; but it was immediately plunged into civil war because many Irishmen who had been fighting Britain since 1916 regarded this treaty settlement as falling short of their ideals of independence. The Irish Free State consisted of only twenty-six out of the thirty-two counties; part of Ireland was excluded from the Free State and remains to the present day in the United Kingdom under the provisions of the Government of Ireland Act 1920, passed by the British parliament.

This geographical partitioning of Ireland was a cruel disappointment for those who had struggled for Irish freedom. There were even some, a minority it may be supposed, who felt that a geographically united

Ireland inside, or associated with, the United Kingdom might have been preferable to a geographically divided Ireland, even if the part separated from Britain had secured political independence. Over the years the word 'independence' had acquired varied meanings in Ireland. Many elements combined to nourish the romantic mythology of Irish independence; and as myths become realities if enough people believe in them, there was disenchantment in the Treaty settlement even for many of those who were defending it in arms in 1922. In the long run, the Treaty may have suffered more from the disillusion of its friends than from the attacks of its enemies. Certainly, this is true for the 1950s. The political separation of Northern Ireland from the rest of the country impaired the social and cultural unity of the island. During the first generation of Partition after 1922 there was a psychological breakdown of communication between the two parts of the island. Dublin ceased to be the accepted capital; and Belfast was becoming increasingly remote from Dublin.

The inspiration of the Irish revolutionaries of 1916 and subsequently, was summarized in the slogan *Sinn Féin,* meaning 'Ourselves'. Those who had accepted this *Sinn Féin* myth expected political independence to bring a great cultural revival, distinctive Irish social development and a tremendous spate of economic recovery. Pearse, Connolly, Mellows and others believed that the flowering of these hopes would end the blight of centuries of British colonial rule in Ireland. The prevailing Irish nationalist economic philosophy had been embodied in this movement of self-reliance. Its great exemplar, Arthur Griffith, argued that *Sinn Féin* meant cultural and intellectual independence as well. Above all, he urged economic development with special emphasis on industrialization which would gradually make Ireland less dependent on imports of goods from Britain and other countries. Economic self-sufficiency, it was said, should be a basis for spiritual freedom and an end to the servility and sycophancy which British rule had implanted in the Irish character. The day of the *shoneen,* who, though located geographically in Ireland, drew his values and inspiration from England, would be ended.

But Griffith the prophet of *Sinn Féin,* and first head of the Free State Government, died soon after taking office and gradually the idealism of his movement gave way to a despondent national mood marked by self-laceration expressed in puritanical political and social legislation, and in economic policies that seemed to have little relevance to the objectives of Pearse and Connolly. The middle class was on the stage, and those who thought that the Irish struggle for independence had other ideals were stranded helplessly in the wings.

Moreover, many patriotic Irish men and women, uncritical of the economic doctrines of *Sinn Féin,* had believed that political independence implied economic independence. Eventually, the dawn of

reality showed them that, even if Partition had never happened, the geographic and economic boundaries of Ireland would not necessarily coincide. Despite the political independence of the Irish Free State there were signs that as part of the legacy of history, Ireland had long since established very close, even inseparable, economic links with Britain. Indeed, in many ways, Ireland and Britain had become a single economic unit. The money of Irish investors flowed out to be invested in Britain, where it secured a better return, and Irish workers sought jobs in Britain, where they got better wages. The existence of a common language facilitated this mobility of people and capital.

All this was very unlike what Irish patriots had expected. It might have been different if the new Government of the Free State had positive economic philosophies or ideologies to match their political convictions. But the new state was dominated by the middle class whose outlook was that of the British middle class, far from that of those who had wished to achieve the apotheosis of the *Sinn Féin* myth. There were, of course, able, independent-minded men in the new Free State Government in 1922, but by and large they were prisoners of the *laissez-faire* liberalism of their education and that of the higher civil servants who advised them. Indeed, what Ministers did was often an expression of their own strength of character and their defiance of their advisers. A treaty with Britain and a declaration of political independence were not enough to achieve the economic and social revolution that the handful of men responsible for the 1916 Rising had dreamt of; long established economic links with Britain were to prove more enduring than political links.

In many ways the Irish Free State after 1922 had a smoother transition to independence than had many countries and, certainly, a smoother one than has been the experience of so many African countries which later emerged to independence. Politically, the new government of 1922 may have appeared a revolutionary one, but the administration it established was inherited directly from British rule. The political structure may have changed, but the civil servants were largely the same. The constitutional framework of the new state was a direct imitation of the British system. The cabinet system resembled the British. Parliament was modelled on Westminster except that a Senate was substituted for the House of Lords. The number of government departments was, of course, greatly reduced but they were direct replicas of British government departments. With the Treaty over 20,000 civil servants were transferred from the British government to the new Irish Free State and so the headquarters of the Irish Government in Merrion Street, Dublin, became a Whitehall, writ small. To the present day Ireland imitates the British administrative pattern.

When Mr De Valera came to power in 1932 he made no change in the structure of the administrative system although in due course he replaced the existing Constitution by one of a republican form. The

73

organization of the Irish public service has changed little since the Irish Free State was established, though some radical changes are expected soon. Very early in the life of the new state, in 1927 in fact, it was recognized that there were many purposes for which the Civil Service as it existed was quite unsuited if the elementary economic objectives were to be achieved. An age of increasing government intervention in economic affairs was dawning, though it was reluctantly accepted in Ireland. As the Irish Civil Service had no experience of operating commercial undertakings or of any of the new activities which Governments in the Twentieth Century were expected to perform, some new administrative agencies were created, usually called 'state-sponsored bodies'. The first of these public enterprises, the Electricity Supply Board, was established to generate and distribute electricity, and this it does efficiently and cheaply; electric power for the domestic consumer is cheaper than in England. Many other such agencies have also been established, especially since 1932, as manufacturing organizations, in public transport and elsewhere.

The first task of the first Government of the Irish Free State had been to establish law and order. The civil war which had occurred when Mr De Valera and his party resisted the Treaty ended in 1923. Over the next ten years the Free State Government took advantage of the Treaty settlement to enlarge the degree of its political independence. In the 1920s Irish Ministers contributed substantially to the deliberations in London which converted the old British Empire into the Commonwealth of self-governing independent states. In those years constitutional advancements were more conspicuous than economic progress in Ireland. The economic and social scene, of course, was changing; yet, it was a far cry from the vision of the earlier revolutionaries, from the aspirations of the *Sinn Féin* mythology. One Minister it is true, the Minister for Industry and Commerce, Mr Patrick McGilligan, had the imagination to initiate and develop a vast scheme of electrification which certainly laid the foundations for much of the industrial and, indeed, agricultural progress that was to be achieved later. It is unlikely that he owed many of his ideas to his civil service advisers. Like the French Revolution, the Irish revolution after 1922 was a bourgeois revolution. Those who remained at home and sought middle-class standards of living were prepared to tolerate the emigration of those who, if they had stayed in Ireland, might have been the agents of social revolution. The new politicians looked on emigration as a 'safety valve' – the means of avoiding social revolution. The dominant elements in Irish society after 1922 were prosperous farmers, successful merchants and professional people. They accepted the socio-economic legacy of a political revolution with which most of them had little sympathy; for them nothing had changed except a transfer of political power from London to Dublin.

Unlike most north-western European countries, unemployment has long been a feature of the Irish economy; so, too, emigration. It is only in recent years that Ireland has come to recognize that these problems are not inevitable or inescapable, and that what other small countries in northern Europe have been able to do might also be done in Ireland if the nature of the problems was correctly understood and if there was a will to find and to give effect to the solutions. Ever since the great Famine of 1847, emigration has been a continuous feature of Irish life and the population fell census after census until 1951 when it showed a small increase for the first time in a hundred years.

The first Free State Government had undertaken a modest pro-gramme of industrial development. Manufacturing industry was en-couraged by a very limited system of selective tariffs, but there was little structural change in the economy. The economists and civil servants still believed in *laissez-faire* as expressing the essential laws of economic life. The Government believed that industry could never achieve a place commensurate with agriculture. Indeed, the myth that farming is, in some transcendental sense, not so much an occupation as a way of life on which Providence has placed a special badge of moral approval, whereas other occupations retain a less sanctified character, still survives in Ireland. It is true, of course, that Irish soil is more than usually suitable for agriculture. It is also true, alas, that markets with the money to pay for Irish agricultural goods have not maintained a demand up to Ireland's capacity to produce these goods. The consequent failure of agriculture to produce jobs at acceptable levels of income for those working on the land has contributed to the emigration of hundreds of thousands who have left Ireland over the last four decades. By and large, in the first ten years of the Irish Free State the economic policies adopted were little different from those that might have been expected if political independence from Britain had never been secured. Economic activity was mainly a matter for private business men and it was not accepted as a responsibility of the state to find work for the unemployed.

Industrial development was accelerated, and quite unselectively, when Mr De Valera's Government came to office in 1932. His Minister for Industry and Commerce, Mr Seán Lemass, later Head of the Irish Government, undertook a rapid programme of industrialization which made extreme use of protective tariffs. In many ways, Mr Lemass achieved what Arthur Griffith had sought to do, and what Griffith's associates in the first Free State Government had left undone because their *laissez-faire* economic convictions were so strong. In retrospect, many of Mr Lemass's early decisions seem almost as starry-eyed as Griffith's economic speculations, but risks had to be taken if rapid industrialization was to be achieved. Mr De Valera's Government has been criticized for neglecting agriculture; but the condition of agriculture after 1932 could hardly be attributed to the Irish Government alone, when the world depression was making agriculture uneconomic everywhere.

75

What Mr Lemass did was to create an industrial revolution in modern Ireland that changed the whole structure of the economy. There were successes and failures. A policy which began as one of declared self-sufficiency ended by creating an industrial economy dependent on imports, because most of the raw materials for manufacturing industry had to be imported. Where private enterprise was unable or unwilling to undertake economic development, Mr Lemass introduced public enterprise to fill the gap. But he did so without ever expressly abandoning an attachment to private enterprise. He never formally declared or formulated his economic philosophy. If he were to do so, he would probably hold in favour of private enterprise reluctantly combined with state capitalism, and argue that in an underdeveloped country, such as Ireland was, private enterprise should be supported by the state until it matured, and that private enterprise, if strong enough and willing, should then be permitted to take over public enterprises. This may be far from socialism, as Connolly or Mellows saw it, but it is, at least, a feasible *ad hoc* approach towards promoting industrial development in a country not noted for insisting on political or economic doctrines, and which remains essentially middle-class in its outlook. It is only now, in 1968, that the system of higher education is being changed to break the middle-class monopoly that it has been since the state was founded.

By contemporary economic and social standards, the first Government of the Irish Free State under Mr Cosgrave and the second Government under Mr De Valera were conservative governments. Their faith rested on private enterprise and the profit motive, though John Maynard Keynes, as he then was, appeared to endorse Mr De Valera's economic nationalism, with some characteristic Keynesian reservations. It is true that public enterprise was encouraged, especially after 1932, but it was done on a purely practical level and had no ideological significance. Apart from individuals with varied doctrinal convictions such as Connolly, Mellows, Peadar O'Donnell, Joseph Connolly, George Gilmore, Noel Browne, Owen Sheehy-Skeffington, Declan Costello, Michael O'Riordan and Frank Edwards, ideology has had little part in Irish politics. Radicalism, either in ideas or policies, has not been a conspicuous feature of Ireland since independence. The Irish Labour Party is a comparatively small party, which up to now has not secured a great deal of working class support. In terms of policy there is no parliamentary Socialist Party although the Labour Party recently, officially, called itself socialist. Speeches during 1968 of two of its members, Dr Noel Browne and Mr Michael O'Leary, and the addition to its ranks in December 1968 of Dr Conor Cruise O'Brien leave no doubt that the party now has some members with profound socialist convictions and the ability to convert them into practice.

Since the great revolutionary Marxist, James Connolly, was executed by the British for his part in the 1916 Rising there has been no socialist leader with the vision and imagination to formulate an economic and social philosophy to inspire a following. Connolly's social and economic convictions were to remain those of a small minority. The Irish, it would seem, are not interested in political theories. Personalities count for more than ideas. The performance of the Irish as a community over the past forty years show that they are complacent and easily satisfied economically and socially. They tend to look backwards. In their distrust of change and in their lack of a sense of history except for their tedious preoccupation with ancient and irrevelant grievances, they must be a heart-break for their political leaders with progressive ideas. In recent years, however, young politicians with ideals and positive objectives have been emerging.

It is sometimes argued that Irish conservatism can be attributed to the influence of the Roman Catholic Church. That Church has certainly a unique place in Ireland. But if Irish churchmen are conservative it is largely because the laity expect them to be. It is the laity who are timid and unadventurous in social and economic matters. Some of the most radical economic and social movements in modern rural Ireland have been sponsored by priests such as Canon John Hayes and Father McDyer and there would be many others if they secured courageous and articulate support from the laity. In present day Irish politics the outstanding anti-clericals are often social reactionaries. Only once in the course of the past forty years had a church in Ireland actively intervened on a political issue to play a reactionary role. In 1951 the Catholic Hierarchy condemned the proposals of Dr Noel Browne, Minister for Health, for a nationalized health service. Individual priests and many laymen deplored the intervention, but the laity was certainly on the side of the bishops. That was seventeen years ago. The intervention of the Hierarchy was unwise, but the balance of unwisdom was not on one side. Nothing like that intervention has occurred since, and nothing of the kind is likely to occur again; the Hierarchy will be too prudent to expose themselves to such vulnerable positions. A new generation of laity has learned a good deal from Pope John, and so too, indeed, have churchmen. Some of the most socially progressive thought in Ireland today is coming from priests who have read Marx and Freud as well as Aquinas.

In 1948 an anti-De Valera Government, a coalition, was formed under Mr John A. Costello, a member of the Fine Gael party with a liberal record and outlook. The coalition consisted of the then conservative Fine Gael party, the Labour Party, a new social democratic party, Clann na Poblachta, a farmers' party and some independents. Historically, the main role of the coalition was to show that an alternative government to either a Fianna Fail or a Fine Gael government was possible. Lack of a unified economic policy was certainly a problem, but the new Government did show that political change was possible and it introduced, perhaps rather fortuitously, elements of economic radicalism which have had a decisive effect ever since. It advocated repatriation of part of the Irish foreign investment in Britain and, in launching this operation, initiated changes, the full implications of which may not have been foreseen at the time. The conventional wisdom of the professional economists expressed abhorrence at what it regarded as reckless liquidation of foreign assets representing the savings of Irish farmers and business men invested in Britain by the Irish banks. The repatriated foreign assets may not always have been used for the most productive purposes if judged by the solemn prudence of hindsight. But Ireland had for long been observing the rules of prudent British economics, accumulating foreign assets and maintaining a 'satisfactory' equilibrium in its balance of payments. And all the time unemployment and emigration had been increasing and the rate of economic growth had been stagnant. Ineffective, but well meaning, management of the economy had gone on for so long that someone would inevitably defy the economic dogmas of *laissez-faire*, which had never been relevant to Ireland. Ironically, the part was most ably played by the Minister for Finance in the coalition Government, Mr Patrick McGilligan, whose role in the first government of the Irish Free State had already established his political identity, but hardly as a radical economist. There was, therefore, economic sense in using Irish savings, as the coalition Government was doing after 1948, for home development, and this became even clearer when sterling, the currency in which Irish savings were invested, was first devalued by Sir Stafford Cripps in 1949. The second devaluation in 1967 confirmed, of course, the correctness of the policy of repatriating Irish sterling investments.

Since 1949 large scale capital investment for development purposes in Ireland has become respectable in the eyes of most of the economists. Experience has taught, it is true, the necessity for distinguishing between various types of investment and for ensuring that investment be as productive as possible, especially as capital is much scarcer in the 1960s than it was twenty years earlier. It is now recognized, however, that the only effective cure for unemployment is to raise the rate of economic growth.

In modified form many of the aims of *Sinn Féin* seem more practical now than they did forty years ago. The visions of Arthur Griffith may not have been entirely illusory. Unemployment and emigration are, indeed, being reduced; but modern Irish economic development owes more to the theories of Lord Keynes than to the inspiration of James Connolly. Ireland remains a complacent middle-class society. To stimulate economic growth a system of economic planning was introduced in 1958. There was a First Programme for Economic Expansion covering the years 1959 to 1963 and a Second Programme from 1963 to 1970. The Second Programme, launched in 1964 in an atmosphere of general expansion and optimism, aimed at a fifty per cent increase in national income by 1970 over that of 1960. Indeed, from 1958 to the middle of 1965 the annual rate of economic growth was over four per cent, an average that had never been achieved before in Ireland, except in artificial circumstances for a very brief period immediately after the second world war. With its industrial base established, Ireland is turning its back on protective measures for its manufactures and taking the course that Britain chose in 1846 with the repeal of the Corn Laws. Emigration is being reduced, but Irish society is still faced with a choice between more jobs for those who, without work, must emigrate or a higher standard of living for those already in jobs, living comfortably and complacently at home. There are signs that young people going into politics, especially the student supporters of the radical 'Just Society' programme of Fine Gael, the principal opposition party, are making an impact on the leaders of that party. It remains to be seen what impact such a programme can make on the electorate.

Efforts are being made to prepare Ireland for participation in the international movement towards free trade represented by the European Economic Community and the European Free Trade Area, and industry both in the private and public sectors is being adapted to meet these competitive challenges. Inducements are being offered to foreign industrialists to provide Ireland with the enterprise that Griffith hoped Irishmen would display for themselves. Since 1959 nearly two hundred industrial undertakings have been set up with foreign capital participation. The concessions offered to foreign industrialists include non-repayable cash grants and full tax relief on profits from exports over ten years. The Government's programme is to create 60,000 new jobs in Ireland by 1970. The emphasis is increasingly on production for export. In 1955 exports of manufactured goods, other than food and beverages, totalled just over £13,000,000. Ten years later in 1965 the total was £81,000,000. Membership of the European Economic Community would open a vast new area for the expansion of Irish exports. As a step towards participation in these more extensive foreign markets an Anglo-Irish Free Trade Agreement came into operation on July 1, 1966. It recognizes the close trading relations which have always existed between Ireland and Britain, but it tries to order these relations in the best interests of both countries. There has, therefore, been a break in recent years with old economic dogmas and the attitudes of disillusion and pessimism. A new spirit of innovation expressed in positive economic planning is using Ireland's own exertions, supplemented by foreign investment and assistance, to seek high levels of economic growth. There is now more confidence in the possibilities of a viable Irish economy which eventually might become part of the European Economic Community, if there were a collective desire by Irish society and by individuals, trades unions and business men to choose national development rather than their own material advancement as immediate objectives. But the defect in Irish nationalism has been its failure to recognize political, social, economic and cultural development as parts of a single process.

The Irish standard of living can be greatly increased; unemployment can be reduced and involuntary emigration can be made unnecessary. These assumptions would provide the realization of the social and cultural aims of those who have striven over the centuries for Irish independence. The economic foundations and, indeed, the framework may seem to be very different from those originally contemplated by the revolutionaries of 1916. But apart from Connolly few of the revolutionaries had dogmatic views on economic systems; they mostly regarded economic systems as bases for a distinctive spiritual, intellectual and cultural development. Nor were these men, least of all Connolly, the Marxist, insular in outlook; they wanted Ireland to take its place among the nations of the earth; they knew, indeed, they hoped, that this would inevitably mean being influenced by ideas and developments from elsewhere.

Ireland is a text book example of the 'open' economy dependent on a high level of foreign trade for its well-being. It reflects, magnifies and sometimes distorts trends prevailing abroad. Because of the extreme mobility of labour from the most remote parts of the country to Britain, the Irish labour market tends to follow the British pattern, even when Irish productivity lags behind. Monetary incomes are often higher than the productivity of the country would seem to warrant; and there is always the alluring temptation of trying to maintain post-imperial standards on a republican national income.

Ireland, of course, has some highly efficient traditional industries, such as brewing and distilling, and a nationalized group including electricity, sugar, peat and public transport. As a rule, the average private industrial firm is small and, sometimes, under-capitalized, but considerable progress has been made in raising managerial and technical standards. The policy of industrial protection, which was the general rule until recently, greatly expanded manufacturing activities and gave employment to thousands of workers who would otherwise have emigrated. Since the decision was taken to apply for membership of the European Economic Community, protection is being dismantled to enable the Republic to face the increasing competition from foreign goods in the years ahead. This freeing of trade will, of course, create serious problems for inefficient firms; it will also offer prospects for firms that are enterprising and technologically advanced. With the Free Trade Area agreement with Britain, Irish firms will have access to a market of fifty million people; if Ireland were in the European Economic Community the market would achieve a further quadrupling.

In the years since 1956 there has been a radical change in the character

The House of Lords, Dublin, designed by Sir Edward Lovett Pearce.
The building started in 1728. It was adapted by Francis Johnson for
the Bank of Ireland after the Union

of the Irish economy. In 1956 it seemed that the limits of profitable expansion of Irish manufacturing industry had been reached. Indeed, more than one economist said so, and this view would have been right if these industries had to rely exclusively on the home market. Only an improved standard of living in Irish agriculture could have increased the demand for industrial goods in the home market, and as population continued to move away from agriculture there did not seem to be much hope for increasing demand from farmers. Since 1956, however, thanks to a series of highly imaginative tax incentives, industrial exports have grown greatly in volume, and it is on manufactured goods rather than on agricultural products, that Ireland's hopes for its economic future now mainly depend. The First Programme for Economic Expansion got under way at the end of 1958. It is still contested whether this Programme was really the cause of the remarkable economic recovery which has occurred since 1958 or whether its association with the recovery has been fortuitous. Over the past ten years, however, the main growth points of the economy have been in manufacturing industry and tourism, though it is true, of course, that home produced agricultural raw materials make a big contribution to industrial production. Over the next five years the principal Irish economic objective is to stimulate an increase in private investment in Ireland, to improve productivity, to promote exports and to establish new industries. The Government will continue to give practical encouragement to private investment from both domestic and external sources by means of tax exemptions, direct grants and other facilities designed specifically for plants producing goods for export. At present, the country is experiencing the momentum of the effects of the export incentives which have been progressively introduced. Ireland is becoming a most attractive haven for the international entrepreneur.

The aim of the second Irish economic plan was to achieve the highest possible rate of national economic expansion feasible with available resources. The plan, or programme as it is called, was based largely on the French model. Private enterprise remained its predominant feature and the planning machinery sought to establish output targets in consultation with representatives of industry and trade unions and to keep under continuous review progress towards the targets set. The assumptions on which the plan was based proved incorrect; in particular, that Ireland would be a member of the EEC by 1970. Late in 1967 it was decided to terminate that plan and to prepare a short-term economic plan on more realistic assumptions for introduction in 1969.

Though Ireland has traditionally been regarded as primarily an agricultural country, this view is likely to change in the decades ahead. Over the next twenty years the volume of agricultural output could double, but the output of industrial goods may well be five times bigger than it is now. This would bring the Republic into line with what is

81

Castletown, Co Kildare, the great house built for William Conolly by Alessandro Galilei and Pearce, 1720–32

happening in other European countries. The tourist industry is fast becoming a most important single element in the economy and represents an outstanding example of what the partnership of public and private enterprise can achieve.

With a few notable exceptions, most Irish manufacturing industries show promise of considerable expansion in production and exports over the next decade. Changes are imminent, however, in the structure of industry. Many firms are too small and must merge with others if they are to survive the competition of international free trade. Mining and quarrying are also likely to become relatively significant and may well triple their output. Since 1960 modern mining methods have been introduced and new deposits of minerals, including lead, zinc, barytes and copper have been discovered. Deposits which, heretofore, were uneconomic to work, may become increasingly valuable if the present upward trend in certain world prices continues. Moreover, if natural gas were discovered in large quantities in the Irish Sea this would further stimulate demand for Irish minerals.

If the present rate of economic development continues Ireland, by the middle 1970s, could be an active participant in the high living standards of the European Economic Community – if it still survives.By retaining its cultural identity it can preserve something, perhaps the essentials, of the *Sinn Féin* myth; and by abandoning political isolation it will be returning to a European tradition from which it derived much of its distinctive character and to which it may yet have some contribution to make.

Parties and Power

Michael Viney and Owen Dudley Edwards

Origins of Modern Irish Politics

An appetite for paradox has long been part of the Irish reputation. The British in particular, having occupied Ireland, decided to be amused by what seemed to them a quaint native taste for illogical behaviour. But what they were dealing with, as they discovered too late, was a hard-learned talent for outwitting the oppressor. A nice example of this was given in the creation of the first genuinely independent Irish Parliament.

Two weeks before Christmas in 1918, the British held a general election. The electorate of Ireland was invited, as usual, to vote its representatives into Parliament at Westminster. The revolutionary Republican movement, whose constitutional arm was Sinn Féin, named candidates in all but two of Ireland's constituencies. Two-thirds of them were in jail, and others were on the run from the British authorities. But, when the votes were counted, it emerged that the people of Ireland had declared for Sinn Féin and national self-determination in 73 seats out of 105. Those elected Republicans still at liberty met in Dublin in January, 1919, and constituted themselves as Dáil Éireann (Assembly or Parliament of Ireland). Using the electoral machinery of their British rulers, they had achieved for themselves a democratically elected Assembly of rebellion. The Constitution they drafted was the armature of an independent Irish state.

These tactics, of course, could prove a two-edged weapon. To employ British-made devices for the acquisition of Irish freedom carried with it the danger of the device imprisoning its new employers. The Irish rebels found that the maintenance of support for themselves among the population (a *sine qua non* to preserve their forces in the guerrilla fighting which broke out in the following year) was best ensured by not quarrelling with such aspects of British administration as had not incurred widespread hostility. During the Anglo-Irish conflict of 1919–21 the Dáil sought to administer the country as though its authority were unquestioned. In practice this meant such things as Dáil-created law courts, dispensing justice to the many country people who took their disputes to them, and being subject to dispersal as illegal assemblies by governmental author-ities should they surprise one of their sessions. Naturally, to increase popular confidence, the justice that was dispensed was on lines long familiar to the people, not in keeping with the ancient but obsolete traditions of pre-Norman law. And when the British forces withdrew, Ireland maintained English law. Even today, the legal systems of England and Ireland are more akin than those of England and Scotland. The difference largely lies in Irish failure to keep pace with English legal reform, although, of course, the Constitution of 1937 has given a further yardstick to justice. But the Irish Constitution has never obtained the place in the legal system that its American counterpart holds, nor was it intended to.

British governmental institutions, and many civil servants of the old régime, remained after 1921. Changes in personnel took place at many levels. But a certain degree of Irish nationalist influence in government had been evident in the years of Liberal rule before 1916. John Redmond, the leader of the Irish Parliamentary Party which Sinn Féin was to displace in 1918, enjoyed the exercise of some patronage within the British-controlled system. Sinn Féin attracted many who had been personally disappointed by Redmond's dispensing of patronage. Independence in certain cases simply meant old jobs for new boys. Awareness of popular conservatism also contributed to a continuity in administrative procedures. Considering how inflamed the rhetoric of the years of rebellion had been, the degree to which the old system was retained was very striking.

To gain even crude insight into the traditions and loyalties which are the dynamics of Irish politics today, one must know at least something of what happened between 1919 and 1923. The facts beyond argument are few enough, for these are the years in modern Irish history that can still arouse the most violent debate of all. In many Irish history books used by children, the story of the nation terminates gloriously with the Proclamation of an Irish Republic by the heroes of the 1916 Rising. The fratricidal scars of civil war are still too tender to probe.

One point may be conceded to David Lloyd George, the British premier during the critical years 1917–22. Whereas most British statesmen had been defeated by the incredible complexity of the Irish question, he may have turned the tables in making it, by his efforts at solution, far more complex than ever before. In 1920 he introduced and passed the Government of Ireland Act, under which two governments and parliaments were set up in Ireland, one in Belfast (for the six counties of Antrim, Down, Armagh, Londonderry, Tyrone and Fermanagh) and one in Dublin (for the remaining twenty-six counties). Both portions of Ireland were to be represented also in the Westminster Parliament, and from the members of both parliaments was to be constituted a council of Ireland. The Ulster Unionists disliked the plan, and their Dublin-born leader, Sir Edward Carson, had even more distaste for it, but it was ultimately accepted. Carson stepped aside, his lieutenant, Sir James Craig, became Prime Minister, and the state of Northern Ireland came into being. George V opened its Parliament in June, 1921.

It was indeed a patchwork solution, for Northern Ireland exists today by virtue of the 1920 act, the greater part of which was rendered a dead letter when Sinn Féin refused to accept it. The experiment in revolutionary representative government in the Twenty-six Counties was enjoying some success; the allied – but not subordinate – guerrilla army assisting Sinn Féin's efforts in the field had produced a brilliant general in Michael Collins, and very effective local commanders. As a result of Lloyd George's manoeuvres a situation obtained whereby nationalist Ireland, which had vainly sought Home Rule for fifty years, now declined a form of it, while the Six Counties (often wrongly styled Ulster, which consists of nine), whose ruling class had threatened to plunge both islands into civil war in 1914 rather than have Home Rule, had accepted precisely that. In doing so, Craig and his associates had obtained a permanent settlement which would ensure a continuation of the economic association between the industrialized Lagan Valley and its British market. That association might have been seriously affected in a nationalist Ireland whose spokesmen preached protectionism for the island. It also ensured that the north-eastern six counties would not have their destiny directed by their fellow Irishmen, the overwhelming majority of whom were Catholic and nationalist. It abandoned the Unionist pockets in east Donegal, Dublin, Cork and other areas, and the old Anglo-Irish landlord class whose power had been broken by land legislation in the late nineteenth and early twentieth centuries. And it left a Catholic nationalist minority in the six counties under the domination of Protestant Unionists whose relegation of them to second-class citizenship would sometimes be underlined by violence against them.

Nationalists had sought to maintain solidarity with their northern counterparts. But they fell victim to an irony of the events of 1918. In the early twentieth century the Irish Parliamentary Party had lost much of the dynamism of Parnell's day; but it had obtained new blood by the acquisition of Joe Devlin's effective political machine in West Belfast, which survived the débacle of the 1918 elections. (Mr De Valera himself, standing for several seats, suffered his sole defeat when he endeavoured to oust the Devlinists.) The North had played a significant part in Irish nationalism and socialism between 1910 and 1920 – Larkin and Connolly had agitated and organized among Belfast as well as Dublin workers; Sean MacDermott, perhaps the major contributor to bringing about the insurrection of 1916, had worked in Belfast; later, unrelenting Republicans including Joe McKelvey and Sean MacEntee were Belfast Catholics. But the fact that northern nationalism in the mass was Devlinist rather than Sinn Féin bred a theoretical concern rather than a practical identification with their northern brethren on the part of the southern Irish. It fostered a curious air of unreality in the approach of Sinn Féin to the North. Mr De Valera and most of his followers seemed to regard the northern Protestants as a different people from those

85

whom he led; this opinion in no way detracted from his belief that the entire island should be united under the rule of himself and his associates.

The first, revolutionary Dáil Éireann, the creation of a single party, Sinn Féin, presented a united front through three years of armed struggle. The perennial Irish tragedy of treachery in the midst of idealism had not been a feature of the 1916 rising and was not a feature to any significant degree now; Collins had reversed that liability by obtaining informers within the British ranks. At the end of 1921, the members of the Dáil were tested on their readiness to compromise in return for peace. Lloyd George offered a treaty. To refuse it was to incur what he termed 'immediate and terrible war', the term 'escalation' being as yet unknown (although that was precisely what was involved since the British forces, the Black and Tans, the Regular Auxiliaries, and the Royal Irish Constabulary were already practising war as immediate and terrible as was within their power). To accept the Treaty was to remain within the British Commonwealth, to acquiesce (subject to a dubiously effective Boundary Commission) in the omission of the six counties from an Irish Free State and to give Britain access to certain Irish ports in time of war. This Treaty was actually signed by Dáil Éireann's delegation to Downing Street, but without referring back to the Dáil, which could still repudiate it. It was on this issue that the Dáil divided. Those who supported the Treaty, led by Arthur Griffith (whose nationalism had originated in a parallel with the Austro-Hungarian dual monarchy), and Michael Collins (who as General thought in terms of his exhausted men and war-worn supporting populace), accepted it as the best possible bargain that could be obtained. Those who opposed the Treaty, of whom Éamon De Valera was the most notable, saw acceptance as betrayal of the 1916 Rising and of the 1918 vote of the people. Symbols had become exceedingly important in the minds of the revolutionary nationalists, and the provision that members of an Irish Parliament under the Treaty would take an oath of loyalty to the English King was singled out for particular attack. By contrast, the Six Counties received surprisingly little mention during the Treaty debates. Outside the Dáil, the most articulate representative voices of the tired nation – the majority of the Press, the Church and the middle class – were in favour of the Treaty. By a majority of only seven in 121 votes, the Dáil approved it, too. The unity of Sinn Féin was in pieces. A civil war between Free Staters and Republicans began on the morning of June 28, 1922.

By the summer of 1923, the military war was ending in Republican defeat. But the results of a general election held in early June 1922 had shown how deeply the people were divided: 58 pro-treaty men were elected, 36 anti-treatyites, and of the others (including Labour) 34. Civil war activity continued sporadically in guerrilla skirmishings and feuds long after hostilities between centrally organized battalions had ceased. And while Dáil Éireann today takes pride in the reasonable, democratic temper of a national parliament, flashes of the old enmities are not unknown. Some of the more vitriolic elder statesmen possess a capacity for wielding words in public with the remorselessness with which once they wielded guns. In keeping with the practice of Michael Collins himself, their public warfare of guns or words contrasts forcibly with their private charm and courtesy. An even more significant indicator of the survival of civil war sentiment is the emphasis which is still placed by heirs of both treatyite and anti-treatyite traditions on the fact that in 1932 when the electorate returned Mr De Valera to power, his defeated opponents relinquished the reins of government without any effort to employ extra-democratic means to exclude their former foes in arms from office. It is the stress on this orderly transfer of power which must seem so odd to the student of normal democratic politics. If politics in Ireland is recognized as the continuation of civil war by other means, the pride in what was done – and was not done – in 1932 becomes more comprehensible. After all, the USA proved unable to accept a similar transfer of power following an election ten years after its own civil war. And the democratic processes were not particularly fashionable in the Europe of the 1930s.

And finally, the civil war era cast very long shadows in the matter of party leadership. The pro-treaty forces were quickly deprived of their leaders of outstanding talent: Arthur Griffith died on August 12, 1922, Collins was gunned down in a Republican ambush ten days later, Kevin O'Higgins was assassinated in 1927. William T. Cosgrave, successor to Griffith as head of the Free State Government, was industrious, reliable and unspectacular. On the anti-treaty side several men of brilliance or of originality of thought were killed, and the survivors were long overshadowed by the lonely, charismatic figure of their leader, Éamon De Valera.

Nature of Parties in the Recent Past

Mr De Valera's party, Fianna Fáil, is, therefore, heir to the civil war divisions, and the same is true of its chief rival, Fine Gael (formerly Cumann na nGaedheal, the pro-treaty party). Under Mr De Valera's leadership, Fianna Fáil was built up from the ranks of those republicans who opposed the Treaty but who decided, in 1927, that abstention from the Free State Dáil no longer served a useful purpose. Despite the idealistic tone of the anti-treaty stand, the decision of 1927 demonstrated that Mr De Valera and his followers were prepared to circumscribe their idealism with practicality. They made the point even clearer by building up a highly efficient political machine. Daniel O'Connell, Charles Stewart Parnell, John Redmond and others had given Irish politics much experience of effective machine-work, an experience Irish emigrants to the USA made use of as they moved all too rapidly into Tammany Hall and similar institutions. Mr De Valera's party political methods possessed much in common with those of the past. Party and voter loyalties were heavily geared to the personality cult of Mr De Valera himself. National ideals were strongly stressed: the British lion's tail was regularly twisted around election time with the same fervour exhibited by Irish-American politicians in Mr De Valera's native Brooklyn in the nineteenth century. Economic and foreign policy achievements were stressed, and aspirations unlikely to be fulfilled (such as draining the Shannon on the lines of the Tennessee Valley Authority) were regularly pronounced imminent. In a time of political extremes, the Fianna Fáil party (notably after its first coming to power in 1932) remained comfortably on centre – slightly left-of-centre on constitutional questions, slightly right-of-centre on social ones. The leader himself possessed a degree of mystery and of the unknown which elevated his party from the ordinary. Like Parnell, he was dry and deliberate in a country whose orators were in general highly exotic. Like Parnell also, he had an appearance of aloofness from the mass of mankind. Irishmen seem by temperament to be happiest among the liberal arts: Parnell's hobby was geology, and Mr De Valera's profession was that of a mathematician. He seems to have carried the precision of his science into daily political life, up to the point, it has been suggested, of applying his findings on the theory of quaternions to the mastery of political conflict.

In personnel, the Fianna Fáil party were largely political neophytes, broadly representing the newer elements in Sinn Féin as opposed to those of political experience but alienated from the old Irish party which had sat at Westminster. Most of Mr De Valera's cabinet colleagues had been fugitives from the Free State Government during the Civil War. The only one of the senior party men to be possessed of notable political forebears, Mr Erskine Childers, is the son of a distinguished member of an English Liberal family who took up the cause of Irish republicanism, opposed the Treaty and was shot by the Free State Government's order. But if Fianna Fáil was not founded by sons of political dynasties, it soon fathered several.

Fine Gael has its dynasties also, but they are in many cases much longer-lived, and much more diversified in their inheritances. The shade of Tory Unionism is there, in the charming and universally liked person of Maurice Dockrell, who, true to his ancestry, cast the only negative vote on the Bill of 1949 to take Ireland out of the Commonwealth and declare her a republic. The descendants of Parnell's followers abound, including James Dillon, son of the last leader of Parnell's party, and the numerous O'Higgins clan, closely related to Tim Healy, most brilliant of Parnell's lieutenants and most venomous of his detractors. Sir Anthony Grattan Esmonde heads an even older political family, stretching back to the eighteenth-century Irish Whig romantic orator Henry Grattan, and including holders of a Parliamentary seat both in Parnell's House of Commons and in the Irish Free State Dáil. The identity of the present leader, Liam Cosgrave, reminds us that new dynasties are not the exclusive prerogative of Fianna Fáil. And, less obviously connected by family ties, there still remains a warmth for certain nuances of the Mussolinarian doctrines with which members of the party's precursor groups were infected *after* Mr De Valera's entry into office in 1932, nuances far less evident positively than negatively, including doctrinaire anti-Communism and hence political Catholicism (to be sharply distinguished, in the Irish context, from *politic* Catholicism to which all the major parties subscribe).

Much of the character of Cumann na nGaedheal/Fine Gael may be ascribed to its having been out of office from 1932 to 1948. Many of its attitudes were then formed in the negative mould of opposition to Mr De Valera. In roughly the same period the American Republican party acquired a similar cast. In both instances individual personalities of widely differing outlook rose to prominence in the opposition party. In both countries the party in power became generally identified for good or ill with a single man, its leader. Fianna Fáil discouraged individuality of intellectual (though not of emotional) expression; Fine Gael had no choice but to encourage it to excess, providing always that such expression, however individual, fell into some variety of conservatism. But both of these laws lost their immutability after Mr De Valera's retirement from politics.

The Labour Party, third largest in size, was founded in 1912 under the leadership of James Connolly, who was shot by the British for his part in the 1916 Rising. The party agreed to stay out of the 1918 election to leave the way clear for the nationalist priorities of Sinn Féin. Labour acted as the 'loyal opposition' until the De Valera forces entered the Dáil in 1927. Then, until 1932, Labour and Fianna Fáil had some points of ideological contact, with particular reference to criticism of social and economic action by the Cumann na nGaedheal government. In 1932, therefore, Mr De Valera was helped into office by Labour support. The Labour party was here following a tradition of Irish politics which considerably antedated the Treaty. The principle was to hold the balance of power between the two major parties in Parliament and extort the maximum concessions from each. Parnell had achieved this in 1885–6, and threw both Tories and Liberals out of office at different times in the process. Asquith's government of 1910–14 was similarly dependent on Redmond and his followers. The Labour party had now the chance of putting Parnell's tactics into action in Dáil Éireann.

But Labour fumbled it. Mr De Valera went to the country again in 1933, asked for election without dependence on anyone's support, and got it. Fifteen years in the political wilderness left Labour avid for office

89

at almost any cost, and in 1948 it quickly joined the rest of Mr De Valera's opponents in forming a coalition government, under Mr John A. Costello. Mr Costello was a Fine Gael leader, but not the head of the party, and he was selected by the coalition forces in preference to his more partisan chief, General Richard Mulcahy. Labour, however, did not supply the dynamism of the coalition, and the image rapidly took shape of the Fine Gael party dictating policies in which Labour acquiesced in its hunger for office. This was particularly noticeable during the second coalition, of 1954–57. There were many reasons, some of which will be considered later, as to why Labour evoked such an image and what, in general, ailed it. The image received some party recognition when Labour leaders declared, after 1957, that the party would not again operate in coalition with Fine Gael. The Parnell tactic had failed, as much as anything else because Parnell's prescription had not been followed. The Irish party never accepted office in a British government, and hence could seek their legislative aims without being fettered by job considerations. By entering the coalition governments, Labour sacrificed its independence of action.

Minor Party Successes and Failures

The same theme, with variations, afflicted the party called Clann na Poblachta whose significant political life was limited to some ten years. Ireland had long had traditions of exotic new parties which founded themselves with great panoply, nominated their members for seats in the Dáil, lost their deposits, quarrelled among themselves, split with themselves and dissolved themselves. But suddenly in 1947–48 the political sky was transformed by the appearance of a new star of ever-increasing brightness, twinkling in a bewildering succession of greens, pinks and reds (and some disillusioned supporters might say, finally settling for yellow). The new party possessed remarkably attractive possibilities. Its name, for one thing, had the comforting ring of pretentious obscurity which characterized the titles of the major parties. (Clann na Poblachta = family, or children, of the Republic; Fianna Fáil = Soldiers of Destiny; Fine Gael = Family of Ireland.) It was led by Mr Sean MacBride, whose father had been a martyr of the Easter Rising, and whose mother, the former Maud Gonne, was renowned in both literary and nationalistic circles. (She was also much beloved by Irish suffragettes of advancing years, one of whom is said to have told Mr MacBride at her funeral, 'Sean, Sean, you'll never be the woman your mother was'.) Mr MacBride was in a position to out-Dev Dev, and he did so by cashing some of the cheques drawn on the unsatisfied aspirations of Irish nationalism by Mr De Valera at election time over the preceding years. Much republican sentiment had declined to support Mr De Valera's entry into constitutional politics, and some portion of this now went to Mr MacBride: if the persons in question be thereby charged with inconsistency, it must be remembered that they had maintained their intransigence for twenty lonely years – an average political lifetime in most countries, if not in Ireland. The MacBride movement also attracted Socialists who had become convinced the spirit of Connolly had been forsaken by his party. It also won some response from persons of little previous political interest whose normal readiness to vote quietly for Fianna Fáil had become eroded by its failure to acquire a more modern image, and who found Fine Gael and Labour no better in this respect. Above all, Clann na Poblachta appealed to a 'lost generation' of Irishmen who had hitherto seen little hope of displacing the older men. We are conscious of a 'generation gap' today; such a gap was a major factor in the Irish political scene of 1947, even if it was not so termed.

Success in by-elections presaged a very bright future for the party. It mushroomed in membership and in voting support, but before its organization could keep pace with its growth, Mr De Valera moved into action and called a general election. Mr MacBride compounded his party's problems by talking of Ireland entering the dollar area: anti-partitionist rhetoric was one thing, but however nationalistic their politics most Irishmen possessed an economic caution too strong to contemplate with enthusiasm a move outside the sterling area. Given time, the electorate might have accepted or forgotten this heresy, but Mr De Valera did not give it time. In the event, Mr MacBride came out of the election with far less support than had been expected, obtaining only ten seats for himself and his followers: so, in a way, Mr De Valera's move was a success. But those ten seats were enough to hold the balance of power, and so, in terms of immediate political results, Mr De Valera was defeated. Clann na Poblachta did not seek to employ its special position for constant bargaining purposes. It may have been the siren song of office, it may have been a recognition that the party needed positive accomplishment as well as negative appeal to remain in the popular favour, but whatever the reason, Clann na Poblachta, like Labour, agreed to join an anti-Fianna Fáil coalition government. It might have been the wrong move even if the party had been fully organized and possessed of ideological cohesion. As matters stood, in fact, the party drew support from all sides of the political spectrum, from Marxists and Americanophiles, from Republicans happiest among their guns to, it was believed, His Grace the Most Reverend Dr John Charles McQuaid, Catholic Archbishop of Dublin. And there were signs that on this structure Mr MacBride was seeking to build a monarchy of the Fianna Fáil pattern.

The coalition government of 1948–51 produced a vigorous record for a time, under the self-effacing leadership of Mr Costello. Mr MacBride, as Minister for External Affairs, flashed from one foreign capital to the

91

next, and Ireland became a Republic in circumstances examined in Conor Cruise O'Brien's essay. Dr Noel Browne, the other Clann na Poblachta minister in the cabinet, virtually eradicated tuberculosis during his tenure of the Department of Health, by means of an ambitious hospital reform programme. But when the young Minister for Health attempted, in 1951, to introduce a 'mother-and-child' scheme (a welfare measure on lines similar to those of Britain's National Health Service), the resultant crises demonstrated the internal weaknesses of Clann na Poblachta as well as those of the coalition government. The measure was opposed both by Irish doctors and by the Roman Catholic hierarchy. The principal hospitals were under clerical direction. Mr Costello deferred to clerical pressure; Mr MacBride supported him against his own party colleague; Dr Browne resigned from office, government and party, and ventilated the entire affair. A divided Clann na Poblachta dwindled in strength at the ensuing election. Dr Browne was re-elected for his own seat with a greatly increased majority, and his votes, and those of his supporters, enabled Mr De Valera to return to office when the new Dáil voted for the new government. As for the Clann, it supported, but did not join, the second coalition government in 1954, withdrew that support to precipitate the election of 1957, and on that occasion was left with a single seat, not Mr MacBride's. The party dissolved some years later.

The same election of 1957 saw the re-emergence on the national political scene of a much more unbending Republicanism than that of Mr MacBride. Sinn Féin still survived as a small party of greatly diminished support. It now went forward with candidates, winning four seats but declining to occupy them inasmuch as it held, and holds, to the original Republican absolute of an independent Ireland of thirty-two counties. Dáil Éireann, representing and ruling a Republic of twenty-six counties, presents an unacceptable compromise. Sinn Féin has been associated with the IRA, an illegal and underground private army which pursued a number of abortive military campaigns against the British authorities in the six counties of Northern Ireland, the last of them a decade ago. Activity in the Republic has taken place more recently at the hands of splinter groups from the IRA, one of which blew up Nelson's Pillar in O'Connell Street, shortly before the golden jubilee of the Easter Rising. The Republican movement, a loosely-knit fraternity of intransigent nationalist idealism, is today in a period of transition from tactics of force to those of constitutional, and predominantly socialist, activity.

A Note on the Constitutional Position

Mention of the IRA in a discussion of modern Irish politics serves two purposes. It brings into focus the political arm of the movement, Sinn

Féin; and it also underlines for us the fact that modern Irish politicians have in some respects less room to manoeuvre than many of their foreign contemporaries. Democratic politics have been somewhat self-consciously on trial during much of the period since 1922. In many other countries, recourse to the gun is a danger raised only by politicians anxious to avail themselves of the luxury of finding exotic issues. In Ireland, the degree of independence which the Free State possessed seemed to owe its existence to the gun, and Irish politicians for many years afterwards could never be quite sure that the gun would not be reintroduced in an effort to redress their failures. Both of the major parties owed their existence to events during the era of the gun; both of them, certainly, had at critical moments given persuasive evidence for the strength of their conversion to democracy, Fianna Fáil in 1927 and Cumann na nGaedheal in 1932. But physical force remained an alternative to men on the extreme fringe of each party. Constitutional development, therefore, involved both a desire to show the effectiveness of democracy, and a certain recurring lack of confidence in its power for self-preservation.

Of the two Constitutions under which Ireland has been governed, those of 1922 and 1937, it was the former whose guarantees of personal liberty suffered more with the passage of time. 'The liberty of the person is inviolable', it stated, 'and no person shall be deprived of his liberty save in accordance with law'. But from 1923 onward legislation was repeatedly enacted to permit trial by military tribunal of political suspects, and also their detention without trial. The oath of allegiance to King George V for parliamentary representatives, against which Mr De Valera and his followers had protested in arms and subsequently in election campaigns, was a part of that constitution, and to prevent popular action leading to its repeal, the referendum and initiative which were also part of the constitution were abolished in 1928. When Mr De Valera came into office, he in his turn made use of the military tribunals whose function had by now been written into the constitution to cover trial of a significant range of offences. The very nature of the legislation in question had long been in use during the days of direct British rule in Ireland; the British might well have been amused, although it must be added that the Cosgrave government at least can never have been wholly confident that Britain would not again resume control of Ireland should the pressure of physical-force elements seem to be beyond the control of the Irish authorities.

Mr De Valera, on the other hand, recognized that his constituents were considerably less ready to maintain the constitutional *status quo*. If he reinvoked military tribunals he also sought to chip away at the stumbling-blocks that made it impossible for the more extreme elements to acquiesce in the existence of the new state. Little by little he removed the constitutional symbols of British power; by 1937 the oath was gone;

and following an adroit exploitation of the abdication of King Edward VIII, the King was disposed of too, save as an instrument for validating the accreditation of Irish diplomatic and consular officials to foreign courts. The Constitution of 1937, adopted by plebiscite, declared Ireland to be a 'sovereign, independent, democratic state'. It also declared the head of state to be a popularly elected president who would hold septennial office. Executive power, however, would be in the hands of the Taoiseach, or prime minister, who was to receive such office by means of a majority vote in Dáil Éireann, which would be the governing house of representatives. In practice the President's work has remained purely ceremonial, even when the incumbent was the formerly autocratic Mr De Valera himself. Nor does the upper house of the legislature, the Senate, whose members are partly nominated and partly elected, possess any more significance than that of a forum of limited practical power. The former Constitution had also possessed a Senate, but it had considerably greater power and force, being reminiscent of the British House of Lords of the same date. (In all but the heredity principle, that is: as Mr Fergus Linehan, the Dublin playwright, has remarked, it is in the lower house of the Irish legislature that the hereditary parallel still obtains.) The present Senate can serve a function in ventilating issues, but with a few exceptions, its personnel do little in this direction. It is in Dáil Éireann, with its 144 members (called, in the Irish language, *Teachtaí Dála,* or TDs), that the real power lies.

Detention without trial is still possible, and has been employed against political suspects within the last twelve years. The referendum is provided for in the present constitution, and has been employed, notably in the matter of the voting system itself. The system of proportional representation has been in use since the establishment of the Irish Free State. The single transferable vote which it allows entitles the elector not merely to vote for his favourite candidate, but also to show his order of preference for the other candidates. By a formula too complex for brief description, a successive reshuffling of votes elects three or more candidates for the same constituency, who may or may not be members of the same party. 'Vote Murphy No. 1' is the kind of slogan painted on walls and bridges and country cross-roads. The Republic has had its share of indecisive elections, and power to make or break a government has sometimes rested with a few independent TDs or with a tiny party. But the electorate has so far remained convinced of the essential fairness of the PR system, preferring the risk of instability to the prospect of monolithic majorities. Before he became president, Éamon De Valera linked a proposal to abolish PR with his own presidential candidature. The people voted 'Yes' for his election, but 'No' on the abolition of PR, thus frustrating his ambition to bequeath to Fianna Fáil the chance of unassailable security in power. In 1968 Fianna Fáil once more set on foot a campaign to abolish PR, which the country answered by an even stronger vote for its retention. This second appeal to the country on an issue decided nine years before seems capable of bringing the referendum into disrepute, and thereby weakening the force of a highly advantageous device for the realization of participation politics. It is a peculiarly necessary device for Ireland, where politicians' uncertainty respecting the viability of democracy has been reflected in the failure to train the nation's young in civics, at least until very recently.

The Major Parties Now

Until the beginning of the 1960s, the parties in the Republic were not distinguished by radically differing political philosophies. The degree of public ownership and State enterprise made necessary by the need for self-sufficiency as a nation and the absence of a large industrial prole-tariat had by-passed the kind of issue most often productive of a Left-Right political polarization. The loyalties of the civil war inevitably promoted traditions of patronage and reward persisting from one generation to the next. In a State of small population and intimate society, with a limited supply of secure or prestigious employment, party patronage was bound to assume a sharply personal significance. Even today, a large section of the Republic's population accepts the fact that personal political favours may be granted on the strength of family loyalties dating back to 1922. The integrity of political life is thus subject to publicly expressed cynicism. Whatever the national political issues of the moment, most of the electorate have voted according to family tradition, and the 'floating' vote has most often been swayed by respect for experience in the exercise of power. Fianna Fáil, the party which has governed longest and whose political organization is the most sophisti-cated, has survived several critical elections through public regard for 'professionalism' in administration.

Mr De Valera led that party for thirty-three years. In the protectionist years up to 1939, he directed the 'Economic War' with Britain and sub-sequently guarded the State's neutrality throughout the Second World War. The following decade saw two coalition governments but in 1957 Fianna Fáil was elected more decisively than at any time since 1944. When Mr De Valera moved into the presidential mansion, in 1959, leadership of the party and the office of Taoiseach fell to Mr Sean Lemass. A middle-class mercantilist with little personal feeling for agri-culture, Mr Lemass set out to develop commerce and industry, and to attract capital investment from abroad. The early 1960s saw a dramatic generation of economic activity, if at the price of inflation and increasing labour unrest.

In the late autumn of 1966, Mr Lemass announced his resignation. An early favourite for succession was his son-in-law, Mr Charles

95

Haughey, then Minister for Agriculture. Mr Haughey typifies one kind of post-revolutionary Fianna Fáil politician: urbanely aggressive, a little too well-groomed for popular trust, but carrying a convincing aura of power. It was widely accepted for some time that his relationship to the Taoiseach would ensure his succession, but this was not to be so. The man eventually chosen by the party was the Minister for Finance, Mr Jack Lynch. An unassertive, mild-mannered barrister of 49, Mr Lynch was one of the few members of the Cabinet likely to command the unanimous loyalty of the party. The selection of a Taoiseach had coincided with a period of acute agrarian grievance, which might well have been aggravated by the choice of Charles Haughey as Fianna Fáil leader. Mr Lynch was enough of an unknown quantity to the public to arouse no strong feelings one way or the other.

Voting support for Fianna Fáil has rested on no clear class identity. During the 1930s, its protectionist policies appealed to the small domestic manufacturer, but since the war and, more particularly, under Mr Lemass's leadership, Fianna Fáil encouraged preparation for free trade, initially with Britain and potentially as a member of the Common Market. While governing a country with more public enterprises than almost any other West of the Iron Curtain, the Fianna Fáil leadership has acted empirically: benevolent to private enterprise when attracting outside capital investment; and murmuring Leftish noises when promising improvements in the social services. The traditional nationalist vote, moved by gratitude to the old Republican symbolism of Éamon De Valera, may be slowly weakening, but its numbers have so far been made up through mistrust of less experienced alternatives. Where a country's two main parties seem to offer no clear ideological choice, the mere practice of power can create its own momentum. Fianna Fáil has thus come to appeal to those who admire the manipulation of power and who might like a little of it for themselves. The resourceful, entrepreneurial Irishman, especially of the rural and less prosperous areas, may be genuinely impressed by the party's air of enterprise, or he may decide that it controls the significant opportunities for advancement and prosperity. In the cities and the market towns, he sees the successful echelons of Fianna Fáil achieving an affluent manner of life which can seem to be the reward of an adventurous opportunism – or simply the legitimate fruit of national independence.

The Fine Gael party had its origins in the urban, bourgeois Ireland which feared the material consequences of separation from Britain. During the 1930s, with Fianna Fáil in power, a section of Fine Gael supporters created a martial force, in opposition to the IRA, which became known as 'the Blueshirts'. But the party itself eventually evaded the neo-Fascist, corporate-State protagonists on its fringes and retreated into an undramatic respectability more in keeping with its social basis of support. Today, the party still draws most of its urban votes

96

*Slea Head, Dingle Peninsula, Co Kerry. A beautiful beach without a crowd –
impossible to find? Not in Ireland!*

from the commercial and professional middle class, which has accepted the self-sufficiency of a separate nationality and would like to protect its interests politically. For the 1965 election, Fine Gael tried to equip itself with a more colourful political image by adopting a programme called 'The Just Society'. This promised a social policy which might more predictably have come from a party of the Left. The incongruity of this programme with the traditional social base of the party may have bewildered the floating voter: Fine Gael gained no new seats. In the 1966 election for the presidency, however, the Fine Gael candidate, Tom O'Higgins, came very close to unseating Éamon De Valera, who was given a majority of only 10,700 votes in a poll of more than 1,100,000. The Fine Gael vote was at least partly one of protest: not against Mr De Valera, but against the manner in which Fianna Fáil conducted the campaign on his behalf. Aggrieved that Mr De Valera should be op-posed in a year of national celebration to mark the 50th anniversary of the 1916 Rising, Fianna Fáil TDs made speeches which provoked many people into casting the first Fine Gael vote of their lives. But for their anger with the style of the Fianna Fáil campaign, they would have been quite content for the elderly Mr De Valera to end his days as head of state. The Fine Gael campaign, showing new organizational strength in the party, projected Mr O'Higgins as a middle-class family man, young by political standards, and this evoked quite inappropriate associations with the Irish public image of the late President Kennedy. When Kennedy visited the Republic, he was received as the ultimate symbol of the 'local boy' made good, and the great wealth of his family was seen as the reward of respectable ambition. Irish regard for social respect-ability has become a political factor. It is a fairly complex emotion, arising only partly from those aspirations predictable in a developing country long harassed by economic insecurity. It is also fed by a feeling akin to embarrassment about Ireland's poor and violent past. Her revo-lutions were led by militant minorities, and while their accomplishment has nurtured a general pride in retrospect, the urban populations, in particular, still hanker after the propriety they feel ought to go with prosperity. 'It's time we grew up' is the catch-phrase expressing both a material wish and a social self-reproach: and the party most likely to gain from confused aspirations to 'respectability' is Fine Gael.

But while support may be mounting for what is generally seen as a party of the Right (especially, perhaps, from recent entrants to the urban lower middle class), there is a sharpening confrontation between two very dissimilar elements in Irish society. James Connolly, the Irish socialist and co-operativist, once wrote of other centuries: 'The Irish Gael sank out of sight, and in his place the middle-class politicians, capitalists and ecclesiastics laboured to produce a hybrid Irishman, assimilating a foreign social system, a foreign speech and a foreign character.' At the time of the 1916 Rising, the 'hybrid' Irishman formed

97

Spectators at the Currach Championships in Galway. The frail lath-and-canvas currach is the traditional craft of the western coast, and races are keenly contested by fishing villages

a social hinterland to the occupying British Ascendancy: a class of real wealth and privilege whose *milieu* was Georgian Dublin and the country mansion. When the Ascendancy departed, the 'hybrid' Irish were left to support the Treaty with Britain and to pick up the social and commercial strings relinquished by their former masters. To the immediate descendants of this social group is now added a swelling generation of urbanized Irish whose regard for technology and the modern devices of capitalism has led to their rejection of what they see as at best an irrelevant, at worst a handicapping, adherence to an outmoded Gaelic culture. This culture is seen as entrenched in the countryside and the small towns, for whose economic ills they may hold it responsible.

This reaction has been fostered by the industrial and technological priorities of Fianna Fáil's economic policy, allied to a courtship of investment in Ireland by multi-national capitalism. In the national demotion of agriculture, both economically and socially, the preoccupations and philosophical modes of traditional Gaelic culture have come to be associated with drift and decline. Ironically, the Fianna Fáil party, while engendering these new attitudes through its development policies, must insist on its monopoly of loyalty to the nationalist cultural tradition and, in particular, to promotion of the cultural ideal of reviving the Irish language. Fine Gael, on the other hand, needs to be less inhibited in political exploitation of the new, commercially-oriented attitudes. Its 1966 policy statement on the language recognized the arrival of a social situation favourable to its historical class image.

Throughout the fight for independence, a dedication to revival of the Irish language was a central ideal. When the State came into being, Irish was surviving as an everyday tongue in a few, remote areas of the North, West and South: the Gaeltacht. It was the new nation's ambition, at that time agreed by all parties, that the Irish should speak their own language rather than English. Irish was given priority in the schools and at least a minimal fluency was demanded for entry to the civil service and other national institutions. Judging it in retrospect, the attempt at revival was intensive but inexpert, and English remains the vernacular of the vast majority of the Irish people. The revival programme has not, however, lessened, and remains a focus of passionate controversy. A section of the population undoubtedly resents what it calls 'compulsory' Irish in the schools. Another section – equally hard to number – is deeply attached to the role of Irish as a cultural card of identity. Beyond these fiercely partisan groups are the people whose sentiment is loyal to the language, but who are confused about the place it should occupy in the national life: these are probably the majority. In its 1966 policy statement, Fine Gael proposed to relax the educational insistence on Irish and replace it by measures of 'encouragement'. This was widely seen, however, as a prelude to relinquishing the language altogether, and it provoked a reaction of suspicious anger which may have surprised the party by its intensity. The renewal of controversy on the language served to dramatize the estrangement of cultural groupings: one predominantly urban, technologically-oriented and seeking its social models in expense-account capitalism; the other predominantly rural, preoccupied with human relationships and communal hierarchies, and defining its heroes in near-mythological terms.

The leaders of 1916 were themselves mostly middle-class, but they envisaged a proletarian Republic. The national anniversary celebrations of 1966 invited reappraisals of the original hopes of the revolutionaries: what had the struggle been *for* and what in fact had come to pass? This led to a renewal of interest in the writings of James Connolly, who of all the 1916 leaders had the clearest picture of the Ireland he wanted to see. And while Connolly's socialist objectives were framed in a very different socio-economic context from the Ireland of 1966, the clarity of his principles was still persuasive. In the rank and file of the Labour Party and among people reluctant to enter the party without a radical reorientation of its policies, the pressure for an avowedly *socialist* party was intensified. By 1968, both the party leadership and its policies had responded.

From the establishment of the State up to 1966, the Labour Party had steadily retreated from the socialism preached by Connolly. Until 1930, the political and trades union branches of the labour movement were united in a single organization, but at a special congress in that year it was decided to make the party a distinct and separate entity. The unions remained as affiliated members, but in 1944 the Irish Transport and General Workers' Union broke away from it. This in turn split the loyalties of the eight Labour members of the Dáil and the Labour movement was not reunited until 1950. Unlike the Labour parties of other countries, the Irish party has lacked a large base of support in urban industry. For most of its history, its strength has rested principally with small farmers and agricultural labourers and it has not succeeded in winning the full support of what industrial population exists. Until the encyclicals of Pope John XXIII, insisting vigorously on liberal concepts of social justice, on the virtue of co-operativism and proletarian self-help, Roman Catholic attitudes in Ireland were still apt to equate socialism with Communism. By most European standards, the trade union rank-and-file are still remarkably conservative, and the Labour Party itself has been led by men philosophically far removed from the kind of socialist active in the British Labour Party or the Left-wing parties of the Continent.

But in recent years the Labour Party has been acquiring increasing support from socialists, if only because they feel they have nowhere else to go. Dr Noel Browne joined it in 1963, after unhappy experiences in Fianna Fáil, and in a short-lived party of his own, the Progressive Democrats. In the former case he left the party when it declined to renominate him after his defeat in 1954; he then won election in 1957, a year of Fianna Fáil national victory, when he ran as an independent in the seat for which Fianna Fáil had denied him its nomination. Independent financial survival ultimately proved impossible for the Progressive Democrats (founded in 1958) and it was then that Dr Browne joined the Labour Party. His decision cost him his seat once more, but he had the consolation, at the 1966 conference of the Labour Party, of hearing the party leader, Mr Brendan Corish, respond to a new militancy in the rank-and-file by declaring, at last, the party's adherence to 'a coherent socialist philosophy'. At the same time the party's decision to offer a candidate in every constituency in the next general election showed its new confidence in the possibility of gaining power.

The political career of Noel Browne holds major lessons for the student of Irish politics both for itself and as a clue to the nature of challenges now confronting the Labour Party which by becoming his home has become the heir to all that he symbolises. On a longterm perspective it may be suggested that the issue at stake in the 1951 crisis was not so much one of Socialism itself as of the public expression of Socialism. What the affair revealed above all else was the gap between Dr Browne's concept of democracy and that held both by his opponents and by some of his friendly critics. Dr Browne, whose political inexperience at once enlarged his moral strength and weakened his capacity for manoeuvre, accepted the principle of consultation of the relevant parties, but maintained that his right and his duty lay in subordinating party political considerations to a point of principle and in taking the argument, in all its complexity, to the people. Opponents and some others took the view that Irish politics simply could not be carried on at this level: relations with the church required delicate private diplomacy, and the assurance that the privacy would be maintained. The suspicion of Irishmen publicising Irish controversies dogged Dr Browne, as it has dogged Irish men of letters. Many who condemned Messrs Costello and MacBride as spineless in their dealings with the hierarchy still felt that Dr Browne had committed the unforgiveable political sin by placing his documented narrative of negotiations before the newspaper-reading public. It was even argued that the public was too new in the ways of democracy to digest the strong diet which depicted politicians and their responses to pressure as these really existed. The public had, indeed, come to consider politicians as a class apart, and politicians' election addresses for the most part did little to suggest either a desire for or a belief in an informed electorate. The politician sought votes of confidence in parties rather than issues. Dr Browne had taken arms against this situation. It was curious that his subsequent history suggested that many voters reached the height of their admiration for him at the points where he was outside any major party, for his defeats all came when he stood as a candidate of Fianna Fáil or Labour. Yet in economic terms it was impossible for Dr Browne to survive as anything more than an increasingly lonely voice when outside a major party; his services as a political educator to the public are unparalleled, yet as his experience of power receded into the past his sense of the current stakes in the power structure must necessarily have weakened also. It may be argued that he had the opportunity to remake Irish politics in 1951 by creating a new socialist party. Yet such an action would have required a mastery of political mechanics which he did not have, and which he clearly was admired for not having. His unyielding idealism, his unquestionable integrity and his martyrdom went to give a picture to the public of a man by his nature at war with the political class. Idealist though he may have been, Dr Browne's simple democratic beliefs seem to have had more in common with the popular spirit in 1951 than those of Mr Costello, who can hardly be blamed for thinking in the traditional terms in which he had obtained his political education, or of Mr MacBride, for whom imprisonment in traditionalist politics was hardly an inescapable heritage. Indeed, Clann na Poblachta may have owed its popularity to a public desire for something on the lines of what is nowadays termed 'participation politics'; if so, it was Dr Browne, its Ishmael, and not Mr MacBride, its Abraham, who took possession of that kingdom.

It may be arguable that as a result of Dr Browne's actions in 1951, Ireland is today less socialist in practice than it would otherwise be. (It is undeniable that because of Dr Browne there are more Socialists, quite apart from those whose lives he saved.) It can be answered that without some public education on the issues at stake, the demand for Socialism could not have been great enough to win what little political response to it that there has been. But without Dr Browne Irish democracy would surely have been in much worse health. Political cynicism could have bitten much deeper, and had much more serious consequences, had he not existed to show that some men of pure devotion to principle could emerge from the democratic process. Politicians, as a class, did not enhance their image as a result of the Browne crisis; but, what was much more important, democratic politics won a much-needed vindication. As the dean of Irish political analysts, Michael McInerney, has argued in his brilliant 'Noel Browne: Church and State' (in the Irish journal *University Review*, vol. V, no. 2 (Summer, 1968)), Dr Browne 'was before, not with history. But his work created a watershed and today history is catching up with him, but only very slowly' (p. 215). That it is doing so is due to his work as a ventilator of political issues in the domestic sphere. It is significant that the other great symbolic figure of the Irish Left should have made a parallel contribution in the arena of world events when he made public the secret machinations that gave rise to his crisis, in 1961. And it was that other man, Conor Cruise O'Brien, who caught the reality of the hostility to such public statements when he quoted Hamlet: 'All which, sir, though I most powerfully and potently believe, yet I hold it not honesty to have it thus set down'.

Contemporary Prospects for the Left

Dr Browne's desperate search for a political home underlines the conflict of possible methods for the Irish Left. Even today he will attract workers who would never ordinarily support a Labour Party candidate, and should he again be returned to a seat in the Dáil he is likely to prove of considerable influence both as a Socialist critic of government and as a yardstick of political morality. But Labour has far to go before the party itself can evoke the activist response of popular idealism which was once roused by Dr Browne. Today he is vice-chairman of the party, yet in 1968 when the party leadership asked him to stand in a by-election the local organization, lacking sufficient pressure from the national leaders, selected an unknown in his stead. The incident reminds us that Labour is still a party deriving much of its electoral strength from local loyalties in rural seats, and as such a conversion of its leaders to Socialism could prove a hollow triumph. On the other hand, the urban roots are being renewed: in 1967 the Irish Transport and General Workers' Union, largest of Irish trade unions with 150,000 members, resolved to affiliate with the party, thereby strengthening the party's organization, war-chest and power orientations.

The new political enthusiasm of the Republican movement represents another aspect of the resurgence of Irish Socialism. The semi-underground Republican leadership in Dublin has begun to take the co-operative movement into account in its planning, while, previous to this, many individual Republicans had already made their mark in assisting co-operative development in depressed areas of the country. The future direction of such thought is as yet unclear. The Special Branch detectives, keeping track of Republicans involved in past campaigns of violence, have been professionally suspicious of the apparent transition from the gun to the economic text book. The political analyst trained in a somewhat different school may prefer to suggest that possible future avenues include peaceful expression through the Sinn Féin party, which has not succeeded in maintaining its 1957 successes, or in a Republican party of open membership and constitutional method. The latter expedient would seem the more fruitful, particularly since the Sinn Féin victories of 1957 owed something to the tactic, long honoured in Irish nationalist politics, of nominating political prisoners currently suffering for their principles. The political benefits of this tactic proved short-term; and the tactic itself implied a close association with the campaign by violence in Northern Ireland, despite the reasonable doubt that exists as to the justice of some verdicts by Northern Ireland courts which made martyrs, and hence candidates, of the accused.

Meanwhile Republicanism may find an outlet in the National Council of Labour, proposed by the Irish Labour Party conference of 1966 as a way of uniting the Left-wing parties of North and South. As we said earlier, Belfast and Dublin possess many common factors in the histories of their labour movements. Labour victories in Dublin city local elections in 1967 support the thesis of a firm urban base of power for Labour at last, while ill-success in the same elections throughout the country indicate that the rural pockets of Labour support under the domination of local personalities are crumbling. Labour's future, if any, in rural Ireland would seem to be linked to movements of protest and reform, such as the co-operatives or the currently embattled National Farmers' Association. The co-operatives also suggest one link between North and South in the future, having been successful on both sides of the border. Recent reverses may also force the Northern Ireland Labour Party to rethink its tactics of putting its Unionist loyalties before all else, much as the Irish Labour Party has been finally led to endorse Socialism despite the risks of being denounced as Communistic.

It is, of course, quite possible that the carpet may be pulled from under all of the actors in the Irish political drama. Irish politicians, like others of their fellow-countrymen, are becoming increasingly conscious of the world in addition to their standard refuges in moments of intellectual bankruptcy – the Flesh and the Devil. The world may very well find its own solutions for Ireland. Now that the payment of political parties by foreign secret services is being restored to the status it once enjoyed in the seventeenth and eighteenth centuries, it is possible that Irish political parties may not be considered beneath the contempt of paymasters in search of friends. Ireland has the advantage for such would-be philanthropists of possessing a myriad of admirable channels for such an activity. Sometimes the great powers may employ subtler methods of influencing domestic politics, which have shown themselves none the less effective. The dubious question of Britain's entry into the Common Market could well re-emerge as a catalyst in Irish politics. Recent kite-flying from the present government has involved a readiness to suggest we are now less nationalistic and less committed to the political theories of nationalism than we have been pretending: this may be the medicine to be prescribed if our politics are to be tailored to the ideas of the USA or Britain, but it is less appropriate if the arbiter of our destinies turns out to be France. Nationalism has in the past proved a useful means of enabling election rhetoric to be substituted for critical social issues, while at the same time it has kept certain forms of dissent alive. But the viability of nationalism and socialism could well prove the turning-points of future debate in a world where the domestic politics of few countries can be regarded as immune from external pressures.

103

Ireland in
International Affairs
Conor Cruise O'Brien

i. Status and Symbols

In the first years of the Irish State, the debate was about identity, legitimacy, symbolism, status. Was the Irish Free State – the creation of the Anglo-Irish Treaty of 1921 – the authentic representative of the historic Irish nation, entitled to speak on its behalf to the other nations of the world? Was the Republic, proclaimed in 1916, still in being as the sole legitimate inheritor of the national tradition? Or was a third conception to be preferred, based on Mr De Valera's theory of 'external association' and combining the requirements of legitimacy and practicality?

This debate – the ideological continuation of the civil war of 1922–23 – underlay all Ireland's early efforts in the international field. The foreign representatives inherited by the Provincial Government from the revolutionary Dáil, were themselves in confusion, and a prey to conflicting loyalties. The first Minister for External Affairs of the Irish Free State, Desmond Fitzgerald, told the Dáil, in January 1923, that 'the former Irish Trade Agent in Paris[1] had now passed into the care of the Irregulars. This is solely due to treachery on the part of the late Trade Agent.' A few months later he spoke with some distaste of Ireland's representatives abroad generally: 'The fact is we began a few months ago without any foreign affairs that we could call foreign affairs, but with a certain number of representatives abroad. The only useful functions they could serve abroad were those of publicity agents. They handicapped themselves with such high-sounding titles as Ambassadors and Colonial [sic] Ambassadors.'[2] Of the two representatives in Italy one was an honest man but 'an avowed adherent of the internal enemies of the State'; the other was 'not an avowed adherent' but 'not an honest man' either. The man in Spain believed his office there could serve no useful purpose 'because Spain had no foreign policy and for other reasons.'[3] The Berlin man was said to be doing 'fairly useful work.'[4]

The disarray of the representatives abroad, as seen by the Minister responsible for their activities, is hardly surprising. These men had

---

[1]*Dáil Debates* II, cols. 1079–80: January 30, 1923 or *Round Table,* March 1960
[2]*Dáil Debates* III, cols. 2388–2402: June 25, 1923
[3]Ibid
[4]Ibid

been engaged in revolutionary anti-British propaganda. They were now required not only to desist altogether from this, but to represent a State committed to the repression of the sort of activities in which they had been engaging.[1] Even those who sincerely gave their loyalty to the new state were virtually disqualified – by reason of their former activities, former contacts and antagonisms formerly aroused – from serving it effectively in the same capital in a radically changed situation.

But even if the representatives abroad could be adapted to a new function, was there in reality any such function for them, in the service of this state which began 'without any foreign affairs that we could call foreign affairs'? The opponents of the Treaty, of course, maintained – in the early years at least[2] – that there was not, since the Irish Free State, not being an independent entity, could have no independent rôle in international affairs. But even some of those who had accepted the Treaty settlement were sceptical about the extent to which that settlement might permit an independent foreign policy. George Gavan Duffy, former Foreign Minister of the Republic, speculated sardonically about the reason for the change from the old description of the Department, to the new 'dominion' language: 'Our foreign affairs have become external affairs. "Don't you think it would sound rather nicer to have external rather than foreign affairs?" "Yes if you say so".'[3] Grattan Esmonde, a conservative Deputy, believed that the representatives of the Free State abroad were absolutely useless: '. . . They have no power, they have no status, they have no position, they have no means of obtaining alternative markets[4] and they are not backed up by the government which sent them out for that ostensible purpose . . . At the present time all ideas, all suggestions, are rejected which are not English suggestions or which are not in accordance with the traditions of the British Treasury.'[5] The suspicion that the whole idea of representation abroad was a sham blended in some minds with the resentment, natural in poor countries, at the social 'airs' of diplomats and at the expense required to maintain them. Martin Corry, a Deputy noted for blurting out things not often uttered in parliaments, complained that 'salaries of £1,500' had to be paid so that the representatives of the Free State abroad 'might squat like the nigger when he put on the black silk hat and the swallow-tail

[1] The Department of External Affairs was at this time a centre for propaganda in favour of the new State – and against its enemies – inside as well as outside Ireland. See *Dáil Debates* VIII, cols. 799–843: July 9, 1924

[2] And to some extent even after Mr De Valera's entry into the Dáil in 1927. See speeches by Mr De Valera and the late Sean T. O'Kelly in *Dáil Debates* XXX, cols. 786–894: June 5, 1929

[3] *Dáil Debates* III cols. 2388–2402: June 25, 1923. Replying, the Minister Desmond Fitzgerald, denied that the British Government 'asked us to call it External Affairs'.

[4] The need to open markets, other than Britain, for Irish products was one of the reasons most regularly adduced in justification of Ireland's offices abroad

[5] *Dáil Debates* VIII, cols. 799–845: July 9, 1924

105

coat and went out and said he was an English gentleman.'[1]

The climate in which the new state began to take its first steps in international affairs was then a harsh one. Snobs despised its representatives for not being able to attain the standard of the British Diplomatic Service: populists despised them for apparently aspiring to these standards. The opponents of the Treaty suspected the foreign service of being part of a façade and a sham: the upholders of the Treaty were in the beginning contemptuous of the foreign service for which they found themselves responsible; some of them seem to have been uncertain as to whether it could serve a useful purpose.[2]

Yet if the climate was harsh it was also stimulating to growth and development. The Department of External Affairs was of necessity the most important political Department of a state whose international status was contested. Cumann na nGaedheal, the party which held power for the first ten years – 1922–1932 – contended, as Michael Collins had done, that the Treaty gave 'freedom to achieve freedom'. It was through the Department of External Affairs that this claim had to be made good. The governing party had the most powerful incentives to make it good. They had, first, the incentive of that basic Irish patriotism which was common to both sections of Sinn Féin, as well as to the old Irish Party. They had also specific and lively personal and party incentives in their desire to refute the Republican case against the Treaty, and to prove that they and their party, far from betraying Ireland's freedom, had worked for it in the most effective way. And they could legitimately hope that, in proving this, they might win over many of the ominously large section of the population which continued to give enthusiastic support to Éamon De Valera, despite the military outcome of the civil war.

The Department of External Affairs, therefore, under the leadership first of Desmond Fitzgerald and then of Patrick McGilligan,[3] set itself, with a skill, pertinacity and tact for which it received rather little credit, to the task of applying 'freedom to achieve freedom'. Specifically it wanted to demonstrate that a country with the status of a dominion – which was the status of the Irish Free State under the Treaty – was not thereby subordinate to the British Government in international matters,

[1]*Dáil Debates* XXVII, cols. 430–500: November 21, 1928. Such sentiments were fairly widespread and tenacious. The present writer remembers – as late as 1943 – an elderly official of the Department of Finance, who whenever he saw the words 'External Affairs' on a file used to mutter '*mothor*-car allowances' – and spit

[2]Above p. 105 At the very beginning, Gavan Duffy referred to 'a section of opinion – official or semi-official – which desires to see our foreign affairs damped down or closed down'. *Dáil Debates* I, cols. 29–30: September 9, 1922

[3]Gavan Duffy had been Minister for Foreign Affairs in the transitional post-Treaty period. Desmond Fitzgerald was succeeded in June 1927 as Minister for External Affairs by Kevin O'Higgins, the Minister for Justice, who was assassinated in the following month. President Cosgrave then himself took over the Ministry briefly. Mr McGilligan became Minister in October, 1927

but exercised its own choices. Aided to some extent by a general trend in the Empire-Commonwealth, but also significantly aiding this trend by its own exertions, the Department of External Affairs was able to make notable progress in the desired direction. We need not here attempt to follow the constitutional evolution in any detail, but a few milestones on the road to an acknowledged right to an independent foreign policy should be noted. In 1923, the Free State entered the League of Nations.[1] In 1924, it registered the Anglo-Irish Treaty with the League, thereby seeking to confer on the Treaty an international status which the British Government had not quite intended: that Government protested against the registration. In 1925 Desmond Fitzgerald, in the Dáil, said that the equality of Commonwealth members was recognized but 'the implementation of that equality' was not quite up to date and there was need for 'progress in that direction', relying on 'the moral pressure of public opinion.'[2] England, he said, was 'our most important external affair.'[3] In this year also the Free State by appointing a Minister Plenipotentiary to Washington became the first country with the status of a dominion to appoint a diplomatic representative to a non-Commonwealth country – an example soon to be followed by Canada.[4] In 1926 the Imperial Conference in London, in which the representatives of the Free State played a significant part, recognized the self-governing members of the British Empire as 'equal in status', though a special position for the United Kingdom was to some extent safeguarded by a reference to dissimilarity of 'function'[5]. The extent of the advance won at the Imperial Conference was hardly clear in Ireland at the time. In the Dáil a Labour critic, Tom Johnson, described it as not an advance at all but 'a retrogression', and – stressing the distinction between 'status' and 'function' – contended that 'these pronouncements concede equality of status within the British Commonwealth but inequality or at least unity in relation to all non-British states and Governments.'[6] The contention was sound enough at the time but soon became obsolete. The gingerly protection provided by 'dissimilarity of function' for the idea of a British tutelage over the international activities of Commonwealth countries soon wore away; indeed it 'was undermined' – in the words of Professor Nicholas Mansergh – 'by the Free State Government within the next few years.'[7] That government took advantage of the 'Kellogg Pact' in 1928 to demonstrate that the idea of imperial unity in international affairs no longer held. Britain had

---

[1] See Section ii below
[2] *Dáil Debates* XI, cols. 1413–1470: May 13, 1925
[3] Ibid
[4] *Round Table* June 1928
[5] *Report of the Imperial Conference*
[6] *Dáil Debates* XVII, cols. 711–770: December 15, 1926
[7] *The Irish Free State. Its Government and Politics* (1934) Chapter XV 'External Affairs' pp. 259–275

accepted the United States invitation – for a treaty to 'outlaw war' – with a reservation touching its imperial responsibilities. The Free State Government took what one of its admirers described as its 'first big step in international affairs'[1] by accepting the invitation *without reservation*. This action proved, according to the same writer, 'the absolute international freedom of the Free State.' This view received further corroboration when, on September 14, 1929, the Free State signed at Geneva, again without reservation, an instrument which the United Kingdom and other Commonwealth countries had signed with a reservation as to inter-Commonwealth disputes.[2] By these symbolic actions the Free State Government was demonstrating the intention asserted by Mr McGilligan: to eliminate 'any possibility of doubt' about 'the supreme and conclusive authority of the Parliament of this State in all matters external and internal concerning its interests.'[3] At the same time Mr McGilligan put the Department of External Affairs – often up to this time described as the 'Cinderella' of Departments – on a more professional basis, introducing regular Civil Service salary scales, raising allowances of representatives abroad, regularizing their designations, and establishing legations in France and Germany. The reorganization followed the rise in recognized status. The situation created by the Imperial Conference, Mr McGilligan explained to the Dáil, 'postulated far-reaching readjustments' in the external relations of the member States with international society at large. Our contribution to the development of these doctrines was positive, persistent and decisive . . . Our Treaty with Great Britain and the Constitution of the Irish Free State gave a new direction to constitutional thought, and set going new forces and new processes in constitutional speculation within the Commonwealth of Nations itself.'[4] The seal was set on this work by the Imperial Conference of 1930 and the Statute of Westminster (1931). 'It might be said', writes Professor Mansergh, 'that with the Imperial Conferences of 1926 and 1930 and the Statute of Westminster, the British dominions have reached complete independence . . . For this development in inter-Imperial constitutional law and practice the Free State is in no small measure responsible.'

It is apparent in retrospect that in these first ten years the Irish State played a more momentous and influential part in international affairs

[1]*Round Table* September 1928. One of Mr De Valera's leading supporters, Mr Sean T. O'Kelly – later President of Ireland – had his own reservations about the pact to outlaw war: 'We do not think it would be right that we should say in advance that we will give up the only means that have yet been used with success to bring that powerful secular enemy of ours to her senses.' (*Dáil Debates* XXIX, cols. 277–320: February 21, 1929)

[2]The instrument was the Optional Clause (Article 36) of the Statute of the Permanent Court of International Justice. Mr Donal O'Sullivan in *The Irish Free State and its Senate* emphasizes the importance of this Irish departure

[3]*Dáil Debates* XXVII, cols. 431–500: November 21, 1928

[4]*Dáil Debates* XXX, cols. 786–894: June 5, 1929

than it was ever to play again. It had speeded up that process which may be called either the evolution of the Commonwealth concept, or the peaceful disintegration of the Empire. It had brought a quite distinct historical sense, fundamentally though discreetly antipathetic, into the explication of those monarchical and imperial 'bonds', which for most other dominions were the metaphorical 'bonds of sentiment' but which in Ireland were felt as real bonds, involuntarily worn. It 'under-mined'—Mansergh's word—an old hegemony, which time had weakened, but which custom, had it not been probed with innovating intent, might otherwise have sustained considerably longer. As it turned out, those who at the time of the Anglo-Irish Treaty sought to defend the integrity of the Empire by insisting on keeping the Irish Free State within that Empire had made a serious mistake. They had clasped – as Boyle Roche would scarcely have failed to observe – a Trojan horse to their bosom.

From an Irish point of view these were remarkable achievements. Yet it is clear that – except for convinced supporters of Cumann na nGaedheal – they left the Irish people cold. Those who had achieved so much were dismissed from office immediately after their crowning achievement. 'The Statute of Westminster received the Royal Assent on December 11, 1931, six weeks before the dissolution which was the prelude to a change of government in the Irish Free State.'[1] There were of course domestic reasons, which we need not discuss here, for Cumann na nGaedheal's loss of support. But there were 'external' reasons also. The solid successes of Fitzgerald and McGilligan in this field were not easy to grasp. They had symbolic significance but lacked dramatic impact. The announcement 'The Optional Clause has been signed *without reservation*' was important but unlikely to make the rafters ring in Roscommon. But the *methods* which had been used to win these valuable but inconspicuous results were themselves conspic-uous, in an electorally unrewarding way. Ministers were seen too often hobnobbing too affably with the British Ministers; heard too often talking too appreciatively about the British Commonwealth, and the results of *Imperial* Conferences. The very effort to expound the signifi-cance of rather abstruse achievements gave an impression of didacticism and intellectual arrogance: an impression which the personality and style of the two responsible Ministers did little to offset. And even if lectures had been acceptable, the prescribed subject – British constitutional law – was profoundly uncongenial to a wide Irish public.

There was also a more substantial 'external' reason for unpopularity. The pro-Treaty party had made much of the clause in the Treaty providing for a Boundary Commission to determine the territory to be administered by the Government of Northern Ireland. It had been

[1]Donal O'Sullivan, *The Irish Free State and its Senate* (1940)

109

widely assumed in the Irish Free State that the Commission would result in the 'giving back' of – at least – the counties of Tyrone and Fermanagh and Derry City. Michael Collins had asserted that this would make Northern Ireland an economically untenable entity.[1] So Irish nationalist opinion, in its perennial state of optimistic confusion about Ulster, was led to believe that the Boundary Commission would result in the disruption, and perhaps in the collapse, of Northern Ireland. So lively had this expectation been that the Minister for External Affairs, Desmond Fitzgerald had stated in the Dáil, in May 1925, that it was 'hard to say whether Northern Ireland (was) an external or an internal affair'[2] – pending the report of the Boundary Commission. This bubble was pricked at the end of 1925, when – with a report in prospect which might have caused the Free State to lose some of its own territory – it became necessary for the Government to rush through a measure confirming the existing boundaries.[3] In retrospect, the Boundary Agreement appears a simple recognition of the inevitable: no subsequent government has been able to achieve improvement on it.[4] But at the time, in the fading light of the hopes which had been both entertained and aroused by the pro-Treaty party, it was bitterly disappointing, and damaging to the party responsible. Even six years later, the real but intangible achievements enshrined in the Statute of Westminster looked wan in comparison with the physical reality of the 'lost counties'. The party which had warned against the boundary clause as a trap seemed to some former waverers more honest, more patriotic and even more competent than the party which at first set such store by the Boundary Commission and then 'accepted partition'. And even the message of the Statute of Westminster, to the extent that it was grasped, was not entirely helpful to the Government. The Statute, after all, meant that the country could now safely support the more vigorous policies urged by Éamon De Valera.[5]

The development in status which primarily concerns us here—the achievement of recognized independence in the conduct of international affairs was complete by 1931, so that subsequent developments in status need only be very briefly mentioned. Mr De Valera, acting on and putting to the test the claims of his opponents about the freedom

[1] It is hard to see why he believed this since Northern Ireland, whatever its size, was to remain part of the United Kingdom

[2] *Dáil Debates* XI, cols. 1411–1470: May 13, 1925

[3] The Treaty (Confirmation of Amending Agreement) Bill approved by the Dáil on December 7, 1925

[4] See Section iv below

[5] The account given here of the decline in the appeal of the pro-Treaty party is mainly based, not on written sources but on early recollections – subject to more mature interpretation – of the repercussions of these events in a politically minded family in which the full spectrum of Irish nationalist opinion was represented: from the ex-Irish-party-pro-Treaty position to the rigid Republicanism of those who broke with Mr De Valera when he 'took the Oath'

achieved by Ireland as 'one of the co-equal partners of the British Commonwealth' proceeded to abolish the Oath of Allegiance hitherto required from members taking their seats in the Free State Parliament.[1] This action unlike those of his predecessors, was not merely symbolic but dramatic as well, as was his general style of demolishing the constitution based on the Treaty. The difference, as Professor Mansergh has pointed out, was that whereas 'the advance had hitherto been made by mutual agreement', Mr De Valera proceeded by 'unilateral denunciation ... The protests of the British Government were not unwelcome.'[2] The status attained by Ireland – the description 'Irish Free State' was now abolished – as a result of Mr De Valera's measures, culminating in the Constitution of 1937, was that of Republic in Mr De Valera's eyes, but not in those of his opponents. A tenuous link was preserved with the Crown, as the symbol of the Commonwealth with which Ireland remained associated. This was not very satisfactory – as the Crown was a symbol which in Ireland inspired more aversion than affection – and the wrangle over status continued until in 1949 Mr J. A. Costello's inter-party Government – a rather miscellaneous coalition of Mr De Valera's opponents – got rid of the Crown altogether, left the Commonwealth, and explicitly declared the country a Republic. The Republic of Ireland Act (1949) had a sour immediate aftermath,[3] but in the longer term it stands out as a salutary measure, removing a divisive symbol, and giving the country a clear and unchallenged status. Symbolism, as Lord Longford has rightly stressed, permeated every aspect of the Treaty controversy, on all sides of the question, and the bitterness of that protracted debate could not be fully removed without a symbolic act, ending – in Mr Costello's words – 'this country's long and tragic association with the institution of the British Crown.'[4]

ii. The League and Europe

The first Government of the Free State made it possible for the country to play a part in international affairs. That Government hardly, however, played such a part itself, with the very important exception of its part within the Commonwealth. It is true that the Free State was elected to the Council of the League in 1930, but its election – to what was regarded as the 'Commonwealth' seat – was a tribute to its activity

[1]Whether Mr De Valera and his followers had themselves taken this Oath is a disputed question into which we must here deny ourselves the intellectual pleasure of entering

[2]*Britain and Ireland* (1942). The fairness and forbearance of this British pamphlet, published at a time when Britain was at war and Ireland was neutral must be noted with respect

[3]See Section iv below

[4]*Dáil Debates* CXIII, cols. 347–724: November 24–26, 1948

in the Commonwealth rather than in the League.[1]

Mr De Valera's party, while in opposition, had been very critical of the League. Mr Sean Lemass – who many years later was to succeed Mr De Valera as Taoiseach – as the party's spokesman on the matter, had been unable to see any advantage in membership of the League'[2] all whose activities were 'wrapped in futility.'[3] These opposition asperities – presumably not unrelated to whatever access of prestige Cumann na nGaedheal might have derived from election to the League Council – ceased to be appropriate when in 1932 Mr De Valera's party, Fianna Fáil, took office and Mr De Valera succeeded, not merely to the seat on the Council, but, as it happened, to the presidency of the Council. His opening speech in that capacity evoked the admiration of even harsh critics in Ireland. It still reflected earlier reservations about the League, and warned against complacency in a measured and realistic way. 'The League' said Mr De Valera 'has no sanctions but the force of world opinion.'[4] In the opinion of a writer who admired Mr De Valera's predecessors and did not then admire Mr De Valera, it was 'a better speech' than any delivered by his predecessors.[5] The writer conjectured that it might have been written by some 'competent clear-thinking person in the Ministry of External Affairs.'[6] Even among Mr De Valera's opponents the theory that he was a muddled, incompetent sort of person, in either internal or external affairs, did not long survive his assumption of office. Two years later in the same columns we find it replaced by the Machiavellian image which was to remain the staple of his opponents during the rest of his active political career. 'His speech appealing for religious freedom in Russia gained him much praise in Ireland, where most people are entirely unaware that he subsequently voted for the admission of Russia to the League and its appointment to a permanent seat on the Council, an action which proved that he is a good diplomatist as well as a good Catholic.'[7] It is hard to see how the knowledge of how he voted could have been kept from the Irish people, but the use of a speech to offset any adverse domestic consequences of a 'difficult' vote remains, of course, an abiding feature of international assemblies and a perennial resource of Foreign Ministers.

[1]The Government claimed to be against the group system and that it sought support on merit alone (*Dáil Debates,* July 1, 1931). It is acknowledged, however that Commonwealth support 'ensured the success of the Irish candidature'. (Donal O'Sullivan, *op. cit.*)

[2]*Dáil Debates* XXXV, cols. 191–198: May 29, 1930

[3]*Dáil Debates* XXXIX, cols. 1262–1283: July 1, 1931

[4]Mr De Valera's addresses to the League are collected in a booklet called *Peace and War*

[5]*Round Table,* December 1932

[6]*Round Table,* December 1932

[7]*Round Table,* December 1932. The Irish correspondent of this periodical was Mr John Horgan, a distinguished Corkman, of wide and generous sympathies which did not, however, at this time quite extend to Éamon De Valera

112

An even more 'difficult' situation, arose in the following years, and was faced with courage and skill. This was the question of the application of sanctions against Mussolini's Italy after its invasion of Abyssinia. The case was difficult because, though the violation of the Covenant was clear – and also the interest of small nations in checking such violations – the aggressor was a nation for which much sympathy existed in Ireland. The Irish people had a traditional affection for Catholic Italy, and a large section of the opposition had a specific admiration for Fascist Italy. General Eoin O'Duffy's Blueshirts imitated the symbolism and militant 'anti-Communism' of the Fascists, and the hitherto eminently constitutional 'party of the Treaty' was for a time so rash as to accept General O'Duffy as its leader. Communism, of which little had been heard in the Dáil while Cumann na nGaedheal was in office, was presented as a burning issue after Mr De Valera had come to power. 'There has been, from the opposite benches' said Mr De Valera in 1936, 'a continued effort since 1931 to try to mend the fortunes of their party, and to build up a case for Fascist organizations on the ground that the Government was sympathetic to Communism.'[1]

Mr De Valera himself was depicted as an Irish Kerensky – not a Communist himself but pursuing policies that opened the way to Communism.[2] The two ex-Ministers for External Affairs were particularly vigilant in their anti-Communism, and disposed to deprecate criticisms of Fascism. Desmond Fitzgerald repeatedly suggested that the Government party might have been subsidized by the Russians.[3] Mr McGilligan spoke in the same vein[4] and also deplored in 1934 attacks on 'the Chancellor of a particular European country . . . scare headlines about barricades, guns and the slaughter of certain people.'[5] What he called 'noteworthy experiments in government'[6] deserved, in his opinion, to be better reported.

It would have been understandable if an Irish Government, faced with opposition of this character, had vacillated on the question of the application of sanctions against a 'Catholic and anti-Communist country.' Mr De Valera, however, addressing the League Assembly on

[1]*Dáil Debates* LXIV, cols. 1194–1228. Fianna Fáil was not sympathetic to Communism but had, while in opposition, shown signs of desiring better relations with the Soviet Union. Mr Tommy Mullins – later secretary of the party – frequently adverted to the necessity of reviving the herring trade with Russia, urged diplomatic recognition (*Dáil Debates* XXXVIII, cols. 745–6) and on one occasion went so far as to refer to 'lying propaganda' against 'the great Eastern democracy if one may so describe it'. (*Dáil Debates* XXVII, col. 475 . . .) Mr Sean Lemass had referred approvingly to Litvinov's proposal to abolish armies (*Dáil Debates*, February 21, 1929) Mr De Valera himself once enquired whether the Free State could not have a representative in the Soviet Union (*Dáil Debates,* June 5, 1929)
[2]This quaint theory was even aired in the *Round Table* as late as December, 1935
[3]*Dáil Debates,* July 11, 1933, June 13, 1934, May 29, 1935
[4]*Dáil Debates,* November 4, 1932
[5]*Dáil Debates,* June 13, 1934
[6]Ibid

Pony show, Co Kerry. (Small English boy, asked what he'd seen on a visit to Ireland: 'I saw nuns.')

September 16, 1935, came out unequivocally and strongly in favour of sanctions: 'Make no mistake, if on any pretext whatever we were to permit the sovereignty of even the weakest state amongst us to be unjustly taken away, the whole foundation of the League would crumble into dust.'[1] Ireland would be faithful to its commitments under the Covenant: 'We have given our word and we shall keep it.'[2]

Mr De Valera's 'sincere, eloquent and outspoken speech' – as an opponent described it – was followed by the introduction in the Dáil of the legislation required to make the proclaimed policy effective: the League of Nations (Obligations of Membership) Bill, 1935. The opposition was now placed in a dilemma, from which it did not entirely emerge until after the Second World War. It had its pro-Fascist tendencies, of recent acquisition and vague character, but it had also a deeper and older commitment, dating from the Treaty and in some cases earlier, to the view that Ireland's destiny and interests were linked with Britain, rendering co-operation with Britain in international matters highly desirable. Now Britain was demanding sanctions against Italy: the 'pro-British' and 'pro-Fascist'[3] tendencies were in contradiction. The result, inevitably, was confusion. On the whole the pro-British elements prevailed, but not without an incongruous admixture of pro-Fascist language. Mr James Dillon, a leading pro-Briton declared, apparently on behalf of his party, that: 'We emphatically endorse the attitude adopted by President De Valera at the League of Nations in connection with the dispute at present existing between the League and Italy.'[4] Mr McGilligan also supported the measure 'so far as it goes' but thought there should have been reference to 'a body of opinion which thinks that if the Fascist State is stopped, and stopped severely in its present course, the Fascist State may suffer and the sufferings of that State may not be confined to the borders of that country'. Some back-bench opposition members were more forthright. A Deputy Kent referred to Mussolini as 'the great leader of the Italian people and defender of our faith in Italy.'[5] Deputy Patrick Belton – soon to become prominent as leader of the Irish Christian Front – thought there might be Jews in Abyssinia – 'there or thereabouts' – who might have something to do with it. Deputy Esmonde thought that 'in this war Signor Mussolini is the

[1] *Peace and War,* December, 1935

[2] Ibid. *Round Table* Mr Horgan, a supporter of the old Irish Party compared Mr De Valera's position to that of John Redmond in 1914. This was a compliment from Mr Horgan's point of view, but might have been ominous as to the degree of popular support which could be expected in Ireland for sanctions against Italy

[3] Both terms are approximate. Members of the pro-Treaty party were not necessarily pro-British *in sentiment*: they were so by their assessment of Ireland's national interest. Those of them who were pro-Fascist tended to believe the reassuring accounts of Fascism given by anti-Communist writers and to reject accurate but damaging reports as 'red propaganda'

[4] *Dáil Debates* LIX, cols. 482–539, November 6, 1935
[5] Ibid

Abraham Lincoln of Africa.' Only these last three voted against the measure. It was clear, however, that the coherence and sense of purpose which had marked the pro-Treaty party's conduct of external affairs while in office had collapsed in opposition and in the changed circumstances of the mid-thirties. Mr De Valera's prestige, on the other hand, rose considerably. The country, a critic admitted, was 'quite solidly behind him.'[1]

The failure of the major powers to apply sanctions caused Mr De Valera, like so many others, to lose confidence almost entirely in the League. To the Assembly, on June 30, 1936 he spoke of 'bitter humiliation' and the 'fulfilment of the worst predictions.' 'Subscribing to what has proved to be a delusion', he said, 'is not the way to secure confidence.' He called for realism and the avoiding of commitments. 'How much nearer', he wondered 'is Europe to the Falls?'[2]

To the Dáil[3] Mr De Valera was even more explicit. Essentially his position was that the failure of the League implied that henceforth neutrality was the most prudent policy for small states. He said that it was clear that the sanctions policy of the League of Nations had failed to do what was expected of it by the founders of the League.[4] The League 'as it was', he said, no longer had 'the confidence of the ordinary people in the world. It does not command our confidence.' 'Should it', he asked, 'be reformed in the direction of imposing military sanctions if necessary? I do not think our people would be prepared for that . . . The small states in Europe have begun to provide for their own defences . . . We must be neutral.'

This was a turning point. Had the anti-Axis powers concerted their action through the League, Mr De Valera's Government was morally committed through his League speech of September 16, 1935, to support them in resisting, within the framework of the League, such obvious cases of aggression against League members as the post-Munich occupation of Czechoslovakia in March 1939 and the invasion of Poland.[5] The failure to use the League – and hence the failure *of* the League – made that commitment inoperative. He had said that if the League were to permit 'the sovereignty of even the weakest state to be unjustly taken away, the whole foundation of the League would crumble into dust.' It had permitted that, in the case of Abyssinia, and thus its foundation had

[1] *Round Table,* December, 1935
[2] *Peace and War*
[3] *Dáil Debates* LXII, cols. 2649–2746: June 18, 1936
[4] This might be thought a diplomatic circumlocution, since the fact was that the founders of the League – Britain and France – had failed to do what they said they were going to do. But Mr De Valera, since he had supported the League – and not Britain and France – no doubt thought it proper to emphasize the failure of the League as an organization
[5] Mr De Valera's implied rejection of military sanctions, it will be noted, dates from after the failure to apply the sanctions he had supported earlier. The language of his address of September 16, 1935, has different implications

crumbled into dust. Henceforward, his course was set towards a policy of neutrality.

The outbreak of the Spanish War set Mr De Valera's Government – and its opponents – a more difficult domestic-cum-international problem even than the question of sanctions against Italy. The war aroused considerable real emotion in Ireland, and also presented a temptation, not strongly resisted, to exploit that emotion electorally against the Government. The Government of Ireland like other governments – except the Fascist ones – continued to recognize the Spanish Republican Government until it had definitely lost the war. As early as November, 1936, however, the opposition tabled and pressed to a vote amid much anti-Communist rhetoric, a motion urging the recognition of General Franco.[1] General O'Duffy recruited an 'Irish Brigade' to fight for Franco, and the fascistoid Irish Christian Front led by Patrick Belton – the authority on the Abyssinian Jews – engaged in violent propaganda in the same cause. In 1937, the Government, supporting the policy of non-intervention in Spain, and to prevent further recruitment for the O'Duffy contingent – which had potentially dangerous domestic implications – introduced the Spanish Civil War (Non-Intervention) Bill. This presented the opposition with a splendid opportunity to appeal to the strongly pro-Franco sentiment which accounts of anti-Catholic atrocities in Spain had evoked in Ireland. It presented the opposition also with a renewal of the dilemma: Britain favoured non-intervention, and did not recognize General Franco, to whom British opinion was generally hostile. This time however – in relation to what was thought of by many in Ireland as a straightforward Communist[2] versus Catholic struggle – the pro-British factor had considerably less weight. It was still present, however, and when mingled with all the pro-Franco rhetoric produced an astonishing medley of vehemence and inconsequence in the Spanish debates. One member of the Opposition Front Bench (Dillon) argued in favour of non-intervention on the ground that if all foreign intervention were stopped the (Franco) 'Government of Burgos would prevail within three weeks.'[3] Another (Mulcahy) argued that non-intervention favoured the Republican Government since that Government 'has been carrying on with increasing Spanish support and less foreign support and . . . the Franco Government has been carrying on with decreasing Spanish and increasing foreign support.' One ex-Minister for External Affairs (Fitzgerald) spoke slightingly of the British Government and British public opinion while the other ex-Minister (Mr McGilligan) said that 'as a matter of fact we are following a British

---

[1] It was defeated 65–44 – a straight Party vote

[2] Atrocities committed by Anarchists and others to whom the Communists were opposed – and whom they afterwards crushed – were generally ascribed to the Communists

[3] *Dáil Debates* LXVI, cols. 643–694: April 9, 1937

proposal, and that in itself is not to be criticized.'[1] Mr Dillon said that he 'and those who are colleagues of mine in this party, detest equally Hitlerism, Mussolini-ism and Stalinism.'[2] One of those who voted with him (Coburn) immediately afterwards opined that if he had a choice between voting for Mussolini and the leader of the Labour Party he would vote 'a thousand times for Mussolini.' Another colleague, the first Minister for External Affairs of the Free State, gave strange expression to his 'equal detestation' of Hitlerism. 'President De Valera', he said, 'made a speech which was applauded by all the Communistic, liberal, pinkish newspapers in Europe. If I remember rightly, he actually implied criticism of the Nazi Government in Germany and their treatment of Jews.'[3]

An independent Deputy of liberal-conservative views, Mr Frank MacDermot, accused opposition speakers in the Spanish debates of trying to 'cash in electorally on Christianity' – a charge which was bitterly resented. It is certain, however, that though what Mr Patrick Belton called 'the fight between Christ and Antichrist' continued in Spain until 1939 the discussions about it in the Irish Parliament lost all intensity after the General Election of 1937, on the eve of which the more fervid statements I have quoted were made. There is no evidence that the statements in question had the electoral appeal that their makers may have assumed them to have. The loudest of all the crusaders, Patrick Belton, was, as the correspondent of the *Round Table* noted with satisfaction, 'obliterated mercifully'[4] in these elections. The premature and rather bedraggled return of General O'Duffy's brigade (or battalion) from Spain 'passed almost unnoticed' according to the same correspondent 'amid the election excitement.'[5] Mr De Valera's Government remained in office, though with a temporarily reduced majority. From this date until the end of the Second World War the opposition in the Irish Parliament no longer seriously attempted to contribute to the shaping of Ireland's policies in international affairs.

By the end of the 'thirties Mr De Valera had gained an authority not possessed by any Irish leader since the fall of Parnell nearly fifty years before. Much of this authority had been won by his activity in international affairs. His speeches at Geneva had caught the imagination of Irish people as his predecessors' had never done. His dignified and measured language conveyed a sense of responsibility and capacity –

---

[1]*Dáil Debates* LXV, cols. 579–867: February 18, 1937
[2]*Dáil Debates* LXV, cols. 598–867
[3]*Dáil Debates* LXV, 598–867. The speaker, Desmond Fitzgerald then introduced a qualification: 'In so far as the action of the Nazi Government towards Jews is unjust, I disclaim it and approve of what President De Valera said.' The people who applauded De Valera were, however, 'pink liberals and Communists in Europe waiting an opportunity of hitting the Germans'
[4]September, 1937
[5]Ibid

and therefore, in those dark days, of reassurance – which was altogether lacking in the discordant, excessive and sometimes incoherent utterances of a dislocated opposition. Members of the Opposition, with their shirts and salutes and their fluctuating insistence on the paramountcy of relations with Britain, had sometimes sounded capable of bringing Ireland in, by accident or design or a little of both, on either side in the coming war, or on both in succession. Mr De Valera on the other hand, with the support of the great majority of the people, set himself, from 1936 on, first to make possible, and then to maintain, a policy of neutrality.

iii. Neutrality and Partition

From very early on the legislators of the new State had showed concern about whether that State would be able to keep out of any future war in which Britain might become engaged. In the early years this concern was linked with the question of *status,* examined in the first section of this essay. Was Ireland's status such that it would go to war automatically, with the rest of the Empire, if England went to war?

Tom Johnson, a Labour member who led what might be called 'the loyal opposition' in the Free State Parliament before the entry of Mr De Valera's party, proposed on February 5, 1926 a motion (which was agreed to) to the effect that the Dáil should be kept informed about 'important developments in international affairs' affecting the Free State either through the League of Nations or through the Commonwealth.[1] He was perturbed by possible implications of the Locarno agreements. Could Ireland remain neutral in a war in which Britain might become involved 'over a treaty . . . to which we are not parties'?[2] He thought that Ireland should persuade other countries through the League that it would not be 'automatically a belligerent' if Britain went to war.[3]

By the time of the next important discussion of the subject – in February 1927[4] – the results of the Imperial Conference had marked a major advance towards the achievement by the Free State of full independence. Possibly because of this (and possibly also because of the 'defence' context of the debate), the emphasis had shifted. The question was now, not whether it would be juridically possible, but whether it would be physically possible, for the Free State to be neutral if Britain were belligerent.

[1]*Dáil Debates* XIV, col. 539 et seq
[2]Ibid
[3]Ibid. The rest of the debate hinged on questions of status later resolved (see Section i). The Government was in difficulty because these questions were still in a transitional stage. Desmond Fitzgerald dealt with the difficulty rather neatly: 'We have done more than anybody else in making it perfectly clear what the position is.'
[4]Debate on the Defence Force Bill, *Dáil Debates* XVIII, col. 384 et seq. February 8, 1927

'We need not blink the fact', said Desmond Fitzgerald, 'that it is quite possible, that in the event of a general attack on these islands – it is perfectly obvious – our army must co-operate with the British army.'[1] The embarrassment implicit in the Minister's syntax was connected with the difficulty of answering, in terms acceptable both to British[2] and Irish public opinion, the question: can the Free State be neutral, if the territory of the United Kingdom, and that alone, is attacked? Tom Johnson now pressed precisely this point. He suggested that 'if we are to conceive ourselves as part of the defence forces of the British islands' then 'if an attack is made upon Britain by air forces from the Continent of Europe, we are by that fact bound up in it . . .'[3] The Minister was constrained to wriggle, stressed that he had been speaking of a *general* attack, then fell back upon a venerable and legitimate device whereby Ministers can evade inconvenient hypothetical questions on major policy issues: 'We would have to come before the Dáil and get the assent of the Dáil as to what the policy of the Government and the Army [sic] would be.'[4] Kevin O'Higgins, then the most authoritative member of the Government, wound up the debate by observing that he was not against the neutrality of the Irish Free State. 'It is a consummation devoutly to be wished.' He added that the possibility of its achievement depended in part on what 'other people' might do.

No one who reads this debate can doubt that the Dáil felt at this early date that, if Britain should be at war, it would be highly desirable, if it were possible, for the Irish Free State to remain neutral. Anyone who may still be of the opinion – rather widely held in Britain and America during the war – that Mr De Valera was solely responsible for developing and 'putting over' the policy of neutrality, should note that this debate took place just before Mr De Valera and his followers entered the Dáil.

Mr De Valera, in the first debate on External Affairs after his entry to the Dáil complained that the desire for neutrality had not been made sufficiently explicit. He wanted it to be made clear 'that if there were to be another Imperial war . . . it is the wish of the Irish people to be neutral in that war'[5] and that the right of war-time control which the Treaty conferred on Britain over the major Irish ports did not have the consent of the Irish people. In office, he laid down the principle that was to be the cornerstone of his war-time policy: 'We have definitely stated that we would not allow our country to be used as a base of

---

[1]Ibid
[2]It had to be acceptable to British opinion if the Free State Government's policy of winning, by negotiation, an accepted status of full independence within the Commonwealth was to be pressed to a successful conclusion
[3]*Dáil Debates* XVIII, cols. 625–678: February 17, 1927
[4]Ibid
[5]*Dáil Debates* XXVII, cols. 430–502

attack on Britain by a foreign power and would do our best to defend our own territory.'[1]

During the period of sanctions against Italy it seemed possible at one point (Section ii above) that Ireland might eventually become involved, with the consent of the Government, in a 'League war'. After the failure of the League, however, the neutrality policy was reaffirmed: 'The small states of Europe have begun to look to their own defence . . . We want to be neutral.'[2] Yet it still seemed to many – including it would seem, Mr De Valera himself – unlikely that this wish could be fulfilled. Even after the 1938 agreement under which Great Britain relinquished its right to the use of the Irish ports in wartime, Mr De Valera seemed pessimistic: 'The truth is, of course, that in modern war there is not any neutrality.'[3] Yet neutrality remained the object of policy. Mr De Valera made it clear that the threat of European war had been the reason for his initiating the discussions that led to the recovery of unrestricted control over the ports.[4] 'Now with due deliberation' declared Mr De Valera 'the Government has set the aim of its policy, in the present circumstance, to preserving a position of neutrality.'[5]

A little earlier, he had indicated – with a realism lacking in some other discussions of the subject – a basic reason for a neutrality policy: 'I think that our people do not differ from the people of any other part of the world in their desire not to get into a war if they can keep out of it.'[6]

It was at this same time, however, that the policy of neutrality began to be linked with the question of partition. Before 1938 – once whatever hopes had been placed in the Boundary Commission had been dispelled in 1925 – it was common ground among the leaders of the main parties that, though the partition of the country was deplorable, there was really nothing that could be done about it. The pro-Treaty party was widely regarded as having 'accepted partition' and did little – until after the Second World War – to counteract that impression. The first Minister of External Affairs even indicated that there was some force in the claim of the Six Counties to 'self-determination'.[7] Mr De Valera repudiated this position,[8] but his own declared position, after he came into power, was similar in its quietistic implications: 'The only policy for abolishing partition that I can see is for us, in this part of Ireland,

[1]*Dáil Debates* LVI, cols. 2119–2216: May 29, 1935

[2]Mr De Valera introducing the Estimate for External Affairs June 18, 1936. *Dáil Debates* LXII, cols. 2649–2746

[3]*Dáil Debates* LXXI, cols. 306–456, April 29, 1938. This is in the context of a rather cryptic statement

[4]*Dáil Debates* LXXII, cols. 639–716: July 13, 1938

[5]*Dáil Debates* LXXV, cols. 1424–1466: May 2, 1939

[6]*Dáil Debates* LXXII, as above

[7]*Dáil Debates* XXVII, cols. 430–502

[8]Ibid: Mr Sean Lemass alleged with more ingenuity than profundity that if self-determination for the Six Counties were admitted as legitimate, County Kerry, which still voted for the Republic, had the right to secede from the Free State.

120

to use such freedom as we can secure to get for the people in this part of Ireland such conditions as will make the people in the other part of Ireland wish to belong to this part.'[1]

1938, however, brought a very significant shift in perspective: from one of seeing the problem primarily in terms of relations between people in the two parts of Ireland to one of seeing it in terms of relations between Dublin and London. On July 13, 1938 Mr De Valera said that two out of the three obstacles to good relations with Great Britain had been removed.[2] The two removed had been the Oath and the control of the ports: the remaining one was partition. At the same time he indicated that if partition was ended Ireland would consider an attack on Great Britain an attack on her own independence.[3]

It is probable that at this stage Mr De Valera, fresh from the triumph of his negotiation with Mr Chamberlain over the ports, did feel more optimistic about the possibility of solving partition – by direct negotiation with London – than he had felt five years before. But even if the 'partition-means-neutrality' position were to fail as a lever against partition – and there it failed totally – its strength as a support for neutrality was considerable. Irish public opinion understood and accepted it readily as such, and it was an argument which any Irish opponent of neutrality, in a discussion amongst Irishmen, would usually find it hard to shake. And to the Irish abroad – especially that critically important section, the people of Irish origin in the United States – it was the most cogent argument available, especially in the period, after Pearl Harbour, when many former friends of Ireland called Irish neutrality into question.

From the point of view of hostile critics, who naturally abounded in Britain and in America during this period, partition was an irrelevancy, introduced to give a cloak of righteousness to a basically selfish position. This is a half truth. The position did have an elementally selfish basis in the desire of the people, in Mr De Valera's words, 'not to get into a war if they can keep out of it.' But this desire, as Mr De Valera said, they shared with other people, and in some of those other people it had been outweighed by other motives. Those countries who went voluntarily to war against Germany did so because they felt their vital interests to be threatened – Britain and France – or because they felt at one, through ties of blood, affection and tradition with another nation that was at war. This was the case of Australia and New Zealand, of English-speaking Canada, and of English-speaking white South Africa. There were those who thought that Ireland should feel in the same way. That Ireland[4] did not in fact feel in the same way was unmistakeably

[1]*Dáil Debates* XLVI, col. 192: March 1, 1933. Many people will wish that this policy for abolishing partition had been honoured in practice as well as in theory
[2]*Dáil Debates* LXXII, cols. 639–728: July 13, 1938
[3]Ibid
[4]That Ireland for which the Dublin Government could speak: the overwhelming majority in the Twenty-Six Counties and a significant minority in the Six

121

clear: in the whole Dáil only one Deputy – James Dillon – favoured entry into the war, and Mr De Valera won two war-time elections, in which his opponents were careful to insist that they too supported the policy of neutrality. Partition was not the reason why the Irish people felt differently from those of the English speaking dominions. It was not the reason, but it was the symbol. The point about partition was not that it was 'an artificial creation' as maintained by the imbecilities of anti-partition propaganda. The point about it was precisely that its roots lay deep in Irish history, and in that area of history which was the reason why Ireland felt differently from 'the other dominions'. The Irish – those who were not of British settler stock – had been a conquered people, and the separate existence of Northern Ireland is proof and symbol of the fact that the conquest has never been entirely undone. The conquest of the natives is the fact that Orange Belfast solemnly commemorates every July, and what it commemorates is what made the rest of Ireland neutral in 1939. For neutrality, though it drew much of its strength from the simple preference for keeping out of the war, was as a British commentator justly observed at the time 'in the last analysis an expression of national feeling.'[1] It was the unambiguous assertion of the will and the capacity of the long-conquered people to conduct the affairs of their recently – and still somewhat dubiously – enfranchised state, in a manner other than that required by their conqueror. In short, it was an expression of freedom.

The entry of America into the war had been expected by some to change Ireland's position radically, and did change it slightly – from 'neutrality' to 'friendly neutrality'. The fact was that Ireland's ties with America, though real and friendly, were not of the same character as those between, say, Britain and Australia. Ireland's ties were not with the American nation as a whole – and certainly not with what was still the ruling class of White Anglo-Saxon Protestants – but with a minority, which was still a somewhat despised minority. This connection was not strong enough to shake the neutrality policy, which had hardened by 1942 and had been fortified by censorship, but it did make it both urgent and very difficult to explain neutrality, and obtain a degree of support for it, from Irish-Americans who were now themselves at war. This situation necessitated heavy emphasis on partition. 'Partition' according to a theory which was outlined in a Dublin periodical shortly after the war – and which the present writer believes to be sound – 'was during the war the only reason for our not plunging immediately into the war on the side of the US which could be appreciated by . . . Irish-Americans and Americans of Irish blood.'[2] The influence of this section in restraining any possible anti-Irish move by the American Government 'could never have been brought to bear if the Partition grievance had not been

[1]Mansergh, *Britain and Ireland* (1942)
[2]The *Leader.* March 29, 1947

kept assiduously to the fore.' This did nothing to 'solve partition'[1] but it may have helped to secure for Ireland 'the necessary protection against great and imminent danger'.

I am not concerned here with the detailed story of the application, as distinct from the formation, of Ireland's neutrality policy.[2] From the point of view of further international options in the post-war world, the importance of the successful conduct of that policy was double. First, it had demonstrated that neutrality for Ireland was possible, and had given the idea of neutrality favourable associations. Second, it had connected the idea of neutrality with the idea of partition, and had invested the need 'to solve partition' with a sanctity and pre-eminence which it had not had before 1938. These factors now operated to keep Ireland out of NATO.

Mr De Valera, who before the war had seen 'no other policy' for abolishing partition than the creation of adequately attractive conditions inside the Twenty-Six Counties, was now led – partly no doubt by the momentum of the war-time insistence on the topic, and perhaps also by a desire to forestall attempts to involve Ireland in future military alliances – to try a policy of seeking to get it abolished by propaganda. While still in office he encouraged this policy discreetly, through supporting the activities of voluntary bodies. Some observers saw quite clearly from the beginning that the attempt to 'reunite Ireland' by propaganda had not the slightest hope of success. 'With the development of the activities of the Anti-Partition League', wrote the *Leader*[3] 'a fresh chapter of futility and disappointment is opening.'[4]

Mr De Valera's government fell in February 1948, on domestic issues. The new inter-party government became identified with the most vehement phase of anti-partition activity. But the initiative in this was taken not by the new government but by Mr De Valera, who now threw his immense prestige as 'leader of the Irish race at home and abroad on the international plane'[5] into a major anti-partition effort, visiting the United States, Australia and Britain for the purpose.

By 'putting an anti-partition girdle round the earth'[6] Mr De Valera

[1]The proponent of the theory thought it 'tended to stabilize' partition, but this is excessive: nothing that the Dublin Government could have done at that time could have made partition more, or less, stable

[2]See articles by T. Desmond Williams in the *Leader* (Dublin) January 31, 1953-April 25, 1953 and in the *Irish Press* (Dublin) June 27-July 17, 1953; also V. P. Hogan, *The Neutrality of Ireland in World War II* (Michigan 1953)

[3]March 29, 1947

[4]The *Leader* also pointed out the fallacy which underlay the idea that the anti-imperialist Labour Government might be prevailed upon to end partition. 'Mr Attlee' the paper pointed out 'did not say that his Government would drive any people out of the Commonwealth who wished to remain in.'

[5]The phrase is that of the *Leader* (April 17, 1948). The *Leader* was not a Fianna Fáil paper and few Irish people (outside Belfast and environs) would have contested its assessment

[6]The *Leader*, July 24, 1948

did not significantly affect either the earth or partition. But he did significantly affect the inter-party government in relation to the options now opening before it. There was now an anti-partition 'wave' and, in the view of a good observer, Mr De Valera was on the crest of the wave, and the inter-party government in the trough.[1]

This was the government which was soon to be faced with the choice of whether or not to join NATO. The leading party in the governing coalition, the party now known as Fine Gael, was that same party which had originally supported the Treaty, and had later in the 'thirties been torn by conflicting sympathies, with Britain and with right-wing movements in Europe.[2] The new distribution of forces in world politics was, however, such that no conflict of sympathies could arise inside this conservative Irish party. Tendency to associate the national interests with those of Britain, anti-Communism, sympathy with Catholic parties and statesmen in Western Europe, traditional respect for the political views of the Irish Catholic hierarchy (including the Irish-American Catholic hierarchy) – all these attractions pulled in the same way; towards involvement on the Western side in the Cold War, and ultimately towards commitment to the Western military alliance. Such a commitment would not, in itself, be necessarily unacceptable to Irish public opinion. Irish public opinion had for a long time been imbued with a sense of the special wickedness and malevolence of Communism and Communists and – in propitious circumstances – might be induced to feel it necessary, in morality and prudence, to join together with other nations to resist any threat from the Godless East. No comparable feeling ever existed in Ireland in relation to Fascism. Irish public opinion, which had responded positively and in simplicity to the Allied propaganda of the First World War, had been disabused by events and by the counter-propaganda of Sinn Féin, so that it later all too easily dismissed reports of what was happening in Nazi Germany as 'British propaganda'. The Irish clergy, which at this time was making anti-Communism a main theme of its contributions to sacred oratory, had said almost nothing about Fascism. In the circumstances a moral pressure to join NATO existed – a factor which had been altogether lacking in the question of Ireland's neutrality in the Second World War. Outside the moral order, three further propitious circumstances existed: the new coalition was led, not by Britain but by the United States; there was no obvious, imminent threat of war; and Russia was farther away than Germany.

In these circumstances the present writer has little doubt that a Fine Gael government, *with a safe majority of its own,* would have taken a strong Cold War line, and would eventually have committed

[1]The *Leader*, May 1, 1948. The *Leader*, for this period, is very near the centre of informed Irish nationalist opinion.
[2]See Section ii below.

itself to NATO. It could, and almost certainly would, have claimed that the great national objective – the reunification of the country – could be pursued most effectively within the framework of the alliance.

Dependence on the smaller parties for a majority in the Dáil made the situation much more complex. Neither the Labour Party, nor the members of the Farmers' Party, nor Mr Sean MacBride's Republican group, had committed themselves to Fine Gael's 'Spanish War' enthusiasms. Yet, given favourable conditions, the cry of 'Christianity in danger' might move them in the direction of a Western commitment. The history of the Irish Labour Party showed that, in conditions where the question 'Christ or Antichrist?' was raised, it had felt a compulsion not to be seen on the side that is indicated as being that of Antichrist. The Farmers' Party were in a similar position. Mr Mac-Bride's party was a more uncertain factor, being national rather than Catholic in emphasis. But its very reputation of 'extremism' might make it sensitive to certain pressures. And Mr MacBride himself was later to show, on a crucial domestic issue,[1] that he did not underestimate – that indeed he seriously overestimated – the positive importance of the 'clerical factor' in Irish politics.

The crucial factor affecting the Government's foreign policy options was Mr De Valera's position. By immediately placing the greatest possible emphasis on partition, as a burning question, he made it far more difficult for the new government to edge towards a Western alignment or alliance. He did so first by the direct impact of his personal authority on Irish public opinion: if 'Dev' was talking about partition in Australia, it would be very hard to convince the Irish people that the Russians presented a dire and urgent threat to Connemara. For, as a result of the war-time experience, the Irish people trusted Mr De Valera's judgement on international affairs far more than they trusted that of anyone else. But Mr De Valera's stress on partition also produced another kind of stress inside the Government. Mr Sean MacBride could hardly be less insistent than Mr De Valera on the urgency of tackling the problem of partition. And Mr Sean MacBride was Minister for External Affairs. Either the Government had to let him have his head on this matter – and thereby itself be carried into emphasizing and magnifying the importance and iniquity of partition – or it would lose his support, thereby precipitating a general election. And in the general election their party would have to fight Mr De Valera, *on an international issue*, involving partition and neutrality. It is entirely understandable that they chose not to risk this, but instead to emphasize partition. And in so doing they were irresistibly propelled in the direction of neutrality, resisting the attraction of the anti-Communist alliance.

[1]The opposition of the Catholic hierarchy to the 'Mother and Child Health Scheme' of Dr Browne precipitated the fall of the inter-party Government in 1951 in circumstances which led to the destruction of Mr MacBride's party.

125

In the autumn of 1948 the Government introduced its Republic of Ireland Bill. This measure had the considerable merit of clarifying once and for all the international status of the Twenty-six Counties. Unfortunately it was presented – and this was just at the end of Mr De Valera's anti-partition tours – also as a measure favourable to the reunification of the country, a matter on which it had no bearing at all. 'We are clearing the decks for action to end partition',[1] said the Minister for Defence, Mr T. F. O'Higgins. And another supporter of the Government, Mr Oliver Flanagan, was of the opinion that 'in the lifetime of this Government, the question of partition will be solved to our satisfaction.'[2]

Mr De Valera supported the measure, without however showing any enthusiasm for it, or evincing any confidence in its efficacy as a cure for partition.

A few months later, the Minister for External Affairs, in answering a question about the Atlantic Pact, then taking shape, committed the Government, in emphatic and unequivocal language, to the full 'partition-means-neutrality' position: 'As long as partition lasts, any military alliance or commitment involving joint military action with the state responsible for partition must be quite out of the question as far as Ireland was concerned.'[3]

The 'state responsible' then proceeded to pass the Ireland Act affirming that 'in no event' would Northern Ireland Act cease to be part of the United Kingdom 'without the consent of the Government of Northern Ireland'. It was made clear that this reaffirmation had been necessitated not so much by the Republic of Ireland itself as by the anti-partition campaign which had preceded it and the predictions which had accompanied it. Because of these predictions, the Irish Government was now obliged to react and did so with excess. The Government joined with Mr De Valera in public protests in the course of which Mr De Valera said nothing particularly memorable, but Mr Costello produced his only too memorable phrase about hitting Great Britain in 'pride, prestige and pocket'. Mr MacBride, who was well fitted to play a useful and acceptable role in the major international organs to which Ireland then belonged – the Council of Europe and the OEEC – was now carried, by the increasing momentum of 'anti-partition' into the unrewarding position (which was, however, required by the Costello doctrine) of administering pin-pricks to Great Britain in the councils of these institutions. Mr Lemass, on behalf of Mr De Valera's party, was then able to rebuke Mr MacBride and the Government of which he was part, for activities contrary to the vital interests of the country, a member of the Sterling Area.[4]

[1]*Dáil Debates* CXIII, cols. 347–724: November 24–26, 1948
[2]Ibid   [3]*Dáil Debates* CXIV, cols. 323–6: February 23, 1949
[4]*Dáil Debates* CXVII, cols. 849–1066: July 13–14, 1949

After Mr De Valera returned to power in 1951 it became apparent that the most momentous international decision of the inter-party years had been the decision that Ireland should not form part of the NATO system. This decision was strictly consonant with the traditions of Fianna Fáil: it was at best dubiously consonant with the traditions of Fine Gael. But Fine Gael, now in opposition, was henceforward debarred from making an issue of 'the defence of Christianity'. In this respect Mr De Valera could serenely follow 'the policy of his predecessors'. And 'serenely' was the word: there was no need to justify, by any verbal militancy on partition, the now uncontested policy of neutrality. To the relief of both the Irish people and their neighbours, 'silence and discretion' characterized the handling of 'the partition problem' by the De Valera government on its return to office. The palmy days of 'anti-partition' were over, and no major party now claims to have any other 'solution for partition' than the substance of that propounded by Mr De Valera in 1935.

In so far as Mr De Valera's 1947 'anti-partition girdle round the earth'[1] was designed to bring the end of partition nearer it was of necessity a total failure. But in so far as it may have been intended to establish a continued policy of neutrality, and to frustrate any alliance-minded tendencies among his opponents, it must be recorded as a brilliant and unqualified success.

iv. The United Nations: Three Principles

The Irish Government decided without enthusiasm[2] to apply for admission to membership of the United Nations in 1946. The application was rejected, through the negative vote of a permanent member of the Security Council, the Soviet Union, because Ireland lacked 'normal diplomatic relations' with that country. Six years later, still without having established such relations, Ireland was admitted, as part of the 'package deal' of 1955. The first session in which an Irish delegation was able to play an active part was the memorable session of 1956 (Suez and Hungary).

The delay in admission was fortunate for Ireland's international repute and also for her self-esteem. By this time Ireland's international status was no longer a matter of internal controversy; neutrality was common ground among the parties; 'anti-partition' had lost its momentum. A domestic consensus existed, adequate to allow Ireland to

---

[1] The *Leader*, September 27, 1952. It is not here suggested that Mr De Valera coldly worked all this out in advance or that he was insincere about the announced purpose of his tour. But a master-politician has an instinct about the probable repercussions of his acts, and Mr De Valera's instinct did not fail him.

[2] See *Dáil Debates* CII, cols. 1308–1481: July 21–25, 1946

play a modest but serious part in the United Nations.[1]

The government at the time of Ireland's entry into the United Nations was the Second Inter-Party, a coalition made up of the participants in the former coalition, but without Mr MacBride. The new Minister for External Affairs, Mr Liam Cosgrave, was a cautious and rather gentle, conservative personality, who was known to dislike the school of oratory which he called 'dying for Ireland' and known therefore to have been made unhappy by the international 'antics' of the First Inter-Party. Mr Cosgrave valued the advice on international matters of Mr F. H. Boland, the very astute and experienced Secretary of the Department of External Affairs, who now was designated as Ireland's first Permanent Representative at the United Nations. Those familiar with Mr Boland's mode of thought and expression will recognize marked traces of these in the 'three principles' which Mr Cosgrave now expounded to the Dáil as guiding his policy at the United Nations. Mr Cosgrave's tenure as Minister was destined to be brief – in fact he represented Ireland only at the first session – but Mr Boland remained for five formative years. The 'three principles' –which were known to command his approbation, and command that also of his successor, Mr C. C. Cremin[2] – continue therefore to be relevant to any study of the Irish position at the United Nations, even though Mr Cosgrave's successor as Minister, Mr Frank Aiken, demurred initially from the last and most significant of the principles.

The three principles were as follows:

1 Scrupulous fidelity to the obligations of the Charter;

2 'We should try to maintain a position of independence, judging the various questions on which we have to adopt an attitude or cast a vote strictly on their merits, in a just and disinterested way.' This implied an effort 'to avoid becoming associated with particular blocs or groups so far as possible.'

3 'To do whatever we can as a member of the United Nations to preserve the Christian civilization of which we are a part and with that end in view to support wherever possible those powers principally responsible for the defence of the free world in their resistance to the spread of Communist power and influence . . . We belong to the great community of states, made up of the United States of America, Canada and Western Europe.'[3]

On these principles, Mr Cosgrave made a significant gloss. He acknowledged a certain difficulty in reconciling with his third principle that fact that there existed a growing desire for self-determination on

[1]Whereas if Ireland had been admitted in, say, 1949, internal pressures combining with the Cold War in the Assembly, would have constrained the Irish delegation to give an 'anti-British-but-anti-Communist' exhibition which would have made the delegation an object of general aversion and even ridicule

[2]With an even more marked emphasis on the third principle

[3]*Dáil Debates* CLIX, cols. 127–226: July 3–4, 1956

Inch Strand, Co Kerry, and the famous gardens at
Glengarriff, Co Cork

the part of subject peoples, a movement which 'with our history' we could not regard otherwise than 'with sympathy'.[1]

Any United States diplomatic analyst could construe this with ease. The third principle meant that Ireland's vote would be as the United States – unquestioned leader of the 'Free World' – required on all important issues. The second principle, as qualified by the third, meant that the Irish delegation would be liable to have to explain – as Latin American delegates so copiously do – the processes of independent reasoning whereby it had coincidentally arrived at the positions favoured by the United States. Nor did the 'gloss' give any ground for anxiety. It meant no more than that the representatives of Ireland would be expected to make mildly 'anti-colonialist' speeches – as did the representatives of the United States itself. As for 'the search for pacific formulas' (also mentioned by Mr Cosgrave) this – when conducted in the light of the third principle – would be likely to lead to the discovery of formulas already framed, but not announced by the United States.

At the first session the Irish Delegation, led by Mr Cosgrave, did nothing to disappoint these expectations. The delegation's interventions were well-prepared, well-phrased and moderate in tone, and its votes on issues of major significance were the same as those of the United States. As regards voting, more than two-thirds of the membership of the Assembly was then similarly committed, so that Ireland's position elicited neither surprise nor censure.

In 1957, the second inter-party Government fell, Fianna Fáil returned to power, and Mr Frank Aiken became Minister for External Affairs; he is still Minister at the time of writing. Mr Aiken was an old and close associate of Mr De Valera's, and he aspired to play a similar part in the United Nations to Mr De Valera's in the League. This required a stronger emphasis on the 'second principle' – independence. 'Such respect as we were able to acquire in Geneva', Mr De Valera had said 'was largely due to the fact that on every question that arose we were able to express our own views independently.'[2]

Stronger emphasis on the 'second principle' implied a challenge to the third, and Mr Aiken had in fact challenged that principle from the moment of its enunciation by Mr Cosgrave. In that debate, Mr Aiken had agreed with the first and second principles, but thought that the third principle departed to some extent from the other two and that the Minister was 'rather tying himself up' in his third point.[3] 'There are sins' he said 'that are common both to the Communistic and to the non-Communistic states.'

For about five years – roughly, from 1957 to 1961 – Mr Aiken,

[1]Ibid
[2]*Dáil Debates* CI, cols. 2429–2156: June 26, 1946. This was the debate on the last Estimate for the contribution to the expiring League.
[3]*Dáil Debates* CLIX, cols. 127–226: July 3–4, 1956

Jerpoint Abbey, Co Kilkenny

with considerable courage and pertinacity, sought to base the actions of his delegation on the 'second principle' and to work in the cause of international peace through the exercise of independent judgement on the issues. He worked for the reduction of Cold War tensions; he urged military disengagement, *pari passu*, in Central Europe; he pioneered the effort to prevent, through United Nations action, the further proliferation of nuclear weapons. And he spoke and voted against the proposition, then rigorously maintained by the West, that the question of the representation of China should not be discussed.

During this period of the relative ascendancy of the 'second principle', the 'third principle' continued to have able advocates within the delegation and to exert a significant influence. There was, of course, a considerable area of common ground for the two principles, in that, since Ireland is a Western country – albeit one with a colonial history – its genuinely independent assessments will often also be 'Western' assessments. The exact delimitation of this 'independent-and-Western' area was at this time the subject of close debate within the delegation itself. 'Third principle' people sought to make the area – in accordance with the logic of Mr Cosgrave's original formulation – virtually coterminous with the whole range of questions before the Assembly. 'Second principle' people sought to define it more narrowly, specifically excluding from it all questions of a colonial or para-colonial character, on which Irish opinion did significantly differ from prevailing Western opinion. During these years the Algerian question provided an annual 'borderline' test of 'second principle' and 'third principle' forces, providing much room for exercise of ingenuity on amendments, paragraph voting and procedural questions.[1]

The tension between the two principles – and between their adherents – increased the effectiveness of the delegation. Major problems received full and careful discussion, and the drafting of statements received thorough critical attention. The Irish delegation carried rather more weight in the Assembly, during this period, than might have been expected from the size and importance of the country it represented.

The relative ascendancy which the second principle held over the third during this period was secured and symbolized by 'the China vote'. The significance of the vote was that this was a subject on which the United States annually exercised heavy pressure to get a majority for its policy, while most delegates privately felt that this policy was contrary to the interests of the United Nations and the prospects of peace. The proposition that the question should not be discussed was at this stage the formal device through which the United States defended its policy of maintaining a Chiang Kai Shek delegation, dependent on

[1]In theory all delegations act on the instructions of their Governments. In practice there is considerable scope for individual judgement on critical 'last-minute' amendments, etc., where there is no time to obtain instructions

the United States, as the representative of China in the Security Council and in the General Assembly. To reject this proposition demonstrated, under pressure, the sincerity of the independent stand and it helped to validate, in the eyes of other delegations (including many who were themselves obliged to cast a 'Formosa' vote) the independence of Ireland's position on other matters.

I have described elsewhere[1] Mr Aiken's resistance to some ingenious forms of pressure applied at the instance of the United States delegation in New York. None the less the 'China' position, and with it the whole of the 'independent' policy, became eroded and eventually collapsed during Mr Aiken's tenure. The rot – from a 'second principle' point of view – began at home in Ireland, where Mr Aiken allowed himself to give a technically correct, but substantially misleading account of what the vote meant. It had been a *vote for discussion*, and he referred to what various countries 'would have said' if a discussion had been agreed to. He would have made an 'effort to discover' whether the Chinese Communists would give 'the usual signed pledge' of good behaviour and whether they would 'give religious freedom to the Chinese people, withdraw from Korea and allow a free united Korean Government under United Nations supervision.'

Here of course, Mr Aiken was seeking to emulate Mr De Valera's course, more than twenty years before, in combining a vote for the admission of Russia to the League with an appeal for religious freedom in that country.[2]

The difference was that Mr De Valera was commenting on a definitive vote, while Mr Aiken was explaining an ambiguous and provisional one, and thereby hypothecating future action.[3]

'Second principle' elements in the delegation, though somewhat depressed by this statement, were able to hope that it was intended purely for domestic consumption – representing what Nkrumah liked to call 'tactical action' – and that, at the United Nations itself, Mr Aiken would continue to hold to an independent position.[4] The period

[1] *To Katanga and Back* (1962)

[2] In fairness to Mr Aiken it should be noted that in 1934 Mr De Valera had to face only some domestic pressure – since Britain and France sponsored the admission of the Soviet Union – while Mr Aiken had to face a combination of domestic and external pressures

[3] Of his explanation, the best that can be said is that it was clearly not addressed to an informed audience. The suggestion that the Assembly had not in fact discussed the question was entirely misleading; and the suggestion about 'the usual signed pledge' is equally so, since China is a founder member and the question to be resolved is not whether China conforms to the requirements of Article 4.1. (applicable to *new* members) but simply whether the government of China is that on Formosa or that in Peking

[4] In the course of this debate Mr Aiken said that the delegation's role should not be that of 'yesmen' to the United States while the Taoiseach said that 'if [Mr Cosgrave's third principle] meant that we were simply to do everything we were told by the leading members of the group I do not think anyone here would have supported it'. (*Dáil Debates*, November 28, 1957)

1961-2 saw these hopes fade and die. The adoption by the United States delegation – under the leadership of the late Adlai Stevenson – of more flexible and sophisticated procedures for excluding China gave Mr Aiken an opportunity of modifying the substance of his position, while not recanting his earlier words. In the spirit of his Dáil explanation, though not of his original stand, he took advantage of this opening. About the same time, changes, reinforcing this trend, took place inside the delegation. Following the resignation of the present writer – in the circumstances related in *To Katanga and Back* – those members of the delegation who had been in the habit of emphasizing the second principle at the expense of the third were dispersed, and the delegation acquired a uniform 'third principle' complexion, which has deepened with the years. The vote of this delegation on major issues is now as solidly riveted to the United States as that of the Cosgrave delegation had been. While talking of 'two Chinas' and incorporating mysterious references to 'the ancient nation of Taiwan' – which would presumably be represented in the General Assembly by the same refugees from the mainland who now represent China – Mr Aiken votes safely in the United States column on this issue. He is discreetly silent on Vietnam, and has given no public backing to the Secretary-General's call for a cessation of the bombing of North Vietnam. His main 'new' project – an elaborate notion about financing of future peace-keeping – is based on an unquestioning acceptance of some more than dubious United States interpretations of the Charter. His statesmanship has drawn from Dean Rusk in 1967 a cordial recognition not accorded to it by any United States spokesman in 1957.

All this represents a signal victory for the policy enunciated by Mr Liam Cosgrave and a signal defeat for the policy once represented by Mr Frank Aiken. Like Mr De Valera in 1948 – but in the reverse direction – the adherents of the Cosgrave principles have succeeded in imposing their international policy on their opponents.

Ironically, this came about at a time when Ireland had greater freedom than ever before to pursue a genuinely independent policy. The first government of the State had won the juridical right to exercise free choices. Mr De Valera had proved that this right could be exercised in practice under the most exacting possible conditions (neutrality). Many of the pressures which had restricted choices in the past had now either vanished or lost weight. The complex dynamism of 'neutrality-partition' which had caused the first inter-party government to lose its international balance had ceased to be relevant. The factors often loosely lumped together as 'clerical pressure'[1] had also considerably

---

[1]'Clerical pressure' more often than not consists mainly of the activities of interested laymen, using the language of piety to encompass purely secular ends, such as return to office or the elimination of a man or measure regarded as politically or financially obnoxious

diminished in significance. Loyalty to the Catholic Church could no longer be easily invoked in justification of support for United States foreign policy. In the light of statements by Pope Paul, for example, it would be impossible to mount a 'clerical' attack, of the 'Spanish war' type, against an Irish Minister for External Affairs who should support the Secretary-General of the United Nations as against the Vietnam policy of President Johnson.

Ireland's position in relation to the United States, also, is one which would easily support a considerable measure of independence. Ireland is not dependent on United States alms, as so many nations are. It does not have extensive and expensive 'world commitments' in the role of deputy policeman. It cannot conceivably pose any threat to the United States, nor can it itself be seriously held to be threatened by international Communism. If the unimaginable disaster of a third world war should descend upon mankind neither the neutrality nor the belligerence of Ireland could have the slightest military significance.

It is true that the vital interests of Ireland are bound up with those of the West. It is also true that on the issue of war or peace, the vital interests of the West are bound up with those of the East. The international policies which have been pursued by the most powerful of the Western governments are far from commanding universal approval in the West, or in the United States itself. There is no reason to believe that blind and dumb acquiescence in these policies has been the best way of serving the West or of showing friendship to the American people.

It is sometimes suggested that a 'cautious' policy at the United Nations – 'caution' here means support for recklessness when indulged in by the United States – is necessitated by Ireland's position as a candidate for admission to the Common Market. The 'independent foreign policy', it is hinted, was a very nice thing in its way, but Ireland's economic interests require that it be dropped, so as to get into the Market. It would be difficult to imagine a more absurd argument, in favour of uncritical support for United States' policies. The United States cannot get Ireland into the Market and France, which can, is not likely to be favourably impressed by displays of subservience to America's supposed interests.

There is a Marxist, or pseudo-Marxist, position which asserts that a country like Ireland, because of its economic system and class structure cannot show any independence on international questions. It is true that these factors preclude certain extremes, but they also leave quite wide room for choice, as experience has shown. There now exists also an overriding factor, the common interest of the species in survival, which transcends class factors. The prime task of an Irish spokesman at the United Nations is to defend Ireland's share in that common interest. He must do so by the exercise of independent

133

judgement, because there is not any other kind of judgement: only different forms of intellectual abdication.

As a result of the efforts of Desmond Fitzgerald and Mr McGilligan in the councils of the Commonwealth; of Mr De Valera at the League, of Mr Aiken in his early years at the United Nations; of a Department of External Affairs which absorbed a considerable part of the talents of the nation and of an army which played a creditable part in United Nations peace-keeping efforts in the Middle East, the Congo and Cyprus, Ireland has acquired an adequate measure of international respect. Her spokesmen find a hearing, when they have something to say. They can exercise a small, but not insignificant influence, on the great movements of public opinion which help to shape world politics. There are some grounds for believing for example that Mr Aiken's original moves for 'relaxation of tensions' helped to lower the intensity of Cold War commitment among Americans of Irish origin; to the extent that this may be so, it would be a minor but not wholly negligible factor in the direction of making the international situation less dangerous. Again – to take an example which this time unfortunately has to be hypothetical – had the Minister for External Affairs of Ireland specifically and publicly supported U Thant's repeated calls for an end to the bombing of Vietnam, his words would have been heard both in the United Nations and in the United States. They would have significantly strengthened the Secretary-General's position – which inevitably came under attack – and they would have given valued encouragement to the peace movement in the United States. Such words would have been entirely within the bounds of Ireland's political range of choice, but to Ireland's shame they were not uttered.

Developments inside Ireland itself – The advent of younger men with new initiatives – permit the hope that a future Minister for External Affairs will return to the emphasis on the second principle which marked the international heyday of Mr De Valera and Mr Aiken. If so Ireland will once again be able to play a small but useful part in strengthening the defences of peace.

Literature in Modern Ireland

Kevin Sullivan

Early in May 1907, James Joyce delivered the second of three promised lectures on Ireland at the Università del Popolo in Trieste, an Italian city then under Austrian rule. The lecture, on the Irish poet James Clarence Mangan, was a revised version of a paper he had read some five years before to his contemporaries at University College, Dublin. His revisions reflect not only the change in Joyce's attitude toward Mangan but the differences – despite obvious parallels between Trieste and Ireland – between his Dublin and his Triestine audience. The latter were cultivated, interested but hardly well informed about literature in Ireland and, it is safe to assume, completely ignorant of Giacomo Clarenzio Mangan. Joyce decided therefore to rough in a general background against which his central figure could be seen in perspective.

'Ireland's contribution to European literature', he told his audience, 'can be divided into five periods and into two large parts, that is, literature written in the Irish language and literature written in the English language.' With a schoolmaster's neatness Joyce then subdivided the first part into two periods, one preceding and the other following the Anglo-Norman invasion of the twelfth century, and the second into three periods: the first encompassing the whole of the eighteenth century (Swift, Congreve, Goldsmith, Sheridan, Burke), the second culminating in the Young Ireland Movement of the 1840s (Davis, Mangan, Ferguson), and the third beginning in the last years of the nineteenth and continuing into the twentieth century as the Irish literary revival.

At this point there is a page missing in the holograph manuscript of Joyce's lecture; a third lecture on the Irish literary revival – promised just before the manuscript breaks off – has not survived.

Even so, Joyce's simple historical outline is today still useful to a reader more interested in broad perspective than in fineness of detail. In the past sixty years, however, perspectives have shifted – more rapidly perhaps than in any corresponding period in literary history – and now reveal a dimension hardly apparent to Joyce in 1907. What is today most obvious is that Ireland's re-entry in the twentieth century into the mainstream of European literature has been effected chiefly through the work of two major writers, William Butler Yeats and James

Joyce himself. The former, still a minor though an important poet and dramatist at the time of Joyce's lecture, came so to dominate the Irish literary scene during the early decades of the century that Joyce, were he sketching his outline today, might – later critics were to do so – designate this period 'The Age of Yeats'. But it is even more certain that Joyce would not have included himself within that 'period'. Another area would now have to be added to the outline indicating, at best only inadequately, his own contribution to literature and his influence on the writers, Irish and others, who came after him.

The dividing line would be about the time of the Second World War. Although Yeats was the older man much of his most important work, like that of Joyce, appeared between 1916 – a date also important for reasons other than literary – and his death on January 28, 1939. (Joyce died two years later on January 13, 1941.) But it is only in point of time, thus stated, that the literary careers of the two men can be said to have run parallel. Their backgrounds, purposes, methods and achievements were strikingly distinct, at times quite opposite, and around each has grown up whole forests (no need to enter them here) of criticism and commentary.

In post-Parnell Ireland Yeats had hoped to concentrate those energies that were no longer viable in politics into a new national literature. Young Joyce scorned the parochialism of this and neither then nor later allowed himself to be associated with the literary movement that took its impetus from the work of Yeats and his contemporaries. As late as 1932, in response to Yeats's kindly offer of charter membership in the newly formed Academy of Irish Letters, he would write: 'I see no reason why my name should have arisen at all in connection with such an academy.' And yet Joyce admired Yeats, and once conceded – a unique concession – that the older man was the greater writer. But the differences were of kind rather than degree. From the beginning Joyce's resources were 'silence, exile, and cunning' and the divisions of his nature, Irish of the Irish, were deeper and more troubled than those that Yeats, transforming private vision into public poetry, projected in his theories of the mask and anti-self. Yeats embodied his age even 'in the foul rag-and-bone shop of the heart'. Joyce exorcised his – 'My people were not their sort out beyond there as far as I can' – continuing to the end as artist 'to refine himself out of existence'. What Yeats was for Ireland during his lifetime, Joyce became for more than Ireland after his death – one of the determining forces in contemporary literature.

But between the distances that separate Yeats and Joyce, between two achievements equally remarkable and utterly different, lies the whole body of modern Irish literature. This is no longer a provincial or colonial literature, no more so now than American literature can be thought colonial. It is part of the literature of Europe and, paradoxically,

136

just to the extent that it has become more European it has become more distinctively Irish.

At the turn of the century while the Irish Revival was still in its infancy there had been much talk of de-Anglicization, a subject to which Douglas Hyde, the moving spirit behind the Irish language revival, specifically addressed himself in a now famous essay. This process of de-Anglicization was intended to operate in almost every area of Irish life – in language (the Gaelic League), in politics (Sinn Féin), even in sports (the Gaelic Athletic Association) – in everything, it seemed, except religion which was anyhow not Anglican but, for an overwhelming majority of the people, Roman. (The de-Romanization of religion in Ireland may be expected – peace to John XXIII and his *aggiornamento* – concurrently with the conversion of the Jews.) The success of these various programmes, never more than loosely co-ordinated, was at best limited, and the ultimate success of the political programme, to which the others could with difficulty be made to relate, was in many ways an historical accident – more the result of British blundering than of Irish statesmanship. If the results then were largely negative this was because the purpose implicit in 'de-Anglicization' was itself less than affirmative. It was not by undoing what the English had wrought but by accepting their own history, divisive and terrible as that history had been, and by relocating themselves anew in the patterns of European culture – all that Europe had made of itself between the rise of the Athenian and the decline of the British empires – that the Irish were to rediscover what Joyce called at the end of *A Portrait* the 'conscience of his race'. This, again, was very like an old thought in the back of Yeats's mind when, reflecting on the purposes that had moved him and John Synge and Lady Gregory in their work, he wrote of 'reuniting the mind and soul and body of man to the living world outside us'. In essence it meant that Ireland, centuries after the rest of Europe, was to be revitalized by the energies and aspirations of the Renaissance, and in literature especially it meant that there could be an end to brogues and blarney and that fresh and compelling voices would be heard again out of Ireland.

A sign of the new orientation in Irish literature can be detected in the biographical sources of its most recurrent theme: expatriation and exile. Ever since Lodwick Barry made his way from Cork to London in 1610, the year his play *Ram Alley* was produced there, Irish playwrights, poets, journalists, hacks had traditionally taken to the same road. The gravitational pull of London was understandable. That capital was the great centre where a writer from the provinces – and Ireland was the most backward of British provinces – could hope to make his mark. In almost every case the writer would also have to remake himself, discard his provincialisms, except those that might be profitably exploited, and adopt the idiom and attitudes of the more complex and sophisticated society in which he found himself. In short, the Irish expatriate in England, even when his subject matter remained Irish – Tom Moore, for example – had to make his way as an English writer. So among Moore's 'Irish Melodies', minor notes in the full scale of English Romantic poetry, are a handful of pure English lyrics, quite Caroline in their purity, far superior to the theatrical effects produced from broken-stringed harps or the unlikely ruins of Tara.

George Moore at the other end of the nineteenth century may be thought an exception, and in many ways he was. After a long sojourn in England where he had won some fame as a novelist, he was drawn back to Ireland by the undertow of excitement created in the stirring tides of the new literary revival. He returned, as he thought, to provide professional guidance to the untutored enthusiasms of his fellow countrymen. But once there, he reports, he fell so under the thrall (the enchantment was to pass) of Cathleen ni Houlihan that he could look back on his career in England and say of his most impressive success there: 'The Englishman that was in me . . . wrote *Esther Waters*.' George Moore is an exception but, like many exceptions, he proves a point.

Besides the two Moores at the beginning and close of the century, there were numbers of other expatriates – Wilde and Shaw are quickest to mind of near contemporaries, as Goldsmith and Sheridan are at a farther remove – who made a success (and sometimes a mess) of things once they had crossed from Kingstown to Holyhead. But Oscar Wilde would have been the first to admit, indeed to insist, that he was more Hellene than Gael, and certainly he could as well have been born in Athens or Alexandria for all the relevance of birth to his exquisite literary attitudes. As for George Bernard Shaw, it is perhaps more a matter of time than of place. It had been said of Shaw that, born out of time, he had the voice, despite his Dublin accent, of a thirteenth century Dominican telling at interminable length his rosaries of burning wit against a multitude of modern meat-eating Albigensians. He wrote a good deal, journalism mostly, about Ireland, or as he thought of it 'the Irish Question', and in one full-length play – *John Bull's Other Island* – he dissolved the question in a perky demonstration of the Irishness of the English, the Englishness of the Irish, and the beguiling foibles of both. But Ireland was always less a theme than a target to Shaw, one of many targets on which he drew his own bull's-eye, then scored with a direct and palpable hit.

All Irishmen, all expatriates – and there are a dozen more who are less well known, and scores not known at all, among the Prouts and Allinghams and Darleys of the nineteenth century – each of these better known writers finds place in a history of English literature. None properly speaking can be considered a writer within the Irish tradition save by the accident or grace of birth. Place of birth, however, as the

Duke of Wellington observed in dismissing the accident of his own Irish origin, is not decisive in this: a man may be born in a stable – but that, said His Grace, does not make him a horse.

It is possible that some or many of these writers never thought of themselves as expatriates (technically they were not) so untroubled was their adaptation to new surroundings. Certainly no one of them – Sean O'Casey may be a later exception – ever thought of himself while in England as an 'exile'. But from the time of Synge onward there were always to be writers out of Ireland, whether for a few years or for a lifetime, whose expatriation carried with it not only the suggestion but, more fatefully, the spiritual dimensions of exile.

The first characteristic of this group – such disparate spirits as Synge, Joyce, Beckett and Behan are among them – is that they did not follow the road to London taken by their Anglo-Irish predecessors, but chose instead the way of earlier Irish exiles – the wild geese of the seventeenth century, the erudite and purposeful monks of the Middle Ages – to the Continent, to France, Germany, and Austria. Unlike those earlier exiles these men were not compelled out of Ireland by religious zeal or political frustrations – except possibly Behan, the last and least of them – but by an uneasy awareness, an instinct almost, of the total irrelevance of politics or religion or any other abstract ideal to their purposes, however dimly foreseen at their going, as artists. And unlike their immediate predecessors, the Anglo-Irish of the eighteenth and nineteenth centuries, they were not content in fleeing the cultural wastes of Ireland to accommodate themselves to the literary market places of England. For England to them was also a wasteland under the governance of idols they could no more accept than they could the harmless 'immortals' of Tir-na-nÓg left behind them in an Irish dream.

What they found in Europe was, though at some considerable remove, closer to what they were accustomed to in Ireland than what they could have expected in England. The atmosphere – in the milieus most of them were to know, it could not be called more than that – was Catholic, not Protestant or reformed, even the prevalence of anti-clericalism, which in Ireland was either underground or inarticulate, being one of the inverse elements of that atmosphere. In Europe, too, as Daniel Corkery has pointed out, memories of old and recent wars, and frequently the visible reminders of them, were – like the ruined towers and devastated stretches of their own country, each with its own blighted memory – quite unlike the serene and lovely countryside of England that for almost a millennium had been preserved in the inviolability of a parkland from the ravages of foreign invasion. What blight there was in the English countryside had been of native doing, and the worst of it done by commerce rather than war; though should an Englishman desire *picturesque* ruins, he could, as Horace Walpole did, arrange to build his own.

139

The people on the Continent who lived this close to history were as restive, many of them – Italian, Slav, Hungarian – under various imperial masters as the Irish had been for centuries under the British. So the society, whatever it happened to be, in which the Irish exile found himself, had, always with the exception of its upper crust which only an explosion could remove, a fluidity, real or potential, very like that characteristic of Ireland and quite different from the rigid social structures that had made England a model of stability. Ireland – 'her lords and ladies gay', Yeats wrote in his last poem, 'beaten down into the clay Through seven heroic centuries' – had been, long before Karl Marx set foot in the British Museum, a classless society, even a middle class not beginning to appear, and then hardly in overwhelming numbers, until well into the nineteenth century. Of course there had always been a crust, known in Ireland as the Ascendancy, but this was generally a pale and at times a ludicrous reflection of the English aristocracy. Ireland, however, had never experienced the rigid stratification of class, from top through middle down to dead bottom, that is one of the wonders of the English social order. For all these reasons, the last reinforced perhaps by the natural bohemianism of many writers, these Irish literary exiles had set out for Europe as the more congenial place of refuge.

The experience of Europe, besides having an individual effect on each of these writers, had certain common effects on them all. The most obvious was language: they all were, or shortly became, multilingual. Synge at one time had thought of becoming a French literary critic and later was to teach himself the rudiments of Irish; Joyce had mastered a dozen languages and in *Finnegans Wake,* some say, created his own; Beckett wrote and published his work sometimes in English, more often in French, and translated (and republished) freely from one language to the other; even Brendan Behan scribbled for French periodicals – 'pieces of pornography' he afterwards called them – and wrote some poetry and an early version of his play *The Hostage* in Irish (*An Giall*). There is also a comic aspect to all this and it is provided, again, by that exceptional man George Moore who had preceded the others to Europe and was also of course bilingual. During his Irish period Moore proposed as his contribution to Yeats's national literary theatre that he compose a play in English – not, he said, in 'that pretty idiom' of Anglo-Irish – that this be turned into Gaelic, that Lady Gregory translate the Gaelic into French, and that he then re-translate the French back into an, not the, original English. Not surprisingly, nothing came of the venture, though Moore's collection of short stories, *The Untilled Field,* later was translated into Gaelic and published as 'a very pretty book' of which, Moore soon complained, 'nobody took any notice'.

But behind Moore's elegant japeries there is a serious intent in the Irish writer's restless preoccupation with language. This goes directly to the conscience of the writer who must grapple obscurely but tenaciously with a profound doubt about being . . . he knows not what precisely, knowing at any time only what he is not. And for the Irish writer this is not simply a metaphysical joke, though he often talks as if it were, but a matter of needing to define himself in a medium which he uneasily suspects is not really his own. In *A Portrait of the Artist* James Joyce epiphanizes this ambiguity in the conscience of the Irish writer by means of discussion on aesthetics between Stephen Dedalus and his dean of studies the English Jesuit Father Darlington. There had been a mild misunderstanding about the word 'tundish'. Then Stephen:

> The little word seemed to have turned a rapier point of his sensitiveness against this courteous and vigilant foe. He felt with a smart of dejection that the man to whom he was speaking was a countryman of Ben Jonson. He thought:

> The language in which we are speaking is his before it is mine. How different are the words *home, Christ, ale, master,* on his lips and on mine! I cannot speak or write these words without unrest of spirit. His language, so familiar and so foreign, will always be for me an acquired speech. I have not made or accepted its words. My voice holds them at bay. My soul frets in the shadow of his language.

It is not enough to dismiss this, as some critics would, with the sane observation that since all language is 'acquired speech' the passage is but another example of the subtle play of Joyce's irony over the solipsistic carapace of Stephen's sensibility. It may be that, it is something more than that. Under the rational surfaces of the best modern Irish writing there is a dark irrational current – in Beckett it is at full flow – that threatens at any moment to break through those surfaces and sweep away all certain landmarks and identities. These writers do not because they cannot, as their English contemporaries may, take language for granted. Their souls do indeed fret under the shadow of language so that the temptation to violence is ever present to them. One result is a literature that is constantly on the verge of nihilism – the accusation has been made – but is as constantly diverted by the play of other f rces into more viable and vital channels.

This attitude toward language left the Irish writer free to experiment in ways that would not have appealed to writers more securely rooted in a clearly defined literary tradition. To writers in the English tradition – as early as Edmund Gosse, as late as V. S. Pritchett, and as different as D. H. Lawrence – Joyce's experiments were an *'olla putrida',* 'a bog of Irish consciousness', a road through an unseemly and uncivilized waste leading nowhere. Some Anglo-Irishmen were even more alarmed: 'Our Romano-Celtic Joyce', John Eglinton wrote, 'nurses an ironic detachment from the whole of the English tradition. Indeed, he is its enemy . . . causing the language of Milton and Wordsworth to utter all but unimagineable filth and treason. Such is Joyce's Celtic revenge.' American writers, beginning with Pound and Eliot, have been more perceptive and sympathetic: many of them were themselves expatriates and given to experiments which often followed or paralleled those of the Irish writer. But the traditionalists, despite their angry rhetoric, were right in suspecting that the direction of these innovations in technique was toward the dissolution of form. They were wrong in dismissing the trend as another example of Irish vagary. For the world, no less than Ireland, had already moved toward a point in time when old certainties were again ready to go into solution, when in literature the tidy formulas of nineteenth century realism (Maupassant, Flaubert) were breaking down under a deeper probing of more obscure levels of reality (Proust, Kafka, Faulkner). The Irish literary exile had preceded most of his contemporaries to that place of spiritual uncertainty.

Samuel Beckett seems to have taken up permanent residence there. 'I wrote all my work,' he reported, 'very fast – between 1946 and 1950.' Actually he began to write in the 1930s and has continued to publish up to the present, but until Joyce's death Beckett had remained very much under the great man's shadow – 'le petit Joyce' he was called in Paris. It was not until 1952 that he was somersaulted backward into fame by the international success, and attendant controversies, of *Waiting for Godot.* The central weight of his fame now rests on the trilogy *Molloy, Malone Dies,* and *The Unnameable.* As a variation on the *Inferno,* the descent here is through progressively denser levels of language toward that silence on the other side of language where the Self, stripped long ago of all disguises and now of all resources, may at last put the question of its own identity. That a void can give back no answer to the romantic heretic is beside the point. More to the point is the progress itself, a *via purgativa,* that leads like the way of the Buddhist or Christian mystic . . . perhaps to annihilation, perhaps to illumination, perhaps to no more than a final re-identification of that separate Self, defined in time and articulated in consciousness, with an eternal flow of impersonal being. However this may be, Beckett owes nothing to formal or systematic mysticism of East or West. 'I'm not interested in any system,' he has said, 'I can't see any trace of any system anywhere.' This is Beckett's limitation, for it is system that enlarged the vision and tested the powers of writers like Yeats and Joyce and was the basis of their major achievements. But if the experience is limited, Beckett's power, 'the passionate pursuit of his own kind of buried reality,' is real: his bums and his derelicts in their passage through time and uncertainty–Godot will or will not come?–are, on this side of silence, in the underground rush of his language toward silence, indestructible. It is in this sense that Beckett is the humanist in spite of himself.

A generation before Beckett, John Millington Synge had successfully carried out a quite different kind of experiment with language. His brief exile in Europe had been cut short by Yeats's advice to go to the West of Ireland where, he was told, there lay buried among the peasantry richer possibilities for literature than an Irishman might find in fin-de-siècle Paris. In going, Synge was really passing from one kind of exile to another. In race, religion, speech, custom and general way of life the Aran Islanders were stranger, more alien than the Germans or French among whom the young Trinity graduate had first sequestered himself. But if he went in among the peasantry like an amateur anthropologist, noting down with interest the peculiarities of their folkways, he returned through his plays as an artist. In Ireland, George Moore had observed, the eighteenth century lasted into the 1870s, but the parts of Ireland explored by Synge were still more remote in time. The English spoken among people long isolated by mountain, bog, and estuary had still the flavour of Elizabethan speech, and the Irish language, where it survived, had for Synge as it had for Yeats the echo of a mediaeval voice. Out of this experience Synge created a new literary language. This may owe something to Douglas Hyde and other scholars and translators of the nineteenth century, and a non-poetic variation of it is to be found in Lady Gregory's 'Kiltartanese', but Synge is nonetheless an original. His renewal of language re-united poetry and speech and made possible again the kind of poetic drama that had disappeared from the English-speaking stage at the time of the Puritan revolution in the seventeenth century. It is this language more than all else that is the source of the abundant vitality of *The Playboy* and of the stark perfection of *Riders to the Sea*.

The genius of Synge established the tone, as Yeats gave direction, and Lady Gregory coherence, to the early Irish theatre. They were soon followed by others, so many others that it would seem the real test of literacy in Ireland was at one time to have written a play. Among the best of these playwrights are Padraic Colum, Denis Johnston, and Paul Vincent Carroll. Quite the best of them, however, is Sean O'Casey who began writing tragi-comedy (*The Shadow of a Gunman, Juno and the Paycock, The Plough and the Stars*), turned in mid-career to technical and ideological experiments (*The Silver Tassie, Red Roses for Me*), and turned back again at the close to comedy and farce (*Purple Dust, Cock-a-Doodle Dandy*). O'Casey is a major figure in the sense that he produced a more considerable body of work than any of the others, and the best of this is generally thought to be the Dublin cycle of plays in which he most closely approximates the achievement of John Synge. The link is again language. O'Casey's proletariat is really a peasantry transplanted from the West of Ireland to the slums of Dublin, and the talk is a melding of urban idiom and softer country rhythms. This is a literary language spoken by no mortal man off the stage, its poetic overtones

143

adapted from Synge for O'Casey's own purposes. In the last group of plays the setting as well as the language is countrified, though what in the Dublin cycle had been an intense fusion of the comic and tragic is now dissipated in an uproar of knockabout farce. The experimental plays of O'Casey's middle period have had their advocates, but history is not yet convinced of their success. For in these plays O'Casey is attempting to manipulate ideas or, to put the matter darkly, ideology. But these ideas are highly unstable elements, not so much charged with emotion as dissolving into it. The result is often a fuzziness of both thought and feeling which, lacking any adequate correlative in language, appears in the plays not as poetry but as a kind of clamorous rhetoric. O'Casey suspected this failing in himself. In the sixth and last volume of his long, lyrical autobiography he wrote:

> Sean had no learning, no knowledge – what he set down were but his feelings moulded with words; there they were and there they'd stay.

So just and honest an appraisal disarms criticism.

There is another kind of Irish literary expatriate who is in no sense an exile and whose experience abroad has only rarely had any significant effect on his work. Indeed, he is less an expatriate than a peripatetic man of letters. He may go to Europe, sometimes to England, but far more frequently to America. His precursors were the poets Padraic Colum and Joseph Campbell who left Ireland around the time of the first World War and spent a considerable amount of their long lives in America. They were followed in the next half-generation by Frank O'Connor and Sean O'Faolain, and more recently by an increasing number of novelists, poets, and short-story writers – Brian Moore, Benedict Kiely, Thomas Kinsella, Richard Murphy, John Montague. The list is a long one. During their stay these writers are commonly in residence at one or a succession of American Colleges where, in their lectures and seminars, they may be thought remote descendants of the wandering Irish Scholar of an earlier age, though it cannot be said that they are much given to works of conversion. The experience of America – a land of criticism in an age of criticism with most of the activity centered around the academy – may be responsible for turning the creative energies of some of these writers in the direction of literary criticism. O'Connor and O'Faolain set the example with their formal studies of the modern novel and the short story. But with the exception of Brian Moore the contemporary Irish writer has not, save obliquely, attempted to use his American experience as matter, theme or setting for his creative work. Language and style seem equally unaffected by the experience.

Whether expatriate, exile or peripatetic, all of the Irish writers mentioned so far have this in common that they wrote for a public that was not primarily, nor intentionally limited to, their fellow countrymen. The reasons for this are various, most of them obvious, and none need be delayed on here. But there is still another kind of Irish writer, usually though not always a stay-at-home, who does not easily fit into any of these categories and who does indeed seem to have written for a specifically Irish audience. He is usually not as well known as some of his more widely travelled contemporaries, and this is unfortunate, for his literary merits are often equal or superior.

In fiction the foremost is Brian O'Nolan. Widely known in Ireland as Myles na Gopaleen, one time pundit in residence at the *Irish Times,* O'Nolan under the name of Flann O'Brien has written in *At Swim Two Birds* a minor masterpiece, second only to *Ulysses,* of the Irish comic imagination. It was recognized as such almost at once by a handful of critics and fellow writers, James Joyce among them, but only recently has it become more widely known outside Ireland. *At Swim* is that rare thing in modern fiction – a radical experiment which, unlike many experiments, is also a joyous book. Its complex parodic structure – a one man symposium on Irish literature – is clearly inspired by *Ulysses,* and it may be that Samuel Beckett took from O'Nolan a hint or two for his own more morbid comedy. But this novel is all unshadowed laughter and since its first publication in 1939 nothing quite like it has appeared in Ireland. Brian O'Nolan himself, whether writing in Irish (*An Béal Bocht*) or again in English (*The Hard Life*) has not surpassed this original achievement.

Among recent Irish poets there are two who stand out from the rest, Patrick Kavanagh and Austin Clarke. Kavanagh is the more original in the sense that his work seems so spontaneous as not to have been inspired or shaped by literary influences of any kind. In post-Yeatsian Ireland this is especially remarkable, for the influence of Yeats, often inhibiting, has been as pervasive in Irish poetry as the example of Joyce, less inhibiting because more inimitable, has been unavoidable in Irish prose. But for Kavanagh

> *Unlearnedly and unreasonably poetry is shaped*
> *Awkwardly but alive in the unmeasured womb.*

Awkwardly at times perhaps but always with a strength that is its own measure. This is the strength Kavanagh took from 'the stone grey soil of Monaghan' where he was bred, a hard hungry land from the like of which generations had fled in the emigrant ships to America. Kavanagh stayed and in one harshly effective novel, *Tarry Flynn,* and in a long powerful poem, 'The Great Hunger', wrote of the life he had known in the unredeemed country and hillsides of Ireland. Reading novel or poem one is brought back a hundred years to William Carleton's *Traits and Stories of the Irish Peasantry* in whom Yeats later had seen 'figures only half-emerged from earth', primal beings no more distinct from

145

nature than roots or stones. The theme of 'The Great Hunger' is not the Irish potato famine but the famine in man's soul and the frustrations in his body. The protagonist, an Everyman of the Irish countryside, is, under his habiliments of clay, brother in frustration to figures from a different life in T. S. Eliot.

> He stands in the doorway of his house,
> A ragged sculpture of the wind.
> October creaks the rotted mattress,
> The bedposts fall. No hope, no lust.
> The hungry fiend
> Screams the apocalypse of clay
> In every corner of this land.

The only exile Patrick Kavanagh was to know was removal from the soil to the publican fastnesses of Dublin. That city soon prompted him to satire, as it had others before and since, but he turned again after a space to his original theme and transformed it in a series of beautiful sonnets from a tragedy of frustration to a lyrical celebration of man's redemption through the acceptance of the ordinariness of natural existence.

> . . . I do
> The will of God, wallow in the habitual, the banal,
> Grow with nature again as before I grew.

Austin Clarke is, after Yeats, the most complete poet of twentieth century Ireland. His work begins under the broad influence of Yeats and matures in a manner as firm and lyrical, and at times as private and obscure, as the later Joyce. In this sense Clarke recapitulates on a small scale the general course of modern Irish literature as it takes impulse and direction from the example of its two chief figures.

Clarke's early background was, like that of Joyce, religious middle-class Dublin. He attended both of Joyce's old Dublin schools, Belvedere and University College, and a few years after graduation, again like Joyce, he took leave of Ireland. After some dozen years in England he returned again to Ireland where he has since remained a more or less permanent resident of Dublin and environs. But this return was not the end of exile for Clarke:

> When I had brought my wife
> And children, wave over wave,
> From exile, could I have known
> That I would sleep in England
> Still, lie awake at home?

The wry complaint is characteristic of more than one contemporary Irish writer.

146

Clarke had begun his career as a poet in the Celtic twilight of the Yeats revival – *The Vengeance of Fionn,* for example, in 1917, or *The Cattledrive in Connaught* in 1925 – but, more especially in his novels and plays, he was to adapt mediaeval materials to an original purpose. This, in brief, was to contrast what seemed to him the artistic and intellectual freedoms of the mediaeval Irish church with the dogmatic Catholicism of modern Ireland. The double vision this required led Clarke inevitably to satire, but though the occasion of his satire is often a public condition or event (censorship, contraception, death by fire of orphaned children), the language is not public, as in Swift or Yeats, but private, almost cautiously so, and even at times entirely personal. 'Celebrations', for example, is a poem that would require the full exegetical apparatus of an American academician to unravel completely. Yet Clarke, like Joyce in *Finnegans Wake,* is rewarding precisely because of the demand he makes upon the imagination and referential world of a reader.

Clarke never attempted to exploit the kind of autobiographical materials that Joyce had already brought to perfection in *A Portrait of the Artist* and *Ulysses.* And yet central to his work is the same preoccupation with a religion in which he does not believe, or no longer believes in quite the way that he once did. It is a mark of his power as a poet that all personal conflicts – essentially religious, but also sexual, social, intellectual, and political – have been transformed in his work into a drama whose underlying theme is, like that of Joyce, 'the conscience of his race'.

In the course of his lecture on Mangan in 1907 Joyce put the rhetorical question: 'If he has never won the sympathy of his own countrymen, how can he win that of foreigners?' In the past sixty years Irish writers have reversed the terms of the question. They have generally won greater sympathy outside Ireland than at home, for they have made themselves part of a larger literary tradition, one with which Mangan struggled blindly to identify himself and this tradition from Homer to the present has in turn magnified the work and reputation of the Irish writer. Like one of its own legendary heroes, modern Irish literature has become itself by becoming more than itself. A conscience – 'the conscience of my race' – has been created in the hard and sparkling smithies worked by Joyce and Yeats, and as the work has continued under their influence, but now under other hands, that conscience may be seen to bear an uncommon likeness to that of our ordinary and unheroic humanity.

The Whores on the Half-Doors

or An Image of the Irish Writer

Benedict Kiely

Knockanure
Both mean and poor,
A church without a steeple,
And ignorant whores
Lean on half-doors,
Demeaning decent people[1] . . .

My first Irish writers were Andy McLoughlin, Alice Milligan, Peadar O'Donnell, Robert Burns, Patrick MacGill and Dean Swift. Andy McLoughlin was never, except to a select circle, as well known as the others. Chauvinistic Scotsmen may be surprised, if you could surprise them, at finding the Bard of Ayr sandwiched between two Donegal men.

The most notable thing, at first sight, about Andy McLoughlin was that he was small and squat, needed badly some decent clothes and a haircut, and that one of his legs was shorter than the other. He was the last bellringer and town crier in Omagh, Co Tyrone, and a sort of laureate too, for he commented, something in the fashion of Dryden, on passing events. He claimed a 'poetic licence' (much as if he had bought it like a dog licence or, more aptly, a gun licence) to call everybody names; and on one occasion when the municipal fathers had passed out a job to a man that Andy, and everybody else except the municipal fathers and the man himself and his relations at home and in the States, thought was the wrong man, Andy wrote thus trenchantly:

Mickey Lynch, you did it dirty.
Have you any eyes to see?
And Alec, what's the matter?
You're our Nationalist MP
McConville and Frank Cassidy,
Ye are not the poor man's friend,
Nor our well-famed bookie:
W. F. Townsend.

[1]There are variant readings. The author, Paddy Drury (1880–1948), a wandering, satirical labouring man, a native of Knockanure in North Kerry, despised his native place and the people in it, but immortalized it in the celebrated patriotic ballad, *The Valley of Knockanure.* (See James N. Healy, *Ballads from the Irish Pubs*, Mercier Press, Cork.) Healy's version differs slightly from mine, which came to me from the late Robert Herbert, Limerick City Librarian.

He had, as I said, but little recognition and died sometime in the 1930s in the poorhouse. But on one occasion he said, and with a gravity not to be laughed at: 'Burns was the best of us.'

Burns is on my list because Burns was, at least before Dunkirk and television, a folklore figure in rural Ulster, just as the darin' Liberathor, Daniel O'Connell, once was in suaver parts of Ireland. Most of the folklore about him indicated that he was a dacent fellow, but dirty. When my mother, now well into her eighties, was bearing her slate and primer to a country schoolhouse, the teacher, a Master Reid, presented her with a volume of Burns with heavy black lines pencilled through the poems she was not to read. Then there was a Popular Underground Burns unknown, as far as I know, even to David Daiches and the scholars in Underground Burns. There was the couplet he spoke to Lord Byron when the Saxon milord walked through a byre that Bobby was sweeping and haughtily ordered the Scottish groom to lift the broom and let Lord Byron by. What was Byron doing in that there byre? Or, for that matter, Burns? There was the quatrain he spoke for a bet when one of a group of drinking companions, a man from Leith, had had as much as his gut could hold and spewed over the table. Leith, I may tell you, rhymes with teeth. There was the quatrain he spoke quick as a shot when he had the girl against the gate and looked over his shoulder and saw a wee fellow watching him and eating a bun. The subject of the quatrain was the wonder of the works of nature. Full quotation is not advisable, but you do from my adroit hints get one popular Irish picture, or image, of the poet.

Patrick McGill, no more than Burns or Dean Swift, I never met. A sort of Irish Gorki, he came out of Glenties in the lovely but barren mountains of West Donegal, to write of the plight of the Irish migratory labourer in Scotland, to serve with the London-Irish in World War I and to write sketch-books of war in the style of Barbusse and, as a way of saying goodbye to all that, to write one fine comic novel of life in Donegal, *Lanty Hanlon*, that reads as if Christopher Mahon had played Pirandello on that meditative man, John Synge, and written another chapter to tell of his life as a likely gaffer. My first of several misadventures with literature and censorship was to be discovered by that incorrigible mother ('Your mother Eire is always young') reading MacGill's *The Rat Pit*, and to have the book impounded, to discover that my mother had actually known MacGill, and that was that. At the moment of impounding I had been trying to work out the connection (as the London telephone girl said to the Canadian soldier) between a young Scotsman, the boss's son, going into a shed with a young Irish girl, a poor potato-picker in the fields of Fife, and somebody in the distance playing Swanee River on the fiddle, and then the girl having a baby and going to hell in the gutters of Glasgow. Music, it seemed to me at the age of nine or ten, had the oddest charms.

149

But no doubt about it MacGill had it in for the priests. Pot-bellied they were, one and all, and purple-faced, and the amount of money one of them would squander on a water-closet for his own carnal comfort and convenience would house, fodder and clean out three parishes. They were not in the least like our own pastor, the reverend Dr McShane, a grey, grave monsignor, who dressed in threadbare suits, had been to the Irish College in Rome, who spoke of Italia Irredenta and Hibernia Irredenta (the Six Counties) and whose polished and literate sermons my mother quoted to the point of distraction. He was known to have called a prominent and pious Dublin politician whom he abhorred because of his civil war record, a murderer. He had also told the enthusiastic and progressive leader of the local drama group who had yearnings towards *The Plough and the Stars* that if Sean O'Casey wrote the stations of the cross you couldn't say them.

Dean Swift is on the list because of an early reading and rereading of *Gulliver's Travels* and the simultaneously acquired knowledge that the learned author had died in the crazyhouse, a something quite compatible, it seemed, with the state of being an Irish writer. Peadar O'Donnell is there because once on the way from Donegal to Dublin he rushed into a room in a house in an Ulster town where two children were painfully struggling with *Elementa Latina*. 'Mensa, mensa, mensam', he said, 'mensae, mensae, mensa.' and he was out the door and away before anybody could answer. That was odd carry-on. He wore a leather motoring jacket and his hair stood up like a bush. Afterwards we were to hear that although he wasn't crazy, he was a Communist.

Alice Milligan, as is only right and proper for a poet who had sung the Fenians of both the old and the new dispensations, and who had walked with the gods, has a very special place on that list. An old clergyman of my acquaintance brought me when a boy to her hallowed door: a stern old puritanical man from a part of the Sperrin Mountains where there had been a priest in the family in every generation for three hundred years. His favourite poet, oddly enough, was Robert Burns but his favourite sliver of Burns was the moralizing passage provoked by the night-rakings of Tam O'Shanter: 'But pleasures are like popies spread – you seize the flow'r it's bloom is shed.'

The old poetess of the *The Fenians* and Abbey playright of *The Last Feast of the Fianna* was then, by courtesy of the church in which her father had been a rector, living, among unkempt lawns and shrubbery gone halfways to jungle, in the rectory, a much decayed building, on the fringe of the lovely little mountain village of Mountfield. 'Divil the much she ever made', said the old cleric, 'hob-nobbing with Yeats and that crew. She dresses, God help her, like Maggy the Rag. If you met her on the road, you'd reach her a penny.' Then he hammered on the front door, called out: 'Alice where art thou?' The door opened and the dear lady appeared, quite literally in wreaths of smoke. There was a jackdaw in the chimney, for whose invasion and occupancy she courteously apologized. We sat in the musty drawing room and listened to her telling us how she had once spent a wonderful day with Miss Gonne and Mr Bulfin (Mr Yeats couldn't make the trip) studying druidic remains in Glencolumcille. The smoke thickened and thickened until the poor old woman could only be seen fitfully, and we were set free to see, from smarting eyes, visions of the woman Homer sung, that statuesque thought from Propertius, going with the walk of a queen along that most wonderful of all Irish western glens. Yet it was saddening to think that to be poor, lonely and smoke-dried should be the lot of a poet in the end of all.

Later it might have occurred to one that there was some connection between an old woman abandoned in a smoky corner and that cracked mirror of the serving maid that a bitter young Dubliner was to see as the symbol of Irish art. But that is not to say that the old poetess was ever anybody's servant: even in the smoke she was proud, and noble.

To make mystic the number of writers I first knew aught of there was a seventh: Brinsley MacNamara. His name was a household two-words, and long ones at that, for horror; and the title of his novel *The Valley of the Squinting Windows* was a handy description for any nest of vipers. Dire tales came through, on the wind, of riot and distress down in the Free State, in the grasslands and lakelands of Westmeath, where a young man had written this holy-awful book calling names to everybody in his village, or so the people in the village thought or said. To aggravate his villainy he had been off prancing around the States with that Abbey Theatre gang from Dublin, disgracing Ireland forever by playacting in a play about a Kerryman who killed his father and was sheltered by the women of Erris and Tyrawley. People were brawling about his book at street corners in the village and arguing about it in courts of law, and a copy of the book was burned on the main street of the village by a butcher, and an old woman (yet another) had been heard to say: 'Thanks be to the Sacred Heart, the trouble's over. The book's burnt.'

That same old Sperrin-mountain priest was, just about that time, congratulating me on some out-of-the-way-brilliant school essay, possibly on the autobiography of an old boot. That was a great theme then, and the roads of the British Isles must have been littered with discarded lonely boots. He said: 'You'll be a writer some day. See that you never disgrace your country the way Brinsley MacNamara did.' It was a remark that in years to come, and over the course of a friendship that was to last until his death, was to inspire in Brinsley touches of that wry humour with which he surveyed almost everything in this curious world.

But you do get the picture. It was damn nearly to be expected that an Irish writer would disgrace his country, his mother and father, his

151

CONOR CRUISE O'BRIEN INTRODUCES IRELAND

wife – if anybody would have him – or his neighbour's wife, if he had a hoor's chance. There was precedent for it, back as far as Eoghan of the Sweet Mouth O'Sullivan and the Gaelic poets of Sliabh Luachra. Why even Maurice Walsh, a Kerryman like Red Eoghan though not, at least, a spalpeen poet with the lust of the world on him, (he was a popular and profitable novelist, then writing romantic novels about the Scottish Highlands to warm the heart of Sir J. M. Barrie at his window in Thrums) even he, God help us, was an authority on whiskey; and it was darkly hinted that he didn't practise. It was never necessary to say what it was that he didn't practise. To be an authority on whiskey and not to practise were two of the salient characteristics of Irish writers.

By other marks, too, you knew them when you met them. There were poverty, blackguardism, anti-clericalism, lunacy, loneliness, and dreams as crazy as those of Shaw's Father Keegan. There was a tendency towards mocking and demeaning the decent people, the tendency displayed by those ignorant whores who leaned on half-doors in the celebrated village that had neither church not steeple. All of this and more of the kind went to make up the image of the Irish writer among, and to, his own people.

If one had not been irrevocably doomed to trying to be a writer all this might have put one off. Who wants in his own country or anywhere else to be regarded as a cut between the village idiot and a tinker who might steal the chickens, or a market-stroller who might steal cherries from maidens or wives from husbands? It seemed odd that this mixture of contempt for, and suspicion of, the writer should exist in the same place as an ancient respect for poetry, ballads, tales and those who could tell them, for the shadow of Robert Burns in the north-east and of Red Eoghan O'Sullivan in the south-west and of many others in between. There was mystery here somewhere. So, in due course up with me to Dublin to find out what it was all about. That was about twenty-five years ago.

In a hilarious *Tourist's Guide to Ireland*, Liam O'Flaherty divided the people of the country into four groups: priests, peasants, publicans, politicians. It is a fair enough categorization and, to be nice about it, you can split the big four into smaller or lesser groups making, say, the civil servants attendant to the politicians. The new middle class of which we hear so much may be peasants aspiring to be publicans, or publicans aspiring to be peasants. But you will not find anywhere a place for writers although it may be a significant symptom of a thwarted natural function that the young men in the mohair suits in the advertising agencies call themselves writers, as signpainters in the trade always called themselves in Dublin.

Not the signpainters, but the modish painters and the sculptors and musicians, can be fitted in somewhere: as servants to the clergy when those latter are stricken by an attack of Art, or as public performers because they don't use words and don't do much harm to anyone and because at times as, say, Edward Delany has so notably done in College Green, they can express and fulfil history and beautify a public square. But the writer in Ireland fits in nowhere except in a pub talking his guts out and doing no writing: elsewhere he is a loner and a drifter. There are no publishers to publish him and give him a fighting chance of making his bread. The work of The Dolmen Press, done mostly in poetry and sometimes in conjunction with a great English firm, is the exception that proves the rule. Like every other country in the world we have a literate minority. Some statistician, or mythological poet, once told me that per head of the population we buy books as well as or better than they do in Britain. But then what is our population? So a writer to get his head at all above the surface must take his wares to London and New York, to be afterwards accused by the Plain People of Ireland of writing for a 'foreign market'. What that hoary accusation really means is that the Plain People of Ireland think that the writer, to line his own pockets, is making a holy show of them before the jeering English: while the writer, driven on by his own personal curse, is merely trying to express himself, his people and his environment, for his own ease of spirit or the satisfying of the demon, for the information or delight or annoyance of all or any who care to read him.

Yet writers are by nature, by sheer necessity, a vociferous and clamant people. As the man in Flann O'Brien's *At Swim Two Birds* said about Fionn MacCool: 'Let him talk, it has to come out somewhere.' Not all the professors from Plato to the late Professor Magennis, high priest of censorship in Ireland in the 1940s and still in these better times an interesting case on Ireland's conscience, can teetotally silence the poet, and poets in Ireland had for patriotic reasons acquired a little extra respect. So many of the 1916 men had been poets, and all the Irish poets, with the two exceptions of Moira O'Neill and Jane Barlow, had approved of and duly mourned the 1916 men. Professor Magennis, by the way, did in his glory outline a prevalent attitude towards the writer when he said that he didn't want to see writers on the Censorship Board because that would be to set Bill Sykes to catch the burglars. He also said of some Irish writers that they were not novelists but only short-story writers padding out with smut to make their wares more marketable in London. He had especially in mind Kate O'Brien, Sean O'Faolain, Frank O'Connor, and if you like irony you can find it by comparing Magennis on the novel in Ireland with the crazy ideas on the same expressed by that most lovable of men Frank O'Connor, in his book *The Lonely Voice*. All of which brings me back to Dublin in the unhappy 'forties.

For the two most clamant voices then in desert or in Dublin

153

were the voices of O'Faolain and O'Connor. Or to be more exact: O'Faolain, in a voice both iron and eloquent, was clamanting on behalf of the two-headed Cork genius begotten by Daniel Corkery on Mother Eire in a state of revolutionary frenzy, a genius that developed to merit the priestly blessing of William Yeats, and that had a definite cousinship with Tchekhov, Turgenev, Babel, Daudet, Maupassant and some others.

O'Faolain and his generation had been committed men, as he pointed out in an article written for the fiftieth anniversary of 1916; and he wondered in the same article if younger writers could be, or were, so committed. Well, at least they could be committed to a considerable admiration for Sean O'Faolain both as a great writer and as a man ready and able to protest against the smug, priestly, self-satisfied Ireland, the Ireland that thought it was better and holier than the 'outside world' (the description was in constant use), the Ireland that seemed to have come out of nowhere, to have appeared like a cherubic changeling in a surplice, in place of the Ireland that the poets and patriots seemed to promise and hope for. The height or depth of that smugness was suggested to me when, as a young newspaper man, I was approached by a Dublin merchant to write a publicity sheet for a project that he and some other god-fearing Dublin merchants had in mind. It was to build on Howth Head (where Joyce had brooded in the bushes and where Yeats and Maud Gonne had watched the white birds soaring over the white foam of the sea) a gigantic statue of the Sacred Heart of Jesus as big, by the holy, as the Christ of the Andes. My immediate thought, fortunately unexpressed, was that it was high time Howth redeemed its reputation, for there had been recently around Howth Harbour a most unholy outbreak of homosexuality that had given rise to a bookful of Dublin jokes, like the one about the man who dropped the half-crown in Howth and had to kick it all the way to Sutton Cross before he had the nerve to stoop to pick it up.

But no: the mammoth statue was to thank the Sacred Heart and Blessed Oliver Plunkett – no mention was made of De Valera – for keeping Ireland out of the war, and it was hoped that all the sailors, including Irish sailors, on all the ships coming into haven from seas doubly-perilous, would see that statue and be inspired by it. At this I demurred to the extent of mumbling that neither the Sacred Heart nor Blessed Oliver Plunkett would thank us for thanking them. Blessed Oliver, who had been an agent and suffered sore for it, would hardly see why Irish men should hide in the corner from anything. The Sacred Heart, too, had had his own sad experience of power politics, and might find it against his principles to have much to do with a group of well-to-do merchants and money-changers congratulating themselves on their own comfort while the rest of the world, including a lot of their fellow-countrymen, were hip-deep in chaos.

Yet, in spite of such revelations of the total decay of the separatist

154

mind, it did take some imaginative effort for writers younger than O'Faolain and O'Connor to understand the extent of the change, the darkening, the altering of the skies from that dawn in which it was bliss, and all that jazz, to be alive, to the dreary early afternoon of the 1940s, with flatulence and headache after six whiskeys and a soggy lunch.

O'Faolain could remember so delightfully the days when he and other youths poured into the mountain valleys of Muskerry to learn Gaelic, and brought gaiety and music with them into places lonely and silent for the rest of the year. But the story that began with that wistful look backwards ended 'with the black back-view of a cleric whose elongated shadow waved behind him like a tail,' a decent fellow, and cheerful, and respected by all, but nevertheless a persecutor and the man who invented sin. In the early stories of O'Connor, in the collection *Guests of the Nation*, even although the title story is a hard tragedy and although tragedy recurs throughout the book, the dominant impression left is that the writer is genuinely enjoying his material: enjoying guns, manhunts, ambushes, attacks on barracks, racing and chasing and battling, with the splendid appetite of healthy youth. The revolution didn't freeze O'Connor's people into rigid sombre contemplation as it did Daniel Corkery's people; instead it set them moving as a windy day might set a streetful of men chasing their hats. In that mood, and for love of life and country and poetry and scholarship, O'Connor made himself a Gaelic scholar; and in post-revolutionary times, when the laughing morning wind had died down into a dismal drizzle, he was to feel the chagrin of having his translation of Brian Merriman's *Cúirt a'Mheadhon Oidhche* (The Midnight Court) banned by the Dublin censorship for being 'in general tendency indecent or obscene'. He was to say ruefully, but with humour and a Munster brogue that never deserted him, that the only compliment his countrymen had ever paid him was to think, some of them, that he was the author of the original poem.[1]

Because he wrote a friendly introduction to a pleasant, harmless, innocent book, Frank O'Connor's name was involved in the most celebrated case of book-banning or persecution in that period. The censoring mind, as George Moore noted in the London that sent Vizetelly to jail for publishing Zola, is also the persecuting mind. Here follows the illustrative story.

Eric Cross was an English research scientist and mathematician. He still is, that is: he still is Eric Cross, a quiet saintly man who lives in the

[1]When Patrick Henchy of the National Library and David Greene of the Institute once suggested a Merriman memorial there were some ignorant puritan protests. Today there has been such a welcome change that, thanks to the work of those and other scholars, there is a Merriman Summer School.

west of Ireland in the sort of rural quietude that he always desired ever since he discovered in the early 1930s that the work he and others were engaged in could be used to make the world safe for germ warfare. So he turned his back on the whole shebang, came to Ireland, got him a horse and caravan and took to the roads; and in a quiet valley in the Muskerry Mountains he met the man of his heart, an old rural philosopher, a tailor who didn't tail much but who lived, with his wife Anstey, in a cabin, on a scrap of land, ten shillings a week pension, and the milk of one black cow; who thought, or knew, that time didn't exist and that the world was well on the way to what he called alabastery. The old man was seventy-seven years of age and walked, albeit agilely enough, on a crutch. No formidable enemy, as you may see, to a nation's morality.

Eric Cross, and he wasn't alone in this, felt the out-of-time enchantment of this old man, his talk, his stories, his wisdom, his humour that had now and again a touch of lively rustic bawdry: the story, for instance, about the sow that ate the eel, or about the weakly father of seventeen who hadn't the price of admission to see the great performing bull, or about what the widower on his way home from his wife's funeral said when he saw the cock treading the hen.

The quiet Englishman on the run from a world of horror was happy to sit in the chimney corner and play Boswell to the talk of the kind and wise old man of the glen, to write it down in a book and to publish it, under the title of *The Tailor and Anstey*, introduced by Frank O'Connor, who was among the tailor's many friends. For how was Eric Cross or Frank O'Connor, or anybody in their sane senses, to imagine that in Dublin a learned professor and senator (the notable William Magennis who had once, begod, considered that a piece by a student called Joyce merited publication in a college magazine) could say that the book was low, blasphemous and obscene, that it was circulated to gratify the English mind, or eye, by allowing it to see 'what the Irish peasant really is when shown up by one who knows him'. The learned windbag, who was then Chairman of the Board of Censorship of Publications, also spoke of the 'foulness' of the tailor's mind. That was in 1943.

Even in that bad year and period it was possible to wonder if Senator Magennis and the owners of the owlish voices who spoke with him were talking of the same book that one had read with some merriment, and with a certain nostalgic longing for the unspoiled and simple life. It was even ordered – with the turn of the screw of idiocy – that the quotations from the book read out in a Senate debate on censorship (in the nation's highest assembly, once dignified by the presence of William Yeats) should be struck from the record, lest perhaps the determined and devoted muckrackers among the Irish should purchase the Senate report for the sake of the dirty reading. A lady senator, who wrote lives of saints for sub-cerebral religious magazines, said that if Dante came back again and really wanted to put the screws on some of his enemies (she didn't put it exactly like that) then he could find no more effective way of doing so than by forcing them to read this diabolical book. It was implied that in conversations at rural hearthsides nobody ever mentioned cows and bulls; and it was impossible not to wonder if these senatorial speakers had not been reared like Marie Louise of the Habsburgs who was married off to Napoleon. In a world where protocol had for centuries taken precedence over commonsense, it was said that she was never allowed to possess a pet animal of the male variety and that all reference to any difference between the sexes was snipped with scissors out of the books she read. A poor preparation for going to bed with Bonaparte, yet an interesting example of censorship.

While all this angry wind was being blown off, on behalf of purity, in the Senate, down in the Muskerry Mountains the desire to persecute had worked itself out in a nasty backhanded way. Some local hooligans, incited by the newspaper reports, tried to make miserable the last days of the poor old tailor. The big English laboratories were not the only places where the rotten heart of man went in for devising methods of germ warfare. Then one afternoon three priests invaded the old man's house, forced him to go down on his knees at his own hearth and burn the book. Dante couldn't have thought of a better one than that. Seamus Murphy, the sculptor, who knew and loved the tailor and immortalized him in red stone, assures me that all this broke the old man's heart and hastened his death.

That to me, or to anybody with half a heart or one quarter of a sense of decency, is a horror story – but instructive. It is a gruesome interlude in the history, normally just ludicrous, of the Dublin censorship, and that it should have happened in a country that prides itself, with good reason, on kindness and tolerance is a sore smudge on our good name: 'The lovely land that always sent its writers and artists to banishment.' Twenty-five years later matters are a bit better. When all the harm was done, *The Tailor and Anstey* was unbanned, and when it was reissued a few years ago and I was reviewing the case for Radio Eireann I asked Francis MacManus, that fine man and novelist, how much he would allow me to say over the air. 'Everything', he said, 'except, for legal reasons, the names of the three black heroes who to defend Irish purity bullied an old man.' To say as much over Irish government radio would scarcely have been possible in the doldrums of the 1940s. Indeed in recent years things looked so lively for a while that after a celebrated swinging folksong and music festival in Mullingar, the young poet, John Montague, jubilated that Puritan Ireland was dead and gone, a myth of O'Connor and O'Faolain; and the young novelist, John McGahern, who had then just received a money award from the Dublin Arts Council seemed inclined to think that O'Connor, and O'Faolain and others had been suffering from persecution mania. But they were at their old tricks yet, and what the Poor Old Woman gave with one fist she made damned sure to grab back with the other, and McGahern's second novel was banned and he was jockeyed out of his job as a teacher in a clerically-controlled school in the archdiocese of Dublin. Now how, in reason, could you have a man teaching in a clerical school who admitted in a novel that an Irish boy might masturbate or hinted that between an adult cleric and a youth there might exist a state of disturbed emotional relationship? 'No book', as a Dublin reviewer once said about a fine healthy open-air novel by Walter Macken, 'to put into the hands of a pure-minded boy.' Ever since, in my own writings, that pure-minded boy has never been out of my mind and some day, when words have really answered to my call I hope to get through to him. He didn't go to school with me, but then I was educated, if that's the word, in a British army garrison town, and as Holloway, the eternal diarist, roared on the first night of *The Plough and the Stars*, at Sean O'Casey: 'If there are prostitutes on the streets of Dublin it was the British Army put them there.' Or words to that effect (see Lady Gregory's *Journals*).

But at least now in the 'sixties there is an open and widespread discussion and criticism that just did not exist in the 'forties, and the most amusing things get said on television programmes, and it is much more generally recognized that censorship is a cod or worse: a sign of sick minds, as O'Faolain has pointed out. It is for sure, a sign of a deplorable fearthought. In the 1940s when my own second novel, a harmless piece, God knows, received the national literary award for being in general tendency indecent or obscene, the editor of a big Dublin daily, for which I then worked, told me, more in sorrow than in anger, that he couldn't give the book to his wife to read. In a better time and under more enlightened editorship the same paper came out strongly against the banning of John McGahern's *The Dark*.

The current determined persecution of the novels of Edna O'Brien is a case that calls for particular study. Is it caused by a hangover (the Irish time lag) from days before women got the vote, from a feeling that while it's bad and very bad for a man to speak out and tell the truth it is utterly unthinkable that a woman (bringing shame on the fair daughters of Erin) should claim any such liberty, especially a woman who had been educated, as the saying goes, at one of the best convent schools. It always did strike me as odd that those strange, most un-Irish un-Catholic clergymen who preach pussyfoot sermons about the dangers of drink ('Fine for Huddersfield,' a London publisher once said to me, 'but out of place in a Catholic city.') seemed to be concerned only that girls educated 'at the best convent schools' should take to swilling cocktails in the lounge bars of Dublin. They never showed any concern about the alcoholic capacity of females who had not had those educational advantages. They wouldn't have the money, I suppose, and couldn't do themselves much harm, except to their bladders, on pints of plain consumed in pubs on the docks. Or was the assumption that the daughter of Erin educated at one of the best convent schools had a prescriptive right to a special sort of vestal virginity? Miss O'Brien has really done something godawful to that assumption.

In my days in UCD I heard two triduums preached to such of the students as, out of fervour or curiosity or because they hadn't the money to go any where else, cared to sit and listen. The preaching was done in Newman's church in Stephen's Green. One decent Jesuit, a writer for the popular press, advised the students that when they went on picnic parties in Dublin mountains they should 'be gregarious' – stay with the herd, in fact, and not pair off in that exclusively Irish sin invented by the priests and called 'company keeping'. Then a rattling Redemptorist, one of the sons of thunder and hellfire, said that just as the pin of the Pioneer Total Abstinence Association was a public declaration of war on the Irish vice of drunkenness ('Then God raised up Father Cullen' – the house of whose birth, by the way, in the town of New Ross is now a licensed premises) so there should also be a purity pin to indicate that the young people of Ireland had declared war on unchastity. It is hard to believe, I know, that two grown men could talk thus to an audience of young men and women at university level, and you will just have to take my word for it that they did, in truth, do so. The possible uses and abuses of the suggested purity pin gave rise naturally to much speculation of a light or trivial nature among students of the male sex, and a friend of mine, a gay Kerryman, once hailed a well-set-up girl from the cattle-country of Meath by asking her where was her purity pin. Whereupon with a smile as broad as a Boyne Valley pasture she replied that she was using it to hold up her drawers.

In her own sweet way Edna O'Brien has been as brutally direct, and it would seem that those moles the censors, or whoever eggs them on to their idiocies, are not able to take it. The persecution of her novels seems to be somewhat pathological, even if it has about it nothing of the horror of that illustrative tale from the Muskerry glen 'where Allua of song rushes forth like an arrow'. It would, too, delightfully seem that in Miss O'Brien the staring eunuchs, 'resembling fakirs in their frog-like and renunciatory sterility,' those holy Joes that hide behind the doors and never want their whining and snivelling brought out into the light of day, may have caught a tartar; and the convent girl with her temper riz may yet do what the strong argument of Sean O'Faolain failed to do. The other day *Esquire* was hailing her (along with Brigid Brophy) as a 'prophetess of sex'. I'm not quite sure what that is, except that to the frog-like fakirs she is, for sure, very much a Cassandra. The only other candidates in our history for that title would be the *Cailleach Béara*, Queen Gormlai, and Grainne of the Ships (Lady Morgan for several reasons fails to qualify, and Lady Blessington is not of the first class), and Ireland, to do her justice, had made heroines out of the lot of them.

The poet who walked through Knockanure and satirized it and its people, in some memory of the ancient Gaelic mode of days when a poem could kill, saw the people as the whores on the half-doors sneering at the poets. The people, adroit and nimble-footed, have switched places. So here, secure on the portion of half-door allotted me, I can lean and meditate on where puritan Ireland, or that part of Ireland that is Puritan, did come from. For much as one would like to agree with John Montague's poem, the puritan, or palsied, part of Ireland is not dead and gone, nor was it, alas, merely a myth of O'Connor and O'Faolain.

There are some wild theorists who would trace it back as far as early hermits and monks, and maintain that there was always that odd strain in the Irish, that a certain sour hatred of life was among the all that ancient Ireland knew. Most unlikely: for if the story of Curithir and Liadain has restraint and penance in it, beauty and passion are also there. In his fine story 'Lovers of the Lake' Sean O'Faolain had made an ancient tale live again in terms that relate to our own time.

It has been argued, too, that Irish priests educated on the continent a century and a half ago were affected by Jansenism and brought it back with them to consummate on Irish soil a most unholy union with the respectability of English Protestant Puritanism. But Emmet Larkin, in New York recently, argued cogently to me that what those Irish priests picked up on the continent was not Jansenism but Gallicanism, that the calamity of the famine punished fearfully the body and spirit of the people so that the wrath-of-God preachers had before them a clear field, that their preaching style came not from France but Italy, the principal preachers being those searing sons of Saint Alphonsus, the Redemptorists. Even in my boyhood it was still possible to see and hear, repeat hear, a Redemptorist father preaching a mission sermon, waving the cross of Jesus in the air and roaring to the congregation: 'Shall I curse the company keepers?' Boy meets girl, indeed. Today, etiquette is calmer.

There is, also, once again, the time lag. Irish novelists in Ireland now face something of what novelists in the larger island faced when George Moore came back from Paris to write *A Mummer's Wife* and *Esther Waters*, or later, when James Joyce had his troubles with the moral British printer. It is a comfort to know that two Irish men had a lot to do with helping the English in this matter, towards a reasonable liberty. A diverting specimen of time lag, or something, is to be observed in Croke Park where the strong men of the Gaelic Athletic Association have been known to stand solemnly before a big game and sing 'Faith of Our Fathers', a hymn written by that effeminate English oratorian and execrable writer, Father Faber, a convert to Catholicism. Wordsworth is said to have said that when Faber went over to Rome, England

lost a poet. He could never have foreseen that Ireland was to gain a sportswriter. Indeed, at Croke Park there can be such a clerical preliminary to a big game, the ball being frequently thrown in by an archbishop, that an American visitor once asked me were they going to say mass or play ball. In stadiums in his own unregenerate land he was accustomed to dancing-girls, not archbishops. But then an Irish woman pointed out to him that if the American fashion were followed in Ireland the pitch might be stormed before the game began.

'Our literature,' a man wrote, 'should be the clear and faithful mirror of our whole world of life, but at present there are vast realms of thought and imagination, of passion and action, of which it is only allowed to give a reflex so obscure and distorted as to be worse than none . . .

'No intelligent man in Ireland can afford to devote himself to honest treatment of any great religious or social, moral or philosophical question.'

Only one word in that quotation have I tampered with: Ireland has been substituted for England. It is to be found in the *Satires and Profanities* (1884) of James Thomson, poet of 'The City of Dreadful Night'.

It is comforting to reflect that, at least, matters are not as bad in Ireland now as Thomson found them to be, nearly ninety years ago, in England. For, helped by that safety valve of publication in London and New York, the Irish writers of this time have done an honest job. So leaning on my half-door I can lift my eyes from the mean street and its squinting windows and see out there sunlight on green fields and enticing roads, and did space permit it would be fun to go that way to compile my Brief Lives of My Contemporary Half-doorists: From Padraic Colum to Thomas Kinsella by way of Austin Clarke, Donagh MacDonagh, Patrick Kavanagh, Robert Farren, Padraic Fallon; from Liam O'Flaherty and Francis Stuart to Pat Boyle, Brian Moore, John McGahern, Aidan Higgins, and the urbane John Broderick; from Elizabeth Bowen and Kate O'Brien to Val Mulkerns and Honor Tracy and Edna O'Brien; from the quietude of Arland Usher to the formidable suavity of Conor Cruise O'Brien. There are, and have been so many others. There are even what a friend of mine, a Dublin theatre man, describes as 'the subversive and underground priests' a small body of intelligent and very brave men.

Out there is all the fun of the fair. If the moles can't appreciate it, well what, anyway, would you expect from moles? The moles, Balor and Mannanan be praised, are in a minority, and Ireland is Ireland through joy and through tears, and hope never dies through the long weary years, each age has seen countless brave hearts pass away, but their spirit still lives on in the men of today.

That splendid peroration, so much more worthy of recital in Croke Park than the works of Father Faber, I cannot, alas, claim for my own.

161

Glencar Waterfall, Co Sligo

The Theatre

Seamus Kelly

Know, that I would accounted be
True brother of a company
That sang, to sweeten Ireland's wrong,
Ballad and story, rann and song . . .

Strangely, Yeats omitted one of his most important future contributions to Ireland from this verse – the theatre. It may be that he felt
that the movement he founded was not new, but only a revival of a long
dramatic tradition reaching back to Congreve and Farquhar, carried
on by Sheridan and Goldsmith, and maintained in Yeats' own time by
Boucicault, Wilde, and Shaw, and yet, if ever a theatrical movement
was founded with a conscious, almost crusading aim, the Irish Literary
Theatre was so founded.

Lady Gregory, in her *Journal*, described its beginning. It was in
the County Galway on a wet day in 1898. Her neighbour, Edward
Martyn, brought young Mr Yeats to luncheon; the talk turned on plays
and Lady Gregory offered a guarantee towards a joint production of
one of Martyn's and one of Yeats's. A few days later the trio wrote a
formal letter to certain people who they thought would be interested.
It said:

> We propose to have performed in Dublin, in the spring of every year
> certain Celtic and Irish plays, which, whatever be their degree of
> excellence, will be written with a high ambition, and so build up a
> Celtic and Irish school of dramatic literature. We hope to find in
> Ireland an uncorrupted and imaginative audience, trained to listen
> by its passion for oratory, and believe that our desire to bring upon
> the stage the deeper thoughts and emotions of Ireland will ensure
> for us a tolerant welcome, and that freedom to experiment which is
> not found in the theatres of Europe and without which no new
> movement in art or literature can succeed. We will show that Ireland
> is not the home of buffoonery and of easy sentiment, as it has been
> represented, but the home of an ancient idealism . . .

In retrospect Lady Gregory wrote: 'Our statement . . . seems now a
little pompous . . .' Be that as it may, the movement which the three
babes in the wood at Coole had started was to make a contribution

162

of major importance not only to the dramatic literature of Ireland, but to the whole world. The 'uncorrupted and imaginative audience' had acquired its 'passion for oratory' from an inheritance of great antiquity. Heroic Gaelic Ireland, though it had no theatrical culture as such, had developed a tradition of bardic poetry which was classic, formal, strictly and deviously disciplined. As the old Gaelic culture declined under suppression, this tradition passed down the generations in the form of elaborate imaginative story-telling by country firesides, and in the narrative poems and songs of the wandering poets of the seventeenth and eighteenth centuries. One of its nineteenth century manifestations was the florid, baroque style of oratory which was the distinguishing mark of the members of the Irish Parliamentary party at Westminster. Yeats and his associates had a potential audience trained to this sort of dramatic expression, if not to the formal conventions of the classic European theatre.

Their first production, *The Heather Field* by Martyn and *The Countess Cathleen* by Yeats, was staged in the Antient Concert Rooms, Dublin, in May 1899. The omens were good. Yeats's play aroused a controversy. It has since become part of the Abbey Theatre's tradition that any play that creates trouble on its first performance is destined for enduring success. After that opening there were five wandering years for the players before they found a permanent stage. They were fruitful years, notable for the first production of a play that had a significant inspirationary influence on the national insurrection of 1916, *Cathleen Ni Houlihan* by Yeats; notable for the discovery of three geniuses, the brothers Frank and W. G. Fay as actors and directors and the unknown John Millington Synge as a dramatist. Then, on December 27, 1904, thanks to the benevolence of Miss A. E. Horniman of Manchester, the first Abbey Theatre was opened. The building had been a morgue, a Mechanics' Institute, and a Savings Bank – it had never been designed for a theatre. Its auditorium was small, holding less than five hundred people, and the back-stage accommodation, especially the scenedocks, was minimal. Yet this toy theatre, over a period of forty-seven years, was to produce a school of dramatists and players unequalled anywhere except, perhaps, in the Moscow Arts Theatre and the *Comédie Française*.

Synge and O'Casey are unquestionably the greatest names among Abbey dramatists – the first a romantic with a bright gift of savage fantasy, the second a realist, an inspired reporter of his own turbulent Dublin, in a way, a theatrical Joyce. Both men had an extraordinary gift for writing in wildly inflated prose-poetry which, though unnatural speech to be issuing from the mouths of their prototype characters, rings credibly from a stage. Both maintained the Abbey tradition that great plays brought troublesome openings. *The Playboy of the Western World* provoked riots on its first production in 1906; so did *The Plough and The Stars* twenty years later. (Contemporary audiences were shocked in both cases to find Irish characters portrayed as denizens of an island of saints and sinners rather than saints and scholars.) But the Abbey throve on trouble. The indomitable Lady Gregory, the languid and willowy Lennox Robinson, even Yeats, for all his ivory tower detachment, grew quite used to dealing with roaring, protesting audiences and to repelling boarders from their stage.

They had trouble with officialdom, too, as when His Britannic Majesty's Lord Lieutenant tried to prevent them from staging the world première of Bernard Shaw's *The Shewing-up of Blanco Posnet* in 1909. Lady Gregory set her jaw, and the play was produced. (It's hard to believe it today, but the attempted proscription was based on allegations of blasphemy from the Lord Chamberlain's office.) Crisis followed crisis in the Theatre's early years. The company had a bloody insurrection, a revolutionary guerilla war, and a civil war to contend with, all in the eight years between 1916 and 1924. Times were lean, but the theatre kept going, even when the centre of Dublin was twice reduced to ruins by fire and bombardment.

On the night of July 17, 1951, the Abbey curtain fell on the last act of *The Plough and The Stars*, a play which ends with insurrectionary Dublin in flames. Four hours later there was no Abbey Theatre, a fire had burned the building to a shell, destroying scenery, costumes, paintings and manuscripts accumulated over forty-seven years. The following night Ria Mooney and the Abbey Players presented *The Plough and The Stars* in the Peacock Theatre, a tiny experimental annexe of the old Abbey. The players were dog-tired and disheartened, but continuity had been maintained. The company were given a temporary home in the theatre attached to Guinness's brewery. Later, they moved to the Queen's Theatre, a shabby nineteenth-century music-hall with a reputation as the home of Boucicault melodrama and, incidentally, Brendan Behan's self-acknowledged theatrical nursery school. This is not to imply that Behan was ever an accepted Abbey playwright. His first plays (including the very first production of *The Hostage* in the original Irish language version) were staged by other Dublin Theatres, but the Queen's was the theatre of Behan's boyhood, where he saw Boucicault and red-blooded variety in turn, and the influence of both is obvious in his plays.

The Irish Government made £250,000 available for the rebuilding of the Abbey under the Funds of Suitors Act; property adjoining the existing site was acquired, and in July, 1966, the new Abbey Theatre was formally opened by the President of Ireland, Éamon De Valera, who admitted publicly that night that he had done a bit of acting himself in his young days.

The modern Abbey has moved far from the poetic ideals outlined in the Yeats-Gregory manifesto of 1898. Standards of plays, presentation and performances have deteriorated over the past twenty-five years, a decline generally associated with the dictatorial managing directorship of Ernest Blythe, a former politician, who gained what amounted to absolute control of the theatre in 1941 and subsequently ousted directors like Frank O'Connor, who were trying to maintain the Yeats tradition.

Contemporary Irish attitude to the Abbey was summarized by Eugene McCabe, one of the country's best new playwrights, when he described it as, '. . . a lovely new chassis, same old engine backfiring now for over thirty years and in no danger whatsoever of exploding.' However, as I write Blythe's retirement is imminent, the new chassis *is* there, and if it be handled intelligently by new and imaginative artistic direction some of the old glories may be recovered and the memories of Yeats, Synge, Augusta Gregory, O'Casey, Lennox Robinson, T. C. Murray, Paul Vincent Carroll, among the dramatists, and of Sara Algood, the Fays, Máire O'Neill, Arthur Sinclair, F. J. McCormick, Barry Fitzgerald, among the players, may again be honoured in their parent theatre; while expatriate Abbey graduates like Cyril Cusack, Siobhán McKenna, Eithne Dunne, Jack McGowran, T. P. McKenna, Rae McAnally may again be seen on the Abbey stage under direction worthy of their internationally recognized talents.[1]

The second major theatrical development in modern Dublin came nearly a quarter of a century after the Abbey's foundation. In 1927 two young actors met in an Irish touring company run by Anew McMaster, a fabulous theatrical figure who travelled the country with a repertory ranging from *Oedipus Rex* to *East Lynne,* from *Othello* to *Trilby.* The newcomers to his company in that year were Micheál MacLiammóir, an Irishman who had learned his trade with Tree at His Majesty's Theatre, London and an Englishman, Hilton Edwards. MacLiammóir, whose talents ran from acting and painting to writing with equal facility in Irish and English, and to talking with freedom, fluency and wit in almost every European language could by now have reached the status of a Gielgud or an Olivier had he chosen to make his professional life in Britain but the gifted young actor was an idolator of

[1]In February 1965 the Irish Government announced that the Articles of Association of the National Theatre Society Ltd (The Abbey Theatre) were being amended to provide, among other things, for the increasing of the authorized share capital of the company. 'A block of shares will be issued to the Minister for Finance, who will appoint a second Government representative to the Board to join the three non-official directors. In addition, thirty shares each are being issued to twenty-five people of standing known to be interested in the theatre and in Irish cultural life generally. The names of those invited to become shareholders have been selected from lists submitted by the directors of the theatre and by Irish Actors' Equity Association.'

The present directors of the Abbey Theatre (1968) are Micheal O hAodha (Chairman), Éarnan de Blaghd (Ernest Blythe), Seamus Wilmot, Gabriel Fallon, and Roibeárd O Faracháin. Two of these have announced their intention of retiring at imminent but unspecified dates. The Artistic Director of the Theatre is Tomás MacAnna, and the Manager is Phil O'Kelly.

Yeats, and deliberately returned to Ireland to try to put into practice his own ideas on the theatre derived in part from Yeats, but capable of fluid extension. Hilton Edwards, who was to become his partner, shared with MacLiammóir a passion for the experimental theatre.

In 1928 MacLiammóir and Edwards founded the Dublin Gate Theatre Studio. Their first productions were offered in the Peacock Theatre, a 101-seater experimental annexe of the Abbey. Here, on a stage not much bigger than a Victorian dining table, they produced *Peer Gynt,* Wilde's *Salome,* and a febrile symphonic surge of expressionistic brilliance called *The Old Lady Says 'No!',* by the most remarkable young Irish dramatist they discovered, Denis Johnston.

'The real business of the Gate,' MacLiammóir has written, 'was with methods of acting, production, design, and lighting . . . We secretly hoped . . . that we would at least discover a way, more evocative than literal, more suggestive than photographic, that might serve as the mould for the Irish dramatist of the future . . .'

The Irish Free State was just six years old and the nation was suffering the post-operative sickness that followed eight years of revolution and a bitter civil war. The Abbey was at its peak, with the three great O'Casey plays newly introduced to its repertory. The cinemas were attracting growing audiences with talking pictures. It was not, one would have thought, the happiest time to start a new art theatre in a small community where there was little wealth. Yet the Gate soon found its own theatre and flourished there for a decade. Irish audiences, accustomed to looking inwards through the Abbey's eyes, found that the Gate turned their vision outwards to the best new plays of Europe and America and to the classics of the world, in presentations that fulfilled everything that MacLiammóir aimed at in his manifesto. Their repertory ranged from Shakespeare and Ibsen to Yeats, Wilde, Cocteau, Aeschylus, Shaw, O'Neill, Tchehov, Strindberg, Auden, Wilder and Stein. Apart from Johnston and MacLiammóir himself, they did not discover new dramatists of any significance, but they awakened Irish audiences to the importance of the theatrical eye as well as the tuned ear, and the disciplined but flexible imaginativeness of Edwards' productions has left every actor, playwright, and director in Ireland today deeply in debt to him and his partner.

In 1936 the sixth Earl of Longford, who had been on the board of the Gate virtually since its foundation, and who had helped to keep it alive with generous financial help, formed a separate company of his own, and an agreement was reached whereby each of the two companies should have tenancy of the Dublin Gate Theatre for six months of the year. From then until 1939 the parent Gate company spent a good deal of time outside Ireland, touring in the Balkans, the near East, the United States and Canada, and playing at least one season at the Westminster in London. During the war and immediately postwar years, they appeared regularly at Dublin's pleasant late-Victorian theatre, the Gaiety. In the intervening years they had fostered such diverse talents as those of Orson Welles (who joined them at seventeen and had his first legitimate stage part as the Duke in a Gate production of *Jew Süss*), James Mason, Geraldine FitzGerald, and Peggy Cummins. Both the principals played in Orson Welles's film of *Othello*, Mac-Liammóir as Iago and Edwards as Brabantio. If the film had done nothing else, it would be worth remembering as the inspiration of a superbly entertaining book by MacLiammóir, called *Put Money In Thy Purse,* which deals with the many misadventures met with during its making. In 1952, the Dublin Gate were invited by the Danish Government to present the Elsinore Theatre Festival production of *Hamlet*, with MacLiammóir as the Prince, Edwards as the King, and Eithne Dunne as one of the best Ophelias that Krönborg Castle has seen.

In recent years Hilton Edwards spent some time as Drama Director of Irish Television, but he came back to the living theatre to direct MacLiammóir in his one-man dramatization of the life of Wilde, *The Importance of Being Oscar,* which has toured the world with great success. Edwards also directed both the first Dublin Festival production of Brian Friel's *Philadelphia, Here I Come,* and its American production, which holds the record for the longest-running Irish play on Broadway. Today, MacLiammóir continues to write books, plays, and commentaries on life in a minimum of two languages with tremendous verve, during and between tours with his one-man shows on Wilde, on Yeats and on the Irish literary tradition. As I write, it is understood that the partners may soon be setting up a new Dublin Gate company at the Gate Theatre, a consummation devoutly to be wished.

The other branch of the Gate, usually called the Longford company, was run by the sixth Lord Longford from 1936 until his death in 1961, very much on the lines of the palace players of a Rennaissance prince. Edward Longford was a man of considerable scholarship, and the company presented his own translations of Molière as well as the Oresteian trilogy in joint translation by his wife and himself. Lady Longford also gave the company some Irish historical dramas, as well as sharply-pointed little comedy-satires on the contemporary Irish scene. These family plays, however, were incidental to the main repertory which included Shakespeare, Sheridan, Shaw, Wilde, Ibsen, and Tchehov, and it is worth mentioning that Edward Longford, in *Yahoo,* wrote the best play yet staged about the turbulent life of Jonathan Swift. Since her husband's death, Lady Longford has continued to administer the Gate Theatre, an eighteenth-century concert hall which was substantially renovated before her husband's death. It nowadays houses the little companies which proliferate in Dublin, appearing in anything from Wesker and Beckett to revue and ballad sessions.

Though the new Abbey Theatre opened in 1966, and its experimental

167

annexe, the Peacock[1], opened in the Spring of 1967, Dublin suffers from a scarcity of theatres today. The old Theatre Royal, where Shaw first saw Henry Irving play, has been demolished to make way for an office block. The Queen's, which housed the Abbey company for fifteen years, is going the same way, while the remaining two commercial theatres, the Gaiety and the Olympia, have both fallen into the hands of speculators, to be reprieved only by a ruling of the Dublin Corporation that they must be maintained as cultural amenities. Were they to go, the total seating accommodation in the professional theatres of what was once a theatrical capital would be in the region of twelve hundred – a meagre proportion for an urban population that is near enough three-quarters of a million, and for a city that has run a successful annual Theatre Festival for the past ten years. Outside Dublin, professional theatres are few and far between. Cork has a substantial all-purposes Opera House which, like the Abbey, was destroyed by fire in the past decade, but was rebuilt more rapidly. Cork is also the home of the Southern Theatre Group, who have a small repertory house where they feature the plays of Ireland's latter-day Boucicault, an effervescent publican from County Kerry called John B. Keane. The southern city's other claim to fame is that it is the only Irish city to have maintained its own ballet company for over ten years, but then Cork claims Alicia Markova for its own, since her mother was born there, and it used to be the ballerina's favourite spot for a restful holiday.

In Galway, there is a State-subsidized Gaelic Theatre, the Taidhbhearc, where Siobhán McKenna learned her trade, and where she played her first *Saint Joan* – in the Irish language. Wexford has a very pretty little eighteenth century theatre, most lovingly restored, but for years past it has been used only on the occasion of the annual Festival of Opera in that town. Belfast, dramatically moribund for many years – although it produced a lively and provocative local dramatist in Sam Thompson – relies for any worthwhile theatre nowadays on the Lyric Players, who keep an art theatre going against heavy odds.

The rest is silence, except that, throughout Ireland, there is an exuberant and vital amateur dramatic movement. Naturally it includes a wide variation of artistic and executive standards, but there is no question whatever that it keeps interest in things dramatic alive, and provide quite a substantial proportion of the acting fodder for Dublin stages. Which brings me to one of the major problems of the con-

---

[1]In the middle 1940s the poet, Austin Clarke, founded the Dublin Verse-Speaking Society, which gave a series of poetry recitals and verse plays in the Peacock Theatre. In 1945 this society became the Lyric Theatre, with the broad aims of preserving Yeats's ideal of a theatre of poetry under the direction of Austin Clarke. They were supported by private subscription, and they staged a number of Sunday night productions of verse plays at the Abbey until the theatre was destroyed by fire in 1951. Their repertory included plays by Yeats, Clarke, Eliot, and Donagh MacDonagh.

temporary Irish theatre – the artists' rewards. With physically small theatres, managements cannot afford to pay Irish actors who are working at home salaries commensurate with their talents.

Irish Television has been a help in putting adequate butter on the bread of Irish actors. So has the existence of Ardmore Studios, near Dublin, where a number of feature films are made. But the Irish actor who wants *jam* on his bread is inevitably forced out of Ireland to earn it on British and American stages and TV studios.

The list of such expatriate artists today includes Siobhán McKenna, Cyril Cusack, Jack McGowran, Ray McAnally, T. P. McKenna, Pauline Delany, Godfrey Quigley, Norman Rodway, Jim Norton, Liam Redmond . . . but I could go on indefinitely. They come back to Dublin for Festivals and for special productions, but most of their work lies in Britain. The brighter young directors, like Jim FitzGerald, have been trying for years to solve this problem by setting up some sort of permanent theatre, where the exiles could try their talents in *nouvelle vague* productions, as well as in established plays, but nothing has come of it. There were hopes that the new Abbey might relax restrictions to some extent, even if only to offering the Peacock Theatre to outside managements. So far, however the only sign of Abbey ecumenism has been the return of Cyril Cusack and Hugh Hunt, two graduate members of the old Abbey, as director and leading player in a very successful revival of *The Shaughraun*, by Boucicault.

It is a pity that actors like those listed (and others besides) should have to work abroad, but it seems to be an economic necessity. It's all the greater pity, since they come of a nation that has been noted for its fine actors back to the days of Sheridan and Keane, and that has given the world such major dramatists as Congreve, Farquhar, Sheridan, Goldsmith, Boucicault, Wilde, Shaw, Synge, O'Casey, O'Neill, Beckett, Carroll, and Behan. Three playwrights still writing in Ireland have talents that have been recognized outside their homeland. They are Eugene McCabe (*King of the Castle*), Brian Friel (*Philadelphia, Here I Come*), and John B. Keane (*The Field*). Others, like Tom Murphy (*Whistle In The Dark*) and Hugh Leonard (*Poker Session,* and *Stephen D.*) have uprooted themselves, though they still hark back to Ireland in their themes, like such more famous expatriates as Joyce and O'Casey.

There is some enlightened big business patronage for the Irish theatre. The Irish Life Assurance Company, for instance, offers an annual award of £500 for a new three-act play, but the fact seems to be that dramatists do not flourish unless there are managements in the same garden – as it were – and unless those managements have the equipment, both artistic, technical, and financial to stage new works adequately. Maybe the day is coming when this will happen. Certainly, everybody in Ireland who is concerned in the theatre and with its future devoutly hopes that it will.

169

Education

Valentine Rice

It is difficult to provide a comprehensive account of Irish education, even at a superficial level, within an article of four thousand words. In order to condense one must omit, and by omission one must inevitably distort. The task is further complicated by the dual role envisaged for the contributions in this volume. They are expected not merely to serve a descriptive function for those who are unfamiliar with this island, but also to embody a critique which may be of interest to those who live here.

Throughout the centuries, the Irish people have manifested a remarkable concern for education. There was a time when men spoke of 'The Island of Saints and Scholars'; our mediaeval Bardic schools were among the most intriguing institutions in the history of education; during the Penal times part of the population maintained an underground system of schools which eventually catered for almost half a million pupils. There have been significant advances since the foundation of the state, but we have not yet succeeded in fully providing for every child in Ireland the best education which his talents allow. And today there is a broadening consensus that we must put our schoolhouse in better order.

The Genesis of the System

The educational manifold of modern Ireland is, in large measure, a nineteenth-century product. In turn, the nineteenth century structures bear the imprint of preceding years. Visitors to Ireland are frequently surprised at the extreme denominationalism of our education: this may best be understood in terms of the logic of unhappy centuries.

The wars of the sixteenth and seventeenth centuries brought the old Gaelic world to an end and effected the English re-conquest of Ireland. The period was remarkable for an unfortunate conjunction of religion and politics which sowed the seeds of centuries of bitterness: the new English were Protestant; the Irish and old Normans remained Catholic. The Tudor policy in Ireland aimed at a complete cultural assimilation of the people of this island and therefore manifested a particular concern for education. When the dissolution of the monasteries removed

170

a major source of schooling, there was legislative intervention by Henry VIII, Elizabeth and James I to found parish and regional schools along English lines. Though many of these schools survive to this day and are among the most venerable of our educational institutions, the Tudor educational policy was largely unsuccessful. Catholics generally preferred to send their children abroad for education or they sought it in private schools when the law turned the other way.

Despite the provisions of the Treaty of Limerick the new rulers of Ireland were uneasy in their estates and so, in the first half of the eighteenth century, the Dublin parliament enacted the penal code, religious in language, primarily political in intent. The educational provisions of this code indicate a significant shift of policy. The total cultural assimilation of the Catholic element was no longer viewed as realistic. Instead, the presence of educated Catholics was considered a political danger, and consequently Catholic schools were proscribed and Catholics were forbidden to go abroad for education. Thus, in the eighteenth century, only Protestant schools were legal, and Catholic education went underground. This was the century of the hedge-schools. Beside fences, in mud cabins, in barns, sometimes in more formal quarters, free-lance schoolmasters offered illicit instruction. The quality of the instruction varied with the teacher. Some were the intellectual descendants of the old bards; some had studied for the priesthood; some were reputed to sow sedition; some were famed for their know-ledge of whiskey. By 1824 there were over 10,000 hedge schools with a total enrollment of over 400,000. By contrast, the 782 parish schools were attended by fewer than 24,000 pupils.

Then, in 1831, the British Government introduced a scheme for a state-supported system of primary education which rapidly brought about the eclipse of the hedge-schools. The arrangements proposed were remarkably liberal for the time. There would be 'combined moral and literary and separate religious education'; a Board of Commission-ers would administer a state grant, and preference would be given by them to applications for support for multi-denominational schools. Within forty years, however, the National School system had become a system of *de facto* denominational schools. A convergence of pressures produced this result. The Church of Ireland was already well-provided with its own system of primary schools. The Presbyterian Synod of Ulster had insisted from the start that the schools should be sectarian and eventually achieved the concession that preference would no longer be given to applications for aid to multi-denominational schools. And the Catholic Church, which originally had found the multi-denomina-tional idea quite workable, became increasingly reactionary toward the middle of the century; this hardening of attitude coincided with the arrival from Rome of Archbishop Paul Cullen.

With the achievement of political independence the old Board of

171

Commissioners was abolished and its functions were vested in a Minister for Education and his Department. The system of National Education was retained intact; the only significant innovation was the insertion of Irish as a compulsory subject in the curriculum. And so today, the National Schools, which are attended by all but some 5,000 of our primary school children, are denominational schools, in receipt of State support. There is an intricate pattern of joint control. There are no School Boards: the function of immediate external government is exercised by the manager, who is almost invariably the local priest, minister or rabbi. When a new school is to be built the parish provides the site and a portion of the cost; the greater part is paid by the state. The manager appoints the teachers, but he can normally appoint only those who have been trained in a training college; these colleges are segregated on denominational lines. The state pays the salaries of teachers in the National Schools, controls the curricula, and exercises a right of inspection.

Curiously, the nineteenth century British Government did not make corresponding provision for secondary as for primary education. In fact, the introduction of the National Schools deprived Catholics in many areas of secondary education, for the old hedge-school masters had frequently provided advanced teaching for their better pupils. As Ireland emerged from the Penal Laws there were in existence several flourishing Protestant secondary schools. On the Catholic side the religious orders and diocesan authorities stepped in to the breach; the Christian Brothers and the Presentation and Mercy orders, in particular, provided from their own resources an inexpensive secondary education for many thousands of boys and girls. Thus, again, the logic of events yielded an essentially denominational framework. And when the State, in 1878, finally decided to subsidise secondary education, it adopted the device of paying grants to pre-existing schools, with provision for similar financing for future foundations. The subsidies were first cast as payments on examination results; since independence they have been paid as capitation grants for 'recognized' pupils.

The Irish secondary schools are academic high schools; instruction in more practical subjects is provided in a parallel system of vocational schools. These are multi-denominational schools, which had their origin in an Act of 1899 which set up local Vocational Education Committees on a statutory basis. The Vocational Education Act of 1930 developed the system and determined that from five to eight members of the Vocational Education Committee should be drawn from the local rating authority. There have also been recently established in the post-primary sector a small number of comprehensive schools. These are controlled by triumvirates representative of Church, State, and Vocational Education Committee. By 1970-71 they are expected to cater for 5,000 pupils.

Reform: the Without of Education

Within recent years education has assumed a new prominence in Ireland, a prominence which to some degree is related to the contemporary discovery of the relationship between education and ecomonic prosperity. A milestone was passed in 1962 when a survey team was set up under the joint sponsorship of OECD and the Department of Education to report on the quantitative aspects of our system. The team produced the massive report, *Investment in Education,* which was by any standards the most scientific and factual document hitherto produced on modern Irish education. The report has been a major springboard for a number of reforms which have been initiated with almost bewildering rapidity. Change is not always a painless process, however, particularly when structures have been built up over a long period of time, and the refashioning of Irish education has not been unattended by controversy.

The Proclamation of the Irish Republic in 1916 promised that the independent nation would cherish equally all of its children. The OECD report demonstrated with statistical precision that forty years of native government had not achieved for all of those children equality of educational opportunity. There has been universal free primary education since the foundation of the State and universal literacy has long been achieved. However, diversity in school size has made it difficult to ensure access to equivalent education. In 1962–63, for example, over 66 per cent of our primary schools were one- or two- teacher schools. We have also had a serious dropout problem. Of the 57,000 children who left primary schools in 1957, only some 40,000 went on to post-primary education. Of these only some 10,000 would eventually sit for the Leaving Certificate examination and fewer than 2,000 would be headed for the universities. The OECD survey also showed that there were marked regional and social differences in the degree of participation in post-primary education. For example, of the population aged 13–17 in 1961, nearly 49 per cent were receiving post-primary education in County Cork while the corresponding figure for County Donegal was 30 per cent; the difference was a function of the relative availability of schools. Similarly, in 1961, professional and white-collar workers constituted 20 per cent of the working population. Their children numbered 65 per cent of university entrants from the Leaving Certificate examination. In the same year manual workers were 25 per cent of the working population. Their children received 2 per cent of university places.

A range of measures has been introduced by the Department of Education to provide greater equality of access to education. In 1965 the Department embarked on a policy for the consolidation of small rural schools. The new comprehensive schools have been erected in areas which have hitherto not been provided with post-primary educational facilities. Arrangements are in hand to coordinate the resources of secondary and vocational schools so as to achieve a regional comprehensiveness of teaching. In 1967 the late Minister for Education, Mr Donogh O'Malley, introduced a scheme for free post-primary education; it is coupled with the provision of free transportation. And in 1968 there was introduced a scheme for university grants and scholarships on a scale considerably broader than what had previously existed.

The scheme for the consolidation of small rural primary schools ran into considerable difficulty in many places due to opposition at grassroots level to central planning. Some of the trouble might have been avoided if a systematic public-relations campaign had been organized to convince parents and school managers of the educational advantages of the larger units. Statements in parliament and in scholarly reports do not seem to have had the desired persuasive effect. If this particular battle is now effectively won, it is largely because the advantages of the consolidated schools which have already been built have begun to be manifest. In areas which still prefer the traditional pattern, the erection of prefabricated schools, which can later be re-located if necessary, would seem to constitute a solution which at once respects local liberties and the Government's legitimate concern for economy.

The details of the scheme for free post-primary education are shaped by the historical forms of our arrangements for secondary education. There are separate provisions for Catholic and Protestant secondary schools. To any Catholic school which undertakes to provide free secondary education the state will pay a supplementary grant of £25 per recognized pupil in lieu of parental fees. Because the Catholic schools are staffed to a considerable extent by religious, fees have traditionally been low. The Protestant schools, on the other hand, are staffed primarily by lay teachers and their fees have been considerably higher. A sum of money was therefore made available to a central church body for distribution in accordance with need.

Though the 1967 scheme was a great personal triumph for the Minister, certain difficulties remain. Some Catholic schools, for example, have found it financially difficult to enter the scheme while continuing to provide their particular kind of education; furthermore, no provision has been made for Catholic boarding schools, and there is consequently some danger that these may increasingly become places of privilege. Among the Protestant community there is considerable unrest because of the operation of the means test: on the other hand, no Protestant school is debarred from benefiting since parental circumstances alone determine the award of the grants. Now that we have put our hand to the plough, it seems inevitable that we must proceed toward a more refined set of arrangements which will make the benefits of free education available to all Protestant children and to every Catholic school.

Reform: the Within of Education

The curricula of Irish primary and secondary schools are subject to a degree of centralized control which is quite unknown in England and the United States. This is not a native arrangement but a tradition inherited from the days of British rule. At primary level the control is direct and is exercised through the regulations in the official *Programme of Primary Instruction*. In secondary schools it is indirect but equally pervasive, and is exercised primarily through the regulations governing the state examinations.

The traditional curriculum of the primary school has been based on a core of Irish, English, Mathematics, Religious Knowledge, History and Geography. The same core has generally been continued in secondary schools, with the addition of subjects such as Science and Latin. In both primary and secondary education, subjects tend to be taken for extended periods of years; the elective subject, taken for shorter periods, is almost unknown.

The current review of our education is not confined to the 'without'; it has also been extended to the 'within'. The Department of Education has under consideration a revised programme of studies for the primary schools; it is to be hoped that this will introduce into the curriculum a new flexibility and continuity with life. New regulations have also recently been announced for the Leaving Certificate course and examination. Several additional subjects have been recognized and all subjects have been cast into five cognate groups – linguistic, scientific, social, commercial, and technological. It is intended that pupils in the final years of the second-level education will be obliged to concentrate on three subjects from within one of these groups. They must also take Irish and another subject.

It is to be regretted that the rationale underlying these changes has not been made public. Consequently it is difficult to be sure that one's evaluation is fair. The regulations seem designed to achieve an improvement of standards while preserving some breadth of approach. One can see too how they can constitute an admirable framework for coordinating the work of schools in a given area: in a country town, for example, the convent school, the Christian Brothers' school, and the vocational school might each concentrate on separate groups. The new regulations involve certain curricular implications, however, with which it is difficult to be in agreement.

Thus, for example, a considerable degree of specialization is required at a time when the British are increasingly questioning their practice in this regard. It is assumed, furthermore, that all students are ready for this at the same time. It can be argued, in fact, that effectively many of our students will henceforth be obliged to choose their careers at the age of fifteen. T̶̶̶̶̶̶̶̶̶̶̶lem seems largely to have b̶̶̶̶ passed: Irish is the only subject which is deemed to be essential. And C. P. Snow might never have raised the problem of the Two Cultures.

Inevitably, one feels that there has been a certain inversion of normal order, due possibly to pressure of time, and that greater emphasis has been placed on the design of the examination than on the design of the curriculum. Unfortunately, in Ireland the shape of the examination determines the content of education. The Minister for Education has stated that at present the regulations have been introduced merely on an experimental and optional basis; one consequently assumes that they possess no necessary finality. It would therefore seem to be a matter of some urgency that we face up to the curricular problem and that we seek to define the appropriate content of a second-level education for Irish students of our time – what measure of specialization, if any, is desirable; whether, for example, our students should have some acquaintance with the literary and artistic achievements of the old Gaelic world, or with the classics of the ancient and modern world; whether they should know something of art and philosophy and economics and the scientific method. When this has been done it will be a relatively straightforward matter to design an examination which will measure what has been accomplished. One suspects that we shall then allow specialization rather than require it, that students will be permitted to choose subjects of special study from the totality available, so as better to accommodate the curriculum to the individual, and that we shall provide for breadth in education through the introduction of some mechanism for the recognition for examination purposes of subjects which have been studied for relatively short periods of time.

Higher Education

There are two universities in the Republic of Ireland – Trinity College, the University of Dublin, and the National University of Ireland, with constituent colleges at Dublin, Cork and Galway. Trinity College was founded in 1592, on the model of an Oxford or Cambridge college; like Harvard, whose origins and subsequent development were remarkably similar, it grew into a university with one college. The National University of Ireland dates from the year 1908, and was founded on three nineteenth-century colleges – the Queen's Colleges of Cork and Galway, founded in 1845, and University College, Dublin, which developed from Newman's Catholic University of 1854. In 1967 the Government-appointed Commission on Higher Education presented a major report based on deliberations and investigations extending over six years. It recommended that the colleges of the National University should become independent universities: they were now of sufficient size to render federal links superfluous; in a_____ n, found, _____ _____ ___. To coordinate the work of all the universities within the state there should be a representative Council of Irish Universities. And to supervise planning and financing there should be a body akin to the British University Grants Committee.

An outstanding anomaly in Irish higher education is the prohibition of the Catholic hierarchy on the attendance of Catholic students at Trinity College. The ban was first imposed in 1875, two years after the university had opened its doors to full academic participation by Catholics. Though Catholics are now coming to Trinity College in increasing numbers and constitute approximately one-third of the student body, the prohibition has had very serious consequences. It has for years deprived Trinity College of its full natural complement of Irish students; it has impeded the achievement of academic cooperation in the capital city; it has helped to create in the minds of many Irish people a tragic suspicion of our oldest university.

The hierarchy's attitude toward the several university institutions in this island seems somewhat inconsistent. It has accepted the colleges of the National University, though these are by law non-denominational; Catholics may freely attend the non-denominational Queen's University, Belfast. They may not attend Trinity College without special permission, however, though it is a multi-denominational university in the Christian tradition. There has indeed been a curious shift in the reasons formally alleged for the prohibition. Until comparatively recently it was based on the College's long association with a Protestant communion, the Church of Ireland. Now, it would seem from evidence presented to the Commission on Higher Education, the hierarchy is unhappy because Trinity College is bound to no church at all. The university is accused of 'indifferentism' because it refuses to take religious considerations into account in the admission of students and the appointment of staff. Yet it is this impartiality which makes it possible for Catholics to teach and study there. And there seems to be no objection to similar impartiality when exercised by Queen's University, Belfast.

Since June of 1967 the hierarchy has rejected three appeals from Catholic staff of Trinity College for the removal of the ban and for the provision of an effective chaplaincy, as specifically required by the Second Vatican Council. The bishops stated that they could not take the steps proposed at a time when the whole pattern of university education in Ireland was under consideration by the Government. One would have thought, rather, that the actions proposed to them would have greatly facilitated the coordination and full utilization of our university resources, while providing for the 1,200 Catholic students at Trinity College an assurance that their bishops would not subordinate pastoral care to other considerations.

It is within the general context of the ecclesiastical prohibition that one may perhaps most usefully advert to the issue of the proposed

177

Ballynahinch, Co Galway

association of Trinity College and University College in a single university. If the ban had not been in operation it is unlikely that the issue could ever have arisen. The student body of Trinity College would have grown to such a size as to render such a union unrealistic; furthermore, there could have been no grounds for allegations of intellectual apartheid in the capital city.

The Government's case for a single university in Dublin has been stated mainly in economic terms. It is indeed true that there has been tragically little academic cooperation in Dublin and that there has been some unnecessary duplication. Over the years both institutions have come increasingly to rely on the state for support, and it seems entirely reasonable that the state should wish to obtain the best academic return for the money which it spends. But it is by no means clear that the best interests of Irish education will be served by forcing our two largest university colleges into a union which a majority of their combined staffs consider to be educationally and administratively unsound.

Those who oppose the government plan argue that this country can ill afford to jeopardize our higher education by tampering so radically with our institutions. They fear for the introduction in Dublin of a cumbersome administrative structure which will impede academic initiative; and they fear that, in place of two campus-universities, we are headed for a large impersonal institution, with fragments in various parts of the city, and consequent alienation of students and staff. And many fear also for the implications for academic freedom of the Government's unilateral 'decision', on the grounds that the basis of academic freedom is the autonomy of the institution.

There is, of course, an alternative – that Dublin should posses two separate and cooperating universities. Arrangements for cross-registration could provide for students of each university access to the specialist teaching of the other. There could be complementary development of areas of specialization, and coordinated purchase and use of expensive equipment. It has emerged in the discussions of the past two years that the heart of the Dublin problem centres on the teaching of Medicine and Engineering. It is difficult to see why whatever satisfactory solution for the teaching of these disciplines is proposed within the context of a single university could not equally well be implemented within a two-university framework. It may be objected that fifty years have failed to produce such coordination. The situation, however, has significantly changed. For now, for the first time since the foundation of the state, we possess a Higher Education Authority.

Northern Ireland

Douglas Gageby

There are people who claim to find a great difference between Northern Ireland and the rest of the country. Note that Ireland is a small island – at its widest, two hundred miles across, and from north to south at most three hundred. It was never divided until the year of Our Lord 1922. Yet you will even find those who make out that for centuries there has been a basis for such a division. There are, of course, people who tell us that the earth is flat.

I was born in Ireland and have lived in it for close on half a century; nearly two decades of that was spent in Belfast. I have been in every one of the thirty-two counties and know some of them well, and in all my travels I have never been conscious of two Irelands. The border that runs around six counties – Antrim, Down, Armagh, Tyrone, Fermanagh and Derry – neither takes them out of Ireland nor puts them into Britain: I cannot see two Irelands, even when looking at extremes such as the Orangemen's celebration on July 12.

I went to see it one recent year after a long gap in time, and chose a small country town. From Dublin, where I live, I had nosed my way up to Belfast, and there drove past mile after mile of small, back-to-back brick houses, the sort of street where my ancestors grew up as mill hands, where my grandfather went out to work at the age of ten. Where he sweated and wrought, taught himself the elements of history and politics along with his fellows and helped bring organized labour into the textile industry. Even in this century things could be grim. My grandfather often told of a curate who abandoned a Belfast parish for the Navy. He said he could not preach the gospel to people who had no fire in the grate and no food on the table; but self-pity is not a fault in Belfast, rather is there a pride in the community skills and adaptability.

Belfast, which grew from twenty thousand in the year 1800 to two hundred thousand by 1880 and four hundred thousand in 1925, is a city that has spawned more unhappiness than can be told, and yet is admirable in its courage and toughness. The scars of the industrial revolution are still there, to a great extent caused by the long hours, the humid atmosphere, the poor food, the hopeless sanitary conditions. You can see it in the pale faces, the rickety walk and the runty stature of many of the older generation, the burden of their history as grievous as the

179

burdens of any peasant from Connemara or County Cork who still lives on tales of the famine.

Belfast can be a friendly place with your own friends, so to speak, a savage place when it becomes the plaything of political or religious *agents provocateurs*. There is in its folklore, attributed to Churchill, a sentence which I have never seen written down. He is supposed to have said at a time of hideous sectarian strife: 'In Belfast they do everything but eat the bodies.' That may stem from the days when, as a Liberal, visiting Belfast at the height of the Home Rule controversy, he came very near to being a corpse before his time, at the hands of an anti-Home Rule mob. Those days are far enough behind, in spite of an addle-headed, money-conscious rump of militant Protestantism, in spite of anachronistic string-pulling by the Orange Order. The North has been trapped in the past in at least this respect where the rest of Ireland has moved on from the old days of faction and Donnybrooking, but it seems to be changing now. The young generation, affluent by comparison, seems to show impatience with the drag of the past and, like youth everywhere, is reaching for the good things of life.

Belfast is not all shipyard gantries, satanic mills and grim squatty houses, painted with sectarian slogans or vast gable-covering pictures of King William of Orange crossing the Boyne. Around the city is a semi-circle of mountains and half an hour from the centre you can be amongst heather and running streams, and game birds will rise at your feet. At night the curlews whistle overhead as they descend to the flats of Belfast Lough.

On that July 12 I drove north through Belfast. A few miles from the city centre there arose just behind a neat tongue of suburban houses a steep wooded slope and then a gigantic vertical basalt cliff, hanging there over the red, green and slate-grey roofs of the modern bungalows and villas . . . rising to a height of eleven hundred feet.

Seen from certain angles this cliff-side of the Cave Hill resembles a profile; some Belfast people call it Napoleon's Nose. Alice Milligan wrote of it:

> Look up from the streets of the city,
> Look high beyond towers and mast,
> What hand of what Titan sculptor
> Smote the crags of the mountain vast?
> Made when the world was fashioned,
> Meant with the world to last,
> The glorious face of The Sleeper
> That slumbers above Belfast.

On the top of that cliff, a natural stronghold known as McArt's Fort, there took place a hundred and seventy years ago one of those para-doxical events that make nonsense of the claim of two Irelands. On an early summer day in 1795 a Dubliner, a Protestant, who had set his heart on emancipating the Catholics of Ireland, who had been made Secretary of the Catholic Association, stood with some friends (not long before he was to make a journey to America) and with them swore that they would never desist until they had 'subverted the authority of England over our country, and asserted our independence.' Tone sought also to unite Protestant, Dissenter and Catholic in the common name of Irishman. Belfast today may be very different from the Belfast of 1795, but Theobald Wolfe Tone, the author of one of the great diaries in the English language, loved it, found it tough but boisterous and assuredly brought a lot of laughter to it.

Further on the way to watch the Orangemen I passed through south County Antrim, where in 1798 the United Irishmen, largely Protestant, rose against British rule and were cut down. Some of them are still remembered and their graves a place of pilgrimage. In days when atrocity is on a massive scale you may still be moved by an extract from an account of the aftermath of the Battle of Antrim:

'As a cartload of dead and dying arrived at the sand pit, a Yeoman officer asked the driver "Where the devil did these rascals come from?" A poor wretch raised his gory head from the cart and feebly answered "I come from Ballyboley". He was buried with the rest.'

It was not far to Cullybackey, County Antrim, in the constituency of Captain Terence O'Neill, Prime Minister of Northern Ireland, who was to speak at the meeting. It is a small, well-scrubbed, prosperous-looking place – population 758. We stand in the main street watching the bands with their banners and flags gathering at the far end, waiting for the sign that the day's business is to start. We keep looking down the street for the sleek car to nose its way along. But the procession starts without any state car.

Half the parade has gone past us when on the other side of the road, not far ahead of the banner which depicts Moses viewing the Promised Land, among the Ahoghill Loyal Orange Lodge 414, there is a familiar face. A smile, bows here and there, nods of the head. Clasping a small plastic mackintosh in his left hand, a gavel tied with ribbons in his right, wearing one of his good suits but hardly his best, bowler-hatted of course, his neck hung with the Orange collarette – a smaller version of the sash – comes Captain Terence Marne O'Neill at the same pad and shuffle as his fellow-brethren. He walks and smiles; his greeting is folksy, with that jerk of the neck which to a northern man is sufficient to show recognition without introducing any note of *plámás* or flattery, as much as to say that he is just one of the boys who sit on the bridge of a summer evening, spitting into the river Main.

He does not look like one of the boys, but he acts on this occasion like one of them and, in common with the rest, as he passes the Orange

Lodge, raises his bowler. Some stop momentarily before edging on. It is now a sun and shower day, and the white clouds sail over the humpy field. (Kindly lent by the brothers Harkness.) On a green lorry is the harmonium to lead us in hymns; district inspectors of the Royal Ulster Constabulary idle around twirling slim blackthorn sticks. The white-washed house on the hill across from us is the house from which President Arthur of the United States came, we are told.

You may think that the talk at The Field, as they call a place where the Orangemen meet at the end of their march, would be mostly politics, but on July 12 the politicians frequently take second place to the men of God. To be sure Captain O'Neill speaks well and other men speak well. But the Reverend Samuel Millar, BA, young, hollow-cheeked, with fashionable long hair, is the star of the day.

He reads the Word of God for us: nothing less joyful than the raising of Lazarus. He reads with what elocution classes call 'feeling', head thrown up to the sky, teeth clenched, and when he comes to the bit 'He groaned in His spirit and was troubled' the Reverend Samuel Millar groans with the Lord. He prays his God to 'bring Thy terrible fear upon Thy people'. He tells us that the Lord could heal the putrifying sores of our souls. We need the strong voice of Christ to rise us out of our sin. 'Can you see the corpse, men and women?'

Men and women? We aren't for long; soon we are a generation of vipers. 'Christ is good. He is good, He is good' he shouts. God loves us; He wants to take the hatred from our hearts. But we have spurned the message of the Gospel; it is not enough for us to follow the Reformed Church, not enough to be Orange, not enough for us to be just hearers of the Word and not doers. And so on. We would be saved, however, by the Fairest of the Ten Thousand, by the Lily of the Valley.

Those who had read their Joyce might take the speech of the Reverend Samuel Millar and compare it with the sermon in *A portrait of the Artist*. There is not so much difference between the northern Presbyterian and the southern Jansenist. Afterwards, the Prime Minister speaks respectfully of him while the Reverend Millar, a young man of thirty, sits with his head in his hands, his fair hair over his face. He has warned us.

There is a corresponding organization for Catholics, the Ancient Order of Hibernians. Their big day is in August. They are less numerous and wield less power than the Orangemen who, in fact, dominate the politics of the Unionist Party in Northern Ireland. Every Cabinet Minister is – must be – an Orangeman – at this date. There are signs that this order, too, changeth.

Northern Ireland means to me many things. It means living in a house on the edge of Belfast; at the age of four or five being awakened in the middle of a summer night with a shout of 'halt!', a pounding of feet across the fields below my window and then a shot. It means, in the days of the middle and late twenties, happy hours on the edge of a vast expanse of fields, where symbolically ran two streams, one blue- or jet-black from the dye-works nearby – the other clear from the mountains and brightened by a pair of kingfishers. In the stream were stickle-backs galore and an occasional trout. Close by was a pond with newts and frogs. Across, a mile away, was an expanse of back-to-back houses, over which soared huge brick chimneys, some belching smoke, many of them not at work.

Our house, on the edge of these miles of fields, was passed daily by men in blue suits, wearing collarless shirts with a white choker tucked in, light-coloured caps and pointed shoes. When there were dogs with them, they were usually whippets. On good afternoons there were foot-ball matches in the field nearest to us. It didn't seem odd to me at the time that on a weekday afternoon there could be a hundred men playing and watching football. Often a circle would form around a couple of struggling players and a roar would go up which was deeper than any-thing that had come from the sidelines.

I saw there one day, and Belfast still means this to me in some ways, two men standing almost knee to knee, blood splashing from their faces as they pummelled each other. The desperation of the trapped, un-employed, unemployable industrial fodder of any big European town at that time.

'Who are you lookin' at?' A harmless enough question but I re-member it in Belfast as the childish expression of this unnatural violence. In tougher quarters of Belfast a young stranger was often assaulted just for 'lookin'. It was the battle-cry of the back-streets.

A green spire across those fields was the church of Ardoyne, whose bells reached us on still days. Those chimes still ring in my ear. (How much life in Ireland hinges around the sound of bells! From Ardoyne in Belfast to the slow, night-through boomings of the clock in Trinity College, to the joyful tunes sprinkled out in the quiet hours from St Patrick's in Dublin.) Religious controversy impinged not at all on a small boy, an only child living on the edge of good open country. At this time in the early twenties, however, it was a searing thing in the life of Belfast. To me, from an early age, Catholics meant very good people. I remember my mother, a devoted member of the Church of Ireland, telling me that Catholics attended to their religious duties regularly, and we would be better if we imitated them.

I had another reason for believing from early on that Catholics had something special. I have a small round scar on my right knee. I don't know how many times I heard my mother tell of the sore which would not heal, and how our maid Julia one day, taking me out in the pram, stopped off at a church. When she came back she told my mother that the lad's knee would be all right, because she had sprinkled it with

183

Holy Water. I was always told that it healed well and particularly quickly.

Still, the feeling that there is a Them and an Us is inescapable, or was in the Belfast of those days. I do not know when I first heard a boy of my own age deliver as a simple fact of life that 'Catholics would stab you in the back'. As you grew up you learned that it was wise when introducing people of different religions to try to send up a danger signal. I remember in Ballycastle being pointedly introduced by a Catholic friend as having been educated at the Belfast Royal Academy, which gave sufficient picture to the company I was meeting. This saved embarrassment.

Did we notice any difference in the Catholic boys around us? The atmosphere of the neighbouring Catholic school has been well described by Brian Moore in his book *The Feast of Lupercal*. As far as I remember they seemed to smoke more than we did. And that uneasy Catholic-Protestant no-man's-land in Belfast has been set down in another book of Moore's, *The Emperor of Ice-Cream,* better than anywhere else I have seen it.

You will be told occasionally in the north, and if you are an innocent soul you may even begin to believe it, that there are two races. The less erudite, indeed, may tell you that a Protestant or a Catholic in the north of Ireland is instantly distinguishable by his face. The wheel is turning in the North, the social deserts are blossoming. Not all the mouthing of the extreme Paisleyites or the extreme Orangemen can disguise this. And what a thought for such people that the infusion of charity today is due to a Pope, Pope John XXIII. The winds have blown from Rome and the winds have blown from all the other countries where barriers, religious and racial, are breaking down and the smoke is clearing away from Belfast and other parts of Northern Ireland.

There is no great liberator here, but a man has stepped forward to do his moderate best in bringing about a new and better feeling, and that is the same Captain Terence Marne O'Neill. He brings no sweeping reforms as yet, but an easier, more progressive approach to community relations.

And here is another of those paradoxes for those who see two Irelands, diverging more and more as the years go on: in one part the head of state has a distinctly foreign name; in the other the name is as Irish as Irish could be. The head of that part of Ireland which at times claims to be more Irish than the rest bears the name De Valera, which is not indigenous, while the Prime Minister of that part of Ireland which occasionally seems to be more British than the British, has the resonant Irish name of Terence O'Neill.

Northern Ireland also means to me a welcoming farmhouse in one of the kindliest and most beautiful parts of this country. It is late evening and we are sitting by the light of an oil lamp, buttering with salty country butter oatcake nearly half an inch thick, and dipping our cups directly into the churn for buttermilk, the greatest thirst-quencher. I remember then going to bed, crunching over cockroaches, my belly swollen, to a cold wing of the farmhouse, the smell of which is still in my nostrils. How much of that smell was apples, how much damp, how much came from the heap of turnips which they used to slice in an old hand-turned machine below my window? How much of it may have been from the manure heap and the hay barn? Outside the farmhouse the winds roared in from the Atlantic. On the beach below the waves never calmed, and half a mile on, chocolate-brown, or Guinness-brown if you like, the Bush river spread its stain through the white and ice-green breakers.

Old William George, old Samuel James and John Alexander are long gone to their rest. William George, whose wife had died young, was much given to helping the Church. When one of the neighbours was asked when William George would be putting up a stained-glass window in memory of Mrs George, he answered – typically warm-hearted to the living but caring little for posthumous reverence: 'Aw, who gives two bites of champ for his ould stained-glass window?' Champ being a simple dish of mashed potatoes and onions.

Northern Ireland is also another house to me. A house on a hill in a calmer part. The outside is black-oiled against weather. The gable-end, the windows and the ledges are painted as if they were a ship of the line. And no wonder; this is Islandmagee (the name a slight misnomer for it is a peninsula about nine miles long and perhaps three wide), where for centuries the men have gone to sea. Holdings are small, the people are a warm and singular race. They speak still with a Scots inflection, with a Scottish vocabulary and they have a covenanting religious fervour. On the Island there are two Presbyterian churches, one Church of Ireland and one Methodist place of worship. There is no Catholic church. Many Catholics were murdered after the 1641 rising.

The house sparkles and shines. Round the walls pictures of steamers, the ships that Samuel Ross and his relatives have sailed in. There is a gleaming cleanliness and a thrift and precision everywhere. For tea there is fish freshly fried; they are called locally blocken and lithe, two of the many terms given to pollock or coal-fish. There is crisp iceberg lettuce, thick Stornoway ships biscuits and at least four or five kinds of bread in the Scottish fashion. Outside on the tiny lawn a hare sits up, cocks an ear and quietly lopes away.

It's a Sunday morning: the roads throng with men in blue, most of them with their jackets in old (now new) long styles, serge to a man. There is hardly a motor car, there may be a trap or two and an occasional bicycle. The Jews must walk to their place of worship, these Presbyterians had to for other reasons. When it came to the sermon they expected their money's worth. After forty-five minutes I flagged,

185

but on the way back, and for the rest of the day, or until the evening and another service took their attention, the Reverend Elliot's interpretation of the word of God was discussed, criticized and re-quoted.

Temperance is not just a virtue to these people, it is the norm. I was up there recently burying a relative and met cousins I hadn't seen for years. Roy is in his fifties and we had both been coming to the Island for the greater part of our lives. He is a quiet, hardbitten sailor, a senior officer in one of the best-known ships in the world. We thought of going to the pub after the funeral – it was to be my first visit ever and he, who knew a thousand pubs in a hundred ports, confessed that he had never set foot in it until the previous summer. Drink and Islandmagee didn't seem to go together.

And while we are on that subject: pub-life in Northern Ireland is going the way of pub-life everywhere else – but in the country districts there are still white-washed rooms with benches round the sides, and sometimes you might think you'd be lucky if your glass wasn't rinsed in a bucket of water. Simple, straight-forward, and the crack is good; Spartan, even verging on the primitive. I know one pub on a main road where you are served civilly and well looked after and when you ask for the Gents you are directed out through a door and down to a shed. There is at first nothing remarkable about this shed; a long bench with two round holes cut in it. If you wonder at the draught there is a simple explanation: under the two holes there is a straight drop of nine feet where there ripples and gurgles a small stream, or a burn. Where the burn runs to I have not yet learned, or had the independence of mind to seek.

St Patrick is not by any means the property of the north of Ireland, though he is said to be buried there, and a huge slab of granite in Saul, County Down, marks the place. In his early days he herded sheep in the North, on Slemish mountain, an odd, pap-shaped protuberance on the plateau of County Antrim. All over Ireland there are footsteps of St Patrick. Even in the grounds of Trinity College, a university founded by Elizabeth to teach the Irish what was what, there is a St Patrick's Well. There is a St Patrick's everything in Ireland. Even on the tip of this odd, austere, Scots Presbyterian-inhabited peninsula of Islandmagee, St Patrick has left his mark.

Between Larne Harbour and Islandmagee two ferries used to run, Hood's Ferry and Templeton's Ferry. There was in the one case less than half a mile and in the other case perhaps three quarters of a mile to be covered. The north winds blow down into the funnel-mouth of the lough that divides the Island from the coast throughout the year. Some of the worst storms may come in August and the breakers mount up, sweep in through the narrow neck of Larne Lough. No man, it is said, has ever been lost on this short, sharp and perilous journey. And why? Because St Patrick himself once made it and he blessed the passage. I remember in the thirties the Belfast papers carried a story of one of the ferry boats having been lost on a bitter night. Was St Patrick to be gainsaid? No. A day later, Sam Hood and his boat were found safe and sound on a beach just down the way – in Scotland. The boat is still seaworthy, I was told recently.

These six counties are as Irish as places down south which used to be called Kingscounty and Queenscounty, or Cork which provides endless men for the British Navy, or Dublin which is almost a foreign capital. They are the same Irish people, that is: a mixture of everything from Celts, Danes, Normans, Saxons, Scots, Huguenots, Germans (or Palatines as we call them), interbred with Cromwellians and all the bits and pieces of soldiery which tramped across the country for centuries. Genetically a mess, but still, as Yeats said, or might have said, indomitably Irish. George Russell (Æ), an Ulsterman, wrote truly of 'one river born from many streams'.

The scenery is the same. Jimmy O'Dea, the great Irish comedian, great in his way as Chaplin or Fernandel, used to say that the grass was as green in Antrim as it is in Kerry. In Belfast he brought down the house with this. I am not sure what sort of reception he got in Tralee, County Kerry. The rivers run with salmon and trout, the Mountains of Mourne sweep down to the sea with a grace which equals that of heaven's reflex, Killarney.

People talk, drink, walk, eat and worship God in much the same way as they do in other parts of Ireland. More of them prefer greyhound-racing to horse-racing, the cloth cap to the grey topper; more of them play soccer and rugby than play Gaelic football; they sin and die in very much the same way. There are a dozen, if not more, dialects of Ulster-English speech, all with the same clipped, machine-gunlike delivery, recognizable anywhere, leagues away from the Queen's English. But northerners have gone away as boys from their home, have roamed the world, become Generals or Field Marshals, Pro-Consuls, entrepreneurs, artists, what you will, and have never seen any reason to modify their ways of speech.

Men of the North are said to be dour and silent as compared with the charming, voluble extroverts from the rest of the island. Anyone who sees a north of Ireland man at his best, and he is often at his best when he is abroad, will know that he, rather than Paddy from down below, is the last stage Irishman. You can see it in Westminster, where the north of Ireland still has the nerve to send twelve Members of Parliament.

There is a wryness and a sharpness about the northern man which I think he shares with men of the west. There is a scepticism, a determination not to be impressed. At the mouth of Belfast Lough there is a tiny hamlet called Port Davy; on the shore stand two rocks, each about the size of one of the neighbouring cottages. They are known locally as the Wren's Eggs. This owes nothing to the famous British habit of understatement.

The northerner is not inclined to be over-deferential. After he leaves school he seldom uses the word 'Sir' unless he is pitched into army life; he regards such flourishes as forelock-touching. He has a lack of social pretence. Some people see the northerners as a tribe of Andy Capps. The businessman who fights his way up into the money does not, as might happen with his Dublin counterpart, turn into a dinner jacket at night when the first hundred thousand comes up. He is likely, at home, to stick to high tea for the rest of his life.

Their reputation with money is of being slightly Aberdonian. It is said of Ballymena in County Antrim that it is the only town in Ireland where no Jew has ever made a living. Certainly Ballymena men do not waste words. People in the North may take slowly to anyone who comes to live among them, partly from a lack of social consciousness of an odd kind, partly that they do not wish to intrude on another's privacy; but when the barriers do go down, they are the firmest of friends.

If I have given a picture of a hard, relentless people, I do an injustice. But no one who lived in Belfast through the 'twenties and 'thirties – and in 1935 a score of people were killed in riots which broke out on July 12 – can forget the legacy of hatred which Ireland's history of conquest and exploitation, of divide and conquer, of plantation and devastation has left behind. In Belfast there was added the cruel facts of a modern industrial revolution. In the past few years religious nonsense has again come to the surface, but, many people think, only to be scooped off like scum.

The hurtful tends to remain in the memory, but the north ties your heart down too. I was reminiscing with a Dublin professional man who had also grown up in the North; he was a Catholic and had lived in a quarter where there were few Catholics. As he said, at parties and other gatherings he would often be 'the only one of me kind'. We brooded over the hard edges of a social life in Ulster and he came up with the conclusion that for all his faults the Ulsterman was the truest friend and the straightest to deal with. 'They'll say it all to your face,' he said. 'Give me an Ulsterman every time.'

People and Places

Dublin: Streets Broad and Narrow
James Plunkett

It seems a long time ago now, those beginnings to the mysterious processes of becoming a Dubliner. I see a child pedalling his motor car (it was one of those grey, chain-driven affairs) around a plot of grass in St Stephen's Green; I see him making a perilous swing of the great iron chains that once stretched between the stone posts bordering the public footpath outside it; I see him sitting on the steps of one of the tall houses of Lower Leeson Street hoping his father would soon come by on his way from work so that they could walk home to dinner together.

But instead the burly, straight-backed man with his walking cane and the sticky-out ends on his moustache marches up the street and does a left-turn-slope-arms in front of him. He has all the impact of a military band. He salutes. He declaims

> *Two cigars*
> *For two hussars*
> *A pint and a bottle of stout*

The child nods solemnly. This is as usual. The man with the waxed moustache stands at-ease, comes smartly to attention, salutes again.

> *Two sardines*
> *For two marines*
> *A pint and a bottle of stout*

The child acknowledges. Another salute.

> *Two bugger-alls*
> *For two Donegals*
> *A pint and a bottle of stout.*

Bugger all meant 'nothing at all'. It was an expression permissible only to the adult male.

Who the old soldier was I'll never know, for cold Sergeant Death must have beckoned him a long time since and by now he has fallen on sleep. The child is a ghost too, a waif-like tenant in remote corridors of the mind to be seen occasionally and always unexpectedly. He used to wait on winter evenings for the arrival of the post office parcels car, listening at a window in Upper Pembroke Street for the clip clop of its two enormous horses. These from time to time brought caskets full of expensive chocolates. They were free gifts sent in return for the coupons saved by his mother out of cocoa tins over interminable periods. We used to count them together every other day. Cocoa seems to have played a large part in my childhood. Fry's had a yellow and red label and Bourneville a brown one. Van Houtens was grey with brown lettering. It tasted bitter and I never cared for it, which persuaded my mother, as with everything else, that it had more nourishment in it and was better for me. The milkman came every day and I brought the can to the door. He measured out two pints and then he gave a tilley for me and then he would put in another little tilley and say it was for the cat. He used to wink when he said that. I used to try to wink back but I was no good at it at all. When I tried to close one eye the other automatically closed too. I concluded that winking was an adult accomplishment. Like whistling. One had to practise and be patient.

That was the Dublin of my childhood. We were poor, but to me not noticeably so. The streets around us were elegant, the houses were tall and beautiful, on warm summer evenings we could meet my father in Stephen's Green and have a picnic on the grass. And not so far away there was the Grand Canal, with green banks on either side and awesome cataracts at lock gates and I could follow it almost all the way by Baggot Street Bridge and Mount Street to the house my grandfather and my aunts lived in.

It was in Irishtown and I had been born there, half way between the proletarians of Ringsend and the highly respectables of Sandymount. My grandfather was a carpenter – and a good one – who prayed every night to St Joseph to make him a good craftsman. In the thirties he was on short time for a while and then out of work altogether, and the indignity of it killed him. During the holidays I spent in that house I learned to love the great sweep of Sandymount Strand, where we swam when the tide was full and when it had gone out played football and rounders and watched the quality exercising their horses. Gogarty has described that great stretch of sand with engagement and tenderness and no wonder. The tide goes out so far you'd think it could never return again. When you looked out to sea there was Howth coloured blue and green with bungalows scattered haphazardly about it and the sun catching their windows. When you looked along the shoreline you saw ethereal spires mounting above the genteel harbour of Dun Laoghaire. And when you turned inland again the Dublin mountains were melting colour into colour, brown bog and green fields and yellow furze bearing here and there the shadows of slowmoving clouds. It was the strand Joyce had made Stephen Dedalus walk a long time before I was born.

'In lassoes from the Cock Lake the water flowed full, covering green-goldenly lagoons of sand, rising, flowing. My ashplant will float away . . . Am I walking into eternity along Sandymount Strand.'

190

Young as I was, I was bothered by this sense of eternity too. It spoke through cloudscapes and seascapes, it lurked behind the beady eye of the grey gull perched lonely on the hull of a wrecked ship, a reincarnated sailor anciently revolving the fate of Phlebos the Phoenician. To the north were the cranes and gasometers, the b & i boats, the furnaces of the Bottle House, the tenements of Thorncastle and Townsend Streets and the drama of tramcars. It was that time of life when one wanted to be a tram conductor.

Instead, one went to school – at first to the nuns, where you could buy a black baby by giving a ha'penny a week to the mission fund. I did it myself for a considerable period, more to be in the swim than in any firm belief that a black baby would ever be handed over. My suspicions were proved correct. Month after month passed by. No black baby turned up. Either the price of black babies was exorbitant or the nun was a fraud. I was about seven years of age and sufficiently a Dubliner to accept the second conclusion. Your Dubliner is tolerant of deception provided it is backed up by ingenuity. I got a kick out of putting the ha'penny in the collection box, because the nubian effigy on the top acknowledged by bobbing his grinning head. The grin was perpetual. He too, of course, was a fraud.

Then came the Christian Brothers. These were a religious teaching order founded by Ignatius Rice to rescue Ireland from British Rule by applying the maxim of the patriot Thomas Davis: Educate That You May Be Free. They brought higher education to the children of the plain people of Ireland who could not afford the fees of Irish secondary schools modelled on the British system. Their aim was that of Padraic Pearse – an Ireland not only free, but Gaelic as well, and they dominated Dublin education. As educationists they were thorough, terrifying, yet at times (in the tolerant, over-all view of the Dubliner) likeable, because they indulged the homely vices. They understood poverty and never embarrassed a child whose parents had to welsh when it came to paying the comparatively infinitesimal school fees. If they felt a good belt on the jaw was sure to implant a veneration for learning in their juvenile charges, they nevertheless made a point of dishing out the cigarettes to you on the special occasion, at the altar boys' party for instance, or after the school concert. Their twin enthusiasms were the Catholic religion and the Irish language: their twin distrusts, British ideas and what they called Anglo-Irish literature. This should have meant works written in English by Irishmen but in fact it did not. Charles Kickham and Canon Sheehan wrote in English but were Irish writers. Anglo-Irish writers were people like Yeats and Joyce, who tended to be either Protestant or lax in their devotion to Kathleen ni Houlihan or both. For them the Church was One, Holy, Catholic, Apostolical and entirely unassailable. The Pope was Infallible, and had their unquestioning obedience, except when he condemned the physical force element in

191

Irish politics. In this matter, through the machinations of British Diplomacy (and who, God knows, knew the wiles of the perfidious Saxon better than they did) the poor man had been misled. But that would be put right. Patrick and Brigid, Kevin and Colmcille would have a quiet word with God about it. The school I attended was in Synge Street, a few doors from the house Bernard Shaw had been born in. But the good brothers, like the Jesuits in Belvedere when reminded of their pupil James Joyce, perferred not to talk about it.

All this time, while my father and his cronies went to soccer matches on Saturday afternoons, and gathered in the pubs on the way home to play the match all over again; while figures like Jim Larkin were fighting a losing battle for Socialism at street corners and in dingy rooms, the Irish Free State was still trying to make up its mind about what it stood for. De Valera had decided at last to sit in opposition in Dáil Éireann, but the guns of the extemists were still paying off old scores. There are two things I remember vividly. One is standing with my grandfather at the door of his house in Bath Street, looking downhill at the spire of Ringsend Church which rose against the glowing sunset of a July evening. A newsboy came towards us shouting 'Stop Press Edition' and the news it carried was that Kevin O'Higgins, Minister for Justice, had been assassinated on his way to mass. The second is my grandmother telling me of going to the hospital morgue to identify the body of my father's cousin Frank Jackson, a Republican who had been riddled with bullets in an encounter on Capel Street bridge. My father and his brothers had fought with the British in France and at Gallipoli; while another branch of the family fought the British in Ireland. The Republican side often found safe shelter in my grandmother's house. It was a strange house, where the speech Robert Emmet made against British domination before he was hanged and beheaded hung proudly on one wall, with my uncle Ross's citation for bravery (he had served in the Dublin Fusiliers) hanging beside it. He had been wounded five times and escaped on three occasions from a German prisoner-of-war camp. He lived to come home, but died in a few years from the effects of a bayonet wound in the stomach. I don't know what the raiding Black and Tans made of all this. They probably concluded that Dubliners were not only dangerous, but mad.

But, of course, they are not mad. It is simply that they believe in taking things as they come. Many of them fought for England and spent their leave at home training others to fight the British in Ireland. And they know that when a few years have passed, the once burning issue is no longer of consequence. Only the sure things matter: football, funerals, something to laugh about, the price of the pint, the world that will come after this one. The rest is a snare and a delusion.

While I sat on those steps under the tall houses and the old soldier recited to me, there were men all around me creating a literary legend.

192

Charm and gaiety come naturally to Irish girls. The candle-bearer is a hostess at a mediaeval banquet at Bunratty Castle, Co Clare

George Moore was calling on Yeats and Yeats was calling on George Russell, and Oliver St John Gogarty was calling on and being called on by practically everybody. When Yeats was made a Senator of the new Free State Gogarty called with the news but got no answer to his knock. So he chalked his message on the halldoor. 'Senator W. B. Yeats!'

Of this great drama of wit and intellect I saw nothing, however, until the last few moments before the curtain came down. In a laneway in Rathfarnham I met a silverhaired man in a wheelchair and as he was pushed past us my friend said: 'That's W. B. Yeats.' It was about a year before his death. On another occasion, near the end of the evening, I turned the corner of a quiet road in Clonskeagh and found myself face to face with a ghost. It was a very tall, very thin old lady, dressed from head to foot in black drapes, with a wolfhound on a lead. Then she passed me, an apparition in October twilight. She was Maud Gonne McBride, once the symbol of Romantic Ireland, now so incredibly old to my young eyes that I thought of Oisin when his foot touched mortal ground and all his years in the blinking of an eye descended with the weight of an avalanche on top of him.

All these have looked at the streets of Dublin and gone their way, leaving in her air a memory of their involvement. Joyce contemplated one of her Martello towers, built at a time when England had to keep an anxious eye on the seas about her for fear of a French invasion, and used it for the beginning of his saga of a Dublin Day. O'Casey saw a tenement, Georgian fanlight shattered, its door permanently open and its breath dank and malodorous, and here Seamus Shields and Fluther Good and Bessie Burgess and Juno and Davoren the poltroon of a poet suffered poverty and were noble or ignoble but found a way always to be stronger than Death, and so armed themselves with laughter and compassion, cynicism and cunning, that Despair gave up and went home. I don't think Yeats ever looked at her at all. He once had a thought that he would like to see a pub, and the poet F. R. Higgins brought him to one. Yeats disposed himself, consented to a glass of sherry and looked about him. When the sherry arrived he despatched it without delay and rose. 'Higgins', he said, 'I have seen a pub – now kindly take me home.'

My own Dublin is different still. I have looked at her from Killakee mountain at night, when all her lights twinkle like diamonds and the beams of the lighthouses flash and make circles about her bay. I have walked the back lanes of Patrick Street and Thomas Street and the Coombe and thought of Emmet's head being held up by the executioner for the mob about St Catherine's to gape at; of rebels plotting in Winetavern and Oliver Bond Streets; of mad Jonathan Swift peering at the excrement in an alleyway and establishing by its shape the nationality of the defiler; of James Clarence Mangan the

193

Fishing near Castlebar, Co Mayo

poet limping along shadowy laneways with his flowing cloak and steeple-crowned hat and a voluminous umbrella under his arm, going the road to drug addiction and cholera and death with those words in his heart that totally rejected all hope. 'I have pleasure in nothing and I admire nothing. I hate scenery and suns.'

I have even looked at her from the top of Nelson's Pillar (a most un-Dublin thing to do – like going to view the Book of Kells in Trinity) but the IRA or someone else who harboured a grudge against the Admiral blew the bloody thing up. Some people say the street looks better without him, but I don't know. Some people also think a multi-storeyed concrete biscuit-box with imbecile windows is better than a row of Georgian houses. These architectural monsters are springing up everywhere, while the City Fathers and the Government do nothing to prevent it. They are even making their appearance around St Stephen's Green. Perhaps soon there will be no Green left to pedal a motor car around and no steps a child may sit on under the tall and friendly houses. This thought makes me sad – for myself, for those who are to come, and for the sake of all those lovable eccentrics of the past whose genius and high talk have hallowed the streets of my city and given dignity to her name.

Youghal
Claud Cockburn

Into the office of the Town Clerk of Youghal, County Cork, stormed three furious Londoners. They had a bitter complaint to make about the place. Indeed, as one of them said, they were 'absolutely blind with indignation'.

Certainly they were not in a state to appreciate, as they roared along the road beside the Blackwater, the scene so lushly described by an earlier, but Irish, visitor.

'Here', this traveller wrote, 'more remarkably than any place I recall, have art and nature blended their best elements in one imposing and delightful prospect. High from the road rise time worn walls, above whose summit hangs a wealth of foliage through which flowers gleam as fresh and lovely as a maiden's eyes. Quaint buildings, many of them houses with rare histories, stand out.'

The description is sixty years old, and is still true enough. However, what the three tourists of the nineteen-sixties had eyes for nothing else but, was a monument. It stands in the middle of a little park where you can sit among the flowers, looking at the salmon boats on the estuary, and out over the Atlantic, with nothing but wide miles of sandy strand between you and Spain, or Newfoundland.

But the enraged trio, like many other British tourists, had been stopped half-dead in their tracks by the inscription staring them in the face from the base of the monument. 'In memory of the Rev Peter O'Neill PP of Ballymacoda. Cruelly flogged by British soldiers in 1798.'

Goggle-eyed, they moved round to the side of the monument. The inscription there reads: 'In Memory of Charles O'Brien, unjustly hanged by British soldiers in 1798.' The two remaining sides are inscribed, respectively, to the memory of another man 'cruelly flogged' and yet another 'unjustly hanged' by British soldiers in that year of Irish revolt.

As though there had been a sudden burst in the waterpipes of history, the unfortunate Town Clerk found himself the victim of a deluge. It would probably have been of small comfort to him to reflect that his situation was symptomatic of problems in that 'new Ireland' of which so much is spoken, and of which ancient Youghal is so notable an example.

The tourists waved Irish travel advertisements. 'It says here,' they shouted ' "Come to the Land of a Hundred Thousand Welcomes." And first thing we see is that bloody insult there in the park.'

Next to the export of cattle, the import of tourists is Ireland's (though not Youghal's) largest money-spinner. The issue raised was not trivial. It has since been a matter of considerable informal discussion among leading citizens. In the interests of 'tourism' should the inscriptions be chiselled out? But those four men really were cruelly flogged or unjustly hanged by British soldiers. Are we for sordid considerations to suppress the grim facts of Irish history? May it not be positively good to draw some people's attention to bygones which, in their typically British way, they wish to let be merely bygones?

It was characteristic of Youghal in particular, and in some degree of the 'new Ireland' in general, that the affair of the statue in the park shocked a different group of people in quite a different way. They were Irish-Americans on a trip to the old country. What jolted them was that any true Irishman should think of the matter as an issue at all; should, even on the most theoretical plane, consider the desirability of somehow modifying the impact of those inscriptions.

In fact a great deal about Youghal filled them with dismay. They thought, and some of them wrote home to tell the sad news, that this town had 'lost touch with the true spirit of Ireland', was even 'betraying Ireland's cultural heritage' etc.

In this they were less perceptive than the late President Kennedy when, a few months before his assassination, he addressed the Irish Dáil. Winds, or at the least heavy squalls, of change were blowing in Ireland as he spoke. The resulting draughts caused a lot of sincere people to conclude that there was a total contradiction between 'the old values' and the 'new Ireland'. The President, excellently briefed, emphasized the potential and necessary continuum of past and present

195

– the fact that it is a slack defeatism to suppose that in order to reach for the future you have to abandon the past. There is a conflict, but it can be made, also, a creative dialogue.

Youghal might have served as a text for the President's speech. It is perhaps melodramatic to note that a couple of hundred years BC the Phoenicians came and made vases out of Youghal clay, which they shipped to Athens to be decorated; that, like so many other enterprises in Ireland, the pottery business shrivelled into insignificance; that it was successfully re-started a half dozen years ago, and now does national and international business in the products of that same clay.

And that was no accident. It was a Cork historian's probing of what had been done in the past which first triggered today's undertaking. It is both a fact and a symbol.

The 'heritage' which the Irish-American visitors dreamed of with vicarious nostalgia, included, ten or a dozen years ago, a very high rate of unemployment. The men wandering in and out of the labour exchange were not in a position to contribute their best to 'cultural values'. Today, as a result of a deliberate, concerted effort by local men, workers have to be brought into town daily from thirty or forty miles away.

Are we thereby betraying something– or are we re-creating it and, at the same time, creating the basis for something new?

Twelve years ago a couple of men bought an old shed on the beautiful but mouldering quayside. They turned it into a carpet factory. Now it employs hundreds. Its exports – and you can't say fairer than this – exceed in dollar value that of the entire export of Irish whiskey.

So neo-capitalism is rampant in Ireland? James Connolly is betrayed? The answer to that is in the hands of, in particular, those enforced emigrants to Britain who, at present in a trickle, perhaps soon in a flood, return to jobs here with ideas of – for example – Trades Unionism more advanced than those until lately traditional in Ireland.

Or is this 'industrialization' destroying the amenities? The answer is 'No' – and a lot of drop-jowled beauty-defenders in Britain might do worse than go to Youghal and look.

The quayside is no less lovely because men and women work there instead of mouldering, Nor has prosperity diminished the austere loveliness of the Main Street, elongated by the squeeze of river and hill; mainly Georgian, but assimilating without difficulty the house Cromwell used for his headquarters and some late Victorian extravaganzas.

Youghal recreated its own personality, its own independence. It has got some prosperity without losing beauty. It could even do without tourists– though that would be a greater loss to the tourists than to Youghal.

In this respect it may be a help in the ever present times of trouble in Britain – not to mention Dublin.

Derry City: Frontier Stronghold

A. R. Foster

Some years ago a distinguished Dublin writer, crossing Craigavon bridge on his first visit to Derry, raised his eyes to the city on the hill, crowned by the cathedral spire, and exclaimed: 'I see that there are two cities in Ireland, Dublin and Derry.' His companion, a Derryman, replied 'You mean Derry and Dublin.' For Derrymen are inordinately proud of their native city, and not without reason.

Derry – Derry Calgach, the wood of the ancient warrior Galgacus, then Derry Columbkille, and later Londonderry by charter of James I, but always Derry to its own people – has had a long and tempestuous history. In the sixth century it became a famous centre of missionary enterprise; in the seventeenth century it was an equally famous acropolis, the defence of which changed the course of European history; in the twentieth it was the chief naval base for warships defending the north-west approaches to Britain against the deadly submarine menace of the Nazis. Thus thrice in our era Derry has been in the full flood of world affairs and has won renown for piety, endurance, and feats of arms.

Derry first rose to fame when Columb founded a monastery there, on the hill overlooking the broad tidal river. He was an O'Donnell, a prince of Tyrconnell, a born leader and a man of strong character, but Columbkille, the 'dove of the churches' as he came to be known from his numerous monastic foundations throughout Ireland, was not, at least in his early days, a man of peace. His quarrels with the High King and others led to grievous battles and, it is said, as a penance he was enjoined to leave Ireland and go into exile.

In 563 with twelve other monks he sailed from Derry and settled in Iona, which he made the centre of a great mission. For over thirty years till his death in 577 he laboured to spread the Christian faith through pagan Caledonia and northern Britain, and with such success that he is acknowledged by Scottish church historians as 'founder of the Scottish nationality and of the Scottish church.' And Irish monks from Iona re-kindled the flame of Christianity all over Western Europe after the fall of the Roman Empire.

But till the day he died Columbkille never lost his love of Derry, about which he had written these words:

> *Were all the tribute of Scotia mine,*
> *From its midland to its borders,*
> *I would give all for one little cell*
> *In my beautiful Derry.*

For many centuries after the days of St Columb the annals of Derry have a sorry tale to tell. Invaders, whether native Irish or marauding

197

Danes or Normans, burned and plundered the abbey again and again, but not till the reign of Elizabeth does the place again become widely significant. The English, realizing the strategic importance of a stronghold on the Foyle, lying at the back of O'Neill's territory and between that and Tyrconnell, occupied and fortified Derry with a strong force under Sir Henry Docwra and held it permanently. Under James I, after the Flight of the Earls, the plantation of Ulster was vigorously undertaken and the county and city of Derry were made the special province of the merchant companies of the City of London. They built the walls, which still stand, laid out the streets and peopled the new city with Protestant settlers from England and Scotland. In the rising of 1641 Derry withstood a siege, and in 1688–9 the city became the heart and centre of resistance to James II and Louis XIV. It was besieged for 105 days, the longest siege in the history of the British Isles, and was at the point of despair and collapse from want of food when at last Kirke's ships came sailing up the Foyle, broke the boom and relieved the city.

This was itself an heroic feat of endurance, but it was more than that. The plan of James was to transport Irish and French troops to Scotland, where he would join his Highland army, invade England and regain his throne. The long delay at Derry held up 20,000 men and frustrated that plan. The invasion never took place and William of Orange had a breathing-space in which to rally his forces for the decisive campaign in 1690. Thus Derry played a leading part in the defeat of absolutism in Europe.

December 18, when thirteen apprentice boys, defying authority, shut the gates in the teeth of a Jacobite army, and August 12, when the city was relieved, are still both celebrated with martial music and gay processions.

On the former date a huge effigy of Lundy, the Governor who was accused of treachery, is burned every year hanging from the tall pillar of Governor Walker on the walls.

Any account of Derry must inevitably look to the past, for the past is still vividly felt there. The politics and religion of the seventeenth century are to a large extent the politics and religion of today. But Derry has, of course, changed with the times. Once the leading city of the North, a Protestant stronghold and symbol of Protestant ascendancy, it has been far outstripped in size and wealth by Belfast, and today out of a total population of over fifty-three thousand, thirty-six thousand are Catholics. The tension between the faiths, which has often led to riots and bloodshed, is increased by the fact that, though Catholics now form sixty-seven per cent of the inhabitants, the city returns a Protestant Unionist member of Parliament and twelve of the twenty members of the corporation. Most of the city's officials are also Protestants. 'One man, one vote' is not the rule in Derry.

Derry has suffered from the partition of Ireland. The border within a few miles of the city has for forty-seven years cut it off from half of its natural hinterland in Donegal, but the recent trade agreement may now enable goods to move again across the dividing line. Meanwhile the shirt-making industry employs most labour. There are some twenty-nine factories, employing about five thousand workers, but most of these are females. Forty years ago there was a promising shipyard at Pennyburn which employed two thousand men, but that venture, like others before it, failed. The NI government has in recent years built factories at Maydown and elsewhere and attracted industrial concerns to start production there. But BSR (Monarch Electric), which employed some two thousand workers, most of them males, has now closed down; Sea Eagle, the anti-submarine base, is to be phased out in three years' time; the old sea route to Glasgow, Burns Laird, no longer exists; and the Great Northern Railway linking Derry with Dublin and Belfast has also been terminated.

Many of the older industries such as coachbuilding, cotton- linen- and woollen-weaving, rope-making and distilling have disappeared, but bacon-curing is still a flourishing trade employing male labour. At the moment the number of unemployed workers is depressing: fourteen per cent of all workers, eighteen per cent of the male section.

Derry is well supplied with colleges and schools. Foyle College, an old foundation (1617) has trained many famous men: George Farquhar, the Restoration dramatist, The Lawrences of India and J. B. Bury, the historian among them.

St Columb's College, a fine school, is its Catholic counterpart. Magee University College, founded in 1865 for the education of Presbyterian ministers, developed into a college for all creeds and claims to have been a pioneer in the higher education of women. Rejected by the new Queen's University in 1908, it was recognized as a constituent college by Dublin University, to which it sent many able students, but it is again threatened with inferior status when the New Ulster University is established at Coleraine. Many people of all creeds regard it as an insult that the city was passed over as a site for the new University and that the claims of Magee, with its honourable record, were repudiated.

In its long history the city has been the home of many remarkable characters. George Berkeley the philosopher, was once Dean of Derry and he is said to have laid out his projected foundation in Rhode Island on the plan of Derry City. There have been notable bishops, both Catholic and Protestant, but the most striking ecclesiastical personage was Frederick Augustus Hervey, Earl of Bristol and Protestant Bishop. A man of great wealth, he was a liberal patron of the arts; he built a splendid mansion at Downhill and filled it with Italian paintings. He fought for the reform of the Irish Parliament and for Catholic Emancipation. In 1783 he led a great parade of the Irish Volunteers which, halting outside the Houses of Parliament, with blaring trumpets alarmed

199

the sitting Commons. The Bishop, who delighted in gorgeous display, sat in an open carriage drawn by six magnificently caparisoned horses and escorted by a squadron of dragoons. He was dressed in a purple robe with golden tassels and behaved like a reigning monarch. He spent his last years in Rome, where he was as well known as he was in London and Dublin.

Derry has had a wonderful past. Today spread out far beyond the ancient walls it preserves the air of a frontier city and something of a siege mentality. Tension is there and an acute feeling of neglect by authority, but Derrymen are tenacious and face the future with the old spirit of, 'No Surrender!'

Bound for Kenmare
Fred Hoyle

I boarded a New York flight at London Airport. That was some years ago, in the days when trans-Atlantic flights nearly always put down at Shannon. It wasn't difficult to guess where the chap sat next to me was heading. Accoutred in the outlandish garb of the fisherman, he carried a great bundle or rods, as an archer might carry his quiver of arrows. Sure enough my companion was making for Kenmare. An hour later when the plane landed I watched him depart, a cheery grin stamped like a trademark across his face.

The plane fretted its way across the Atlantic. Within a few hours I would be enmeshed in the restless commotion of New York. Which is the true reality I wondered, the thrash and roar of traffic along crowded Manhattan avenues or the quiet Kenmare river with the splash of salmon making bright the pools? At that time my idea of an answer was ill-formed, but already I had the beginnings of a concept which has clarified itself over the intervening years. I mean the extent to which so many of us live today in a trash culture, a culture that encroaches more and more on worthwhile things in order to create an excessive affluence. Affluence is like food, too much of it leads to mental fat.

From the beginnings of such thoughts I passed to the memory of a great September in Kerry. It started with the mist down, as so many brilliantly coloured days do. We started from the house of Padraig Browne in Dunquin. The mist was lifting by the time we had crossed over to Dingle and were approaching Anascaul. Our immediate objective was the Ballaghisheen, because Paddy had never crossed it, whereas I had. Learning of this sad situation only a few days before, and feeling no doubt that an Englishman should never be permitted to stand where he had not on Irish soil, he instantly resolved to set the matter to rights. Hence our trip in his big Dodge, really too large for the narrow roads ahead of us.

200

We had a tough time of it getting through Killorglin, the streets being chock-a-block with cows. Is there anywhere else in the western world where a cow is judged more important than a car – at any rate on market day? Then on to Glencar, and so to our famous pass.

Paddy discoursed the while on Gaelic folklore. While he talked I determined some day to write an Irish story using one of the old tales as a basis. The following summer I did in fact carry this project through, and the book *Ossian's Ride* appeared in due course. By an odd inversion of locale the story was actually written in the Scottish Highlands, which I suppose explains why it came out as Ossian instead of Oisin. I remember checking the final manuscript with Paddy, and I well remember the gales of laughter with which he approved of Ireland becoming a technologically advanced country, with England hanging on a long way behind.

Down a long winding lane to Waterville, a detour into Ballinskelligs Bay, then over the Coomakesta, and a long stop at Derrynane. The colours lighting up the sea and sky had become overpowering, blue, white, green and gold. What is the physics of this colour business? A traveller from England on a grey day must feel that England is the brighter country, the Irish fields appear rather drab. Yet let the sun blaze out, and all is changed. The hitherto drab fields take on a brilliance which cannot to my knowledge be matched anywhere in the world. Why? The secret lies I suspect in the multitude of tiny water droplets always to be found in our humid atmosphere. Air blowing over the sea for hundreds of miles develops a uniformity – the droplets separate out according to their respective sizes. I think it must be this well-ordered air that really does the trick. Then after passing for a while over land the air becomes stirred and mixed by the time it reaches England – and the vivid colouring becomes weakened and frequently lost.

The day hadn't finished with us yet. After high tea in Kenmare, back once more to the Dingle peninsula. It was nearing sunset as we drove uphill from Ventry between long rows of red-berried trees. We didn't glimpse the vast clouds slashed across the western sky like a crimson canopy until we reached the hilltop above Dunquin. We stopped to gaze out over the sea until the last of light was gone.

I stumbled off the plane. Immigration and Customs loomed ahead, and after that – traffic, lots of it. But of course I exaggerate. We all know that big cities are fine, as long as you don't want to stop.

The Wexford Festival

Compton Mackenzie

It was in the early spring of 1951 that in response to an invitation from Dr T. J. Walsh I went over to Wexford to give a talk about operatic gramophone records. Dr Walsh was anxious to form a society for the enjoyment and study of opera through the medium of the gramophone.

My tongue always runs away with me when I am addressing an Irish audience because the Irish response to a speaker with the gift of the gab is such an unfailing encouragement. After I had talked in the old gaol, as I remember, I suddenly wondered why I had made that fierce crossing to Rosslare to persuade the people of Wexford to listen to gramophone records when they had a theatre in which the operas of Balfe had been performed in the town where they were composed. Why not revive a Balfe opera?

Two or three months later Dr Walsh wrote to tell me that there would be an opera festival in Wexford at the end of October of which I had been elected President and of which the Bishop of Ferns was to be the Patron. Appropriately the opera chosen to inaugurate the Wexford Festival was *The Rose of Castile* by M. W. Balfe, and I look back to that first production as a feat that I should hardly be exaggerating to call a miracle. Dr Walsh who had an impresario's ear and eye for a singer had persuaded even Italian singers to appear: the chorus consisted of the boys (and girls) of Wexford directed by a Franciscan friar. The authorities extended the hours in which spirits could be drunk until 3 a.m. It was the only real festival in Great Britain or Ireland.

In 1952 Donizetti's *L'Elisir d'Amore* was the opera, and the success of the first festival had so deeply impressed the town councillors of Wexford that the narrow streets were illuminated for the first time. How wise they were to appreciate the chance to bring that old theatre to life and rouse to enthusiasm audiences who had not applauded Italian opera in the Theatre Royal, Wexford for over a century. Dublin was still inclined to regard the Wexford Festival with an air of indulgent condescension but Dublin surrendered in 1954 and I had the pleasure of seeing the first opera train from Dublin arrive and hear the visitors welcomed by the Mayor and the town band. The opera that year was the enchanting *La Sonnambula* by Bellini. It was beautifully conducted by Bryan Balkwill and admirably produced by Peter Ebert.

The success of the 1954 Festival fired Dr Walsh and his aids and abetters to put on two operas for each future week of the Wexford Festival. By now, besides the opera in the Theatre Royal, there were opera films in the cinema, concerts by the Radio Éireann Symphony Orchestra, recitals of Chamber Music to which, as time went on, would be added Festival Forum when a panel of four speakers would stand up to the questions sent in by the audience, conducted tours round the lovely countryside, exhibitions of paintings, and even a Late Night Revue by the Dublin University Players.

But the greatest festival of all was the festival of talk that was continuous throughout the week. For me one of the many delights of Ireland is what always seems, and indeed what always is, the spontaneity of the occasion, whether it be talking about the world or driving a motor-car. Where else but in Ireland could one find oneself at four o'clock in the morning sitting up in an hotel room with a Franciscan friar, a pretty singer of folksong, and a university student discussing everything under the moon with a large melon for refreshment? Where else but in the very narrow streets of Wexford would it be unnecessary to have one way streets because all the drivers can see the other drivers' point of view?

Let me close with the message of greeting I have been honoured by being asked to send each year for the Wexford Festival, so wisely held in the last week of October when the weather of southern Eire can be so perfect. This was sent in 1966 from France:

> I always deeply regret it when I am unable to enjoy the Wexford Festival in person; this year I have an additional regret at my inability to be with you because I have never had the good fortune to hear either of the operas which are being given, and I have always particularly wanted to hear *Lucrezia Borgia.*
>
> I consider the Wexford Festival a most precious link between the past and the present, for there never has been a time in history when such a cultural link was not needed. I shall be with you in spirit and I hope that St Luke's little summer will bring you golden weather for your unique Festival.

Tyrone : the Rough Field

John Montague

The parish in which I was brought up lies in Tyrone, what a Belfast poet (John Hewitt) once called 'the heart land of Ulster'. A seventeenth century survey, on the other hand, describes it as 'cold mountainous land' which may explain why it escaped resettling at the time of the Plantation. Across the road from our house were the crumbling remains of stables, a halt on the old Dublin–Derry coach road. And with its largely Catholic population (MacRory, MacGirr, Farrel, Tague) Errigal Kieran could still be taken for a parish in Southern Ireland, artificially marooned. Most of the place names were pure Gaelic: Garvaghey (The Rough Field), Glencull (The Glen of the Hazels), Clogher (The Golden Stone). On a clear day, working at turf on the top mountain, one could see straight down to North Monaghan.

But there were defiant differences. The post-van which came down the road was royal-red, with a gold crown on either side. And the postman himself was an ex-Serviceman who remembered Ypres and the Somme, rather than 1916 or the Eighteenth day of November. In school we learnt the chief industries of Manchester, but very little about Cuchulainn or Connemara. And none of the farmers had enough Gaelic to translate the names of the townlands. A dark-faced fanatical priest tried to teach us some after school hours. I thought him a fear-

203

some bore until I greeted the last Gaelic speaker in the area after mass one Sunday, and saw the light flood across her face.

The ordinary life of the people, however, took little stock of racial or religious differences; they were submerged in a pre-industrial farming pattern, where the chief criterion was 'neighbourliness'. True, there were social differences which betrayed the historical cleavage. The depressed class of farm labourers were largely Catholic, just as the majority of the stronger farmers were Protestant. There were also the sexual fantasies which emerge when, as in the American South, two cultures rub uneasily together. Pedigree bulls were mainly owned by Protestants: indeed, there was a curious legend that Catholic bulls were rarely as potent. And when I went to fetch the local gelder for our young bulls, it seemed oddly appropriate that he should take down his cloth-covered weapon from beside a stack of black family bibles.

But in the seasonal tasks that pushed the wheel of the year the important thing was skill, based on traditional practice. Turf-cutting, which began in late spring, revealed all the instinctive layers of a craft. First there was the stripping of the bank, the rough sods being saved for the back of the fire. Then the three-man team moved in, one to cut (using the traditional slane or flanged spade), one to fill (grasping the wet turves in rows) and one to wheel (emptying the barrow sideways, so that the turf fell uncrushed, but open to the sun). At mealtime, they sat around the basket in a circle, their hobnailed boots shining with wet, and talked of great teams of the past.

But turf-cutting was not as delicate a task as building a stack. To begin, a circle of stones and whins was laid, 'to let the air in under her'. Upon this the stack rose, the builder riding with it, to catch and place the sheaves forked to him, until he slithered down to round the conical roof of thatch. One of our hands, slovenly enough in other ways, was held to be a master builder. In winter, when the thresher came, his stacks unpeeled in smooth slives, like an orange.

Such tasks determined the character of the people, hard-working, frugal, completely escaping the traditional view of the Celt. Kitchens were usually well lit, with a dresser of delph along one wall, a curtained settle bed in another, a shotgun or fiddle resting on a third. But the centre was the great blackened tent of the hearth, where the crook swung, supporting a hierarchy of pots and pans. From this fire to the dairy, with its meal bins and churns, the farmer's wife bustled, until the men came tramping in for their evening meal.

The hearth was also the focus of the strongest custom in Ulster farming communities, the habit of dropping in, for a visit or *ceilidh,* after milking time. One rarely knocked, your approach being heralded by the dog's bark, the shadow crossing the window. Sometimes a worn pack of cards was produced, for a game of 'twenty-five'. Sometimes a song was called for, but the district was not rich in balladry, except for a version of the north-country 'Barbary Allen' and one or two patriotic songs, like 'The Mountains of Pomeroy'.

It was at such times that one came closest to the secret life of the countryside. Starting from practical details, the chat drew a thick web of speculation over local affairs: who was 'failing fast', who was threatening 'the law' on some neighbour, who was going to give birth (inside or outside the blanket, a third of the children in the local school being illegitimate). Fact soon drowned in fancy: how so-and-so had broken his leg after ploughing down a fairy fort, how a B-Special's hair had turned white because he arrested a priest on his way to a dying man, how Father Mackey had put a poltergeist in a bottle.

For behind the flat surface of daily life beat memories of a more resonant past, now half-regretted, half-feared. When I was five I was brought to my first wake and remember the neat row of clay pipes beside the snuff and porter. But by the time I was going to secondary school my aunt had given up plaiting the rushy St Brigid's Crosses which used to hang over the lintel in kitchen and byre. Even barn dances had become a thing of the past, although I made the last one in the Fintona area famous when, climbing to get a swig of poteen from the local fiddler, I fell straight through the loft into a nest of squealing pigs.

For a long time Carleton's Tyrone survived in the remote areas, under the shadow of the mountains, but since the war, the rate of change has become relentless. The replacing of the hearth fire by a stove dealt a blow not merely to turf-cutting and breadmaking (most farmers' wives now buy shop bread) but also to the practice of ceilidhing. The battery wireless was an endearing faulty messenger from outside, but with the arrival of electric light and television the Rough Field has become a part of the twentieth century. The old coach-road is now a magnificent highway, running straight as a die through the built-up valley. The public-house, surrounded by cars, looks like a roadhouse; the shop sells ice-cream to children from the pre-fabricated village where the road workers and lorry drivers (formerly farm labourers) live.

But one must avoid seeing all this through a haze of nostalgia. The last time I was back I was talking to a strong farmer in his byre. Behind us the milking-machine hummed, the pans and cylinders swaying under the cow's udder. He was lamenting the decline of neighbourliness, how farming had become mechanized, how the young had no time for anything but cars and dancehalls. Then a smile crossed his face, and he described how the oldest crone in the district had come down to see his television set. 'She had a stick in either hand, and her bent over like a hoop. She came into the kitchen – we had to pull back the dogs off her – and she said she be to see the picture box. She sat in front of it for an hour and then rose to go, saying that a wee man you could turn on like that would be a great comfort on a cold winter's night.'

Tourism

Basil Peterson

In the early 'sixties a very remarkable film entitled 'Yeats Country' and produced by Patrick Carey was seen in many countries. A survey in colour of that part of County Sligo associated with the life and works of the poet W. B. Yeats, it introduced thousands of people to that range of delicate shading, subtle colour contrasts and misty profiles against a high lucent sky which entrance the newcomer to this small but variegated land.

These are the eternal qualities which make Ireland such an attraction for visitors and no one who has seen the purple mantle hover over a Wicklow glen at the fall of a summer's night or who has heard the intense silence of a lonely western bog can fail to be moved by their sheer contrast to the tumultuousness of urban civilisation.

But this is not all for, in these heady times, nothing, not even the face of the land, remains the same for long. People change and, in doing so, change the land on which they live. Too often they destroy rather than improve and regard a momentary profit or convenience as better than the perpetuation of lasting values. This situation is now being faced in Ireland where, through deliberate official encouragement, tourism has become our largest single export.

The growth of tourism in Ireland during the past ten years has been almost phenomenal. It started in a small way after the Second World War when the hungry British came to Ireland for better and more varied food and, in doing so, discovered the attraction of the land and its people. It grew steadily during the years in which continental Europe was licking its war wounds, but in the late 'fifties a point was reached when the growing facilities and counter-attractions of continental Europe – now eagerly seeking tourists – began to drain away the number of tourists coming from Britain. Something had to be done.

It was realized that tourism had become a highly organized business, that the attractions of the land had to be sold to visitors in their own homes and that standards of accommodation and recreational facilities had to be improved. A country which had a reputation – not fully deserved but certainly not wholly undeserved – for a lackadaisical approach to life and a carefree attitude to the maintenance of accepted standards of living had to organize itself to cater adequately for the visitors which it sought while at the same time preserving those attractions which brought the tourist to its shores.

The organization and promotion of tourism was placed in the hands of a new state-subsidized body, Bórd Fáilte Éireann – the Irish Tourist Board – and this body was provided with funds for the purpose of advertising Ireland abroad and of stimulating development at home by the grading and registering of hotels and guest houses and by making funds available for capital development and improvement.

For a while all went well until two new factors intruded. It was found that Bórd Fáilte Éireann, an urban body, was insufficient in organization and in staff to keep properly in touch with the more remote parts of the country – and these the most dependent on tourism – and with the small tourist bodies which were trying to develop their own localities. As with all centralized organizations, it cost the small man a lot of time and trouble to get his demands through and his requirements met.

Then, in the early 'sixties, came the age of the motorist. Quite suddenly more and more people in western Europe became car owners and began searching desperately for road space on which to enjoy a holiday. The roads of Britain, and especially of England, had become so crowded that motoring for pleasure became almost impossible and British motorists turned with delight to the only country left in western Europe which could offer carefree motoring, through entrancing scenery, on an extensive road network possessing a density of only six cars to the mile. This has become, perhaps, the most popular form of holiday in Ireland, since it is now easy for motorists to hire cars if they do not want to ship their own. Aer Lingus, for example, with its frequent flights to Dublin, Cork or Shannon from points in England and Scotland, makes a wide variety of holiday arrangements which include the provision of a car from the moment of arrival. The motorists pouring into Ireland every summer have made entirely new demands on accommodation and services.

These two factors compelled a drastic revision of Irish tourism organization as it then existed and in 1964 a sweeping change was introduced. The territory of the Republic was divided into eight tourist regions – of which the City of Dublin constituted one – and in each of these regions a professional manager was installed with the necessary staff and supported by a Board of Directors representative of local tourist interests and of local governmental bodies. At the same time local authorities were given legal power to allocate a portion of their rates to the new regional bodies. Bórd Fáilte Éireann remained the central tourist body charged with advertising abroad, the grading of accommodation and the making of capital grants for tourist development. Its representative sat on all the regional boards.

The immediate effect of this reorganization was quite remarkable. Instead of having to deal with a remote body in Dublin people dependent on tourism now possessed a tourist authority in their own region which existed specifically for the development of tourism in that region and to which access was immediately available. The young managers appointed went about their work with remarkable fervour and, despite initial handicaps and an ingrained reluctance on the part of some people to respond to the new stimulus, succeeded in quite a short time in gaining the co-operation of the majority of the people in their region and in infusing a new spirit and interest in tourism in areas where it had previously been regarded as of little or no importance.

The physical geography of Ireland has always had an effective influence on tourist development. In the old days the traditional tourist areas were those parts of the country – mainly in its western half – where, if the scenery was beautiful, the people were impoverished. These areas needed tourists in order to give to their inhabitants an increased income and so raise their standard of living, and the very fact that these people followed an outmoded but colourful way of life made them, as well as the land from which they gained an inadequate living, attractive to those coming from the great urban complexes of Europe and North America.

The seeking out by visitors of these traditional tourist areas was all to the good but it was realized that the midland and eastern areas of the country possessed their own attractions: attractions which had been largely overlooked in the past. The introduction of regional management revived interest in the development of these other areas and both the rich farming counties of the east – which had hitherto ignored the possibilities of tourism – and the flat bogland counties of the midlands became aware that they too had much to offer the visitor and much to gain from him.

The midland counties, a region of lakes and sluggish rivers, found a small gold mine in the variety and number of both game and coarse fish which could be found in their waterways, and their possession of the greater part of the Shannon river brought to them an ever-increasing number of pleasure craft seeking on unfrequented rivers and lakes that outlet which the visiting motorist sought on the Irish roads. Not only British but also continental Europeans now come in increasing numbers to fish and to cruise on waters which are both extensive and unpolluted and which offer a welcome contrast to the conditions which they encounter in their own countries.

At the same time, in the farming counties of the east, another new tourist outlet appeared. In these regions, apart from some long-established seaside resorts, tourism was almost wholly disregarded and, in the beginning, local authorities proved more than reluctant to subscribe in any adequate manner to the regional coffers. It took patient persuasion and much time to demonstrate to them that the tourist cake was not cut entirely in favour of the west and that they and their

208

Roads empty enough to allow you to look at the landscape
(top: *the Twelve Bens, Co Galway), and a haunting past*
(bottom: *churchyard at Aghador, overlooking Killarney, Co Kerry*)

countryside had much to offer to the visitor who preferred a rolling land of lake and wood to the wilder and more barren vistas of the west. This attitude was reinforced when it was discovered that the modern tourist, again seeking to escape from the artificialities of urban living, preferred to live with and among local people rather than subject himself to the standardized conveniences of hotels. Thus the farmhouse holiday came into being and, especially in the richer farmland areas, proliferated.

Bórd Fáilte Éireann have encouraged the farmhouse holiday but rightly insist on certain basic standards of accommodation and services. These are more readily available in the eastern part of the country than in the more impoverished west and so the people of the eastern parts have found a new source of revenue in their farms and the housewives have gained an outlet for new human contacts. Even in the west, however, the farmhouse holiday has caught on and grants are available to those willing to improve their houses to the required standard of sanitation and comfort.

This, the farmhouse holiday, is but one aspect of the expanding variety of Irish tourism. Both public and private monies have been expended over a large range of building and improvement running from luxury hotels to small farmhouses. In addition, the year 1965 saw the introduction of probably the most ambitious and certainly the most successful activity of the new dispensation. It was realized that the new mobile visitor – usually touring with his family – would need accommodation in a number of places during his tour and that he would soon become disillusioned with his holiday if, on arriving somewhere in the evening, he was compelled to spend tiring hours in a search for accommodation.

To counter this a network of Information Offices – more than a hundred of them – was set up throughout the territory of the Republic. These, linked to each other by telephone, provided not only the standard tourist information regarding their locality but also a room reservation service by the use of which the visitor could obtain accommodation not only in the locality of the Information Office but even further on, at the place which he intended to reach that day. Every port of entry into the country now has its Information Office and the visitor can, if he is so inclined, be fed from there into a smoothly-operating system which will cater for his needs during his stay in the country. So successful, and necessary, has this service turned out to be that the number of Information Offices was increased for 1966 and will undoubtedly continue to grow.

Popular response, both financial and emotional, to the establishment of the new regional organizations has tended to follow a geographical line from west to east. In the west, where people are only too fully aware of what tourism means to their standards of living, the response was enthusiastic and financially satisfactory. As one moved east,

209

The round tower at Ardmore, Co Waterford: an architectural development unique to Ireland

however, the response lessened and reached its nadir in the City of Dublin; itself a designated tourist region.

One would have to be well steeped in Irish history and politics to obtain a grasp of the influences which dictate the attitude of the city and people of Dublin to the rest of the country. *Sui generis* might well be the motto of Dublin when one contemplates it vis-à-vis the rest of Ireland. It is the capital of the nation, it draws its increasing population and most of its revenues from the countryside and, unlike such cities as Copenhagen which are economic entities in themselves, it would wither away without the food, the trade and the money which rural Ireland pours into it. Yet, Dublin has an unhappy knack of, at times, dissociating itself from the rest of the nation and of assuming that its specific requirements should override anything to the benefit of the country as a whole.

In the tourist context, Dublin has not only made available for tourist purposes a smaller percentage of money than any other region; it has also sought, for its own selfish reasons, to destroy a tourist amenity which is the property of the whole country and which is developing a steadily increasing tourist income.

From the Port of Dublin the Grand Canal runs across the centre of Ireland to the Shannon and, on the way, puts out a branch to the River Barrow, thus giving access to the Waterford and Wexford river systems. This canal is the vital feeder of the whole Irish inland waterway system as increasing numbers of British cruising craft cross the Irish Sea to Dublin in order to gain access to the Shannon and its lakes. Dublin however, with a lofty disregard for what is of benefit to the rest of the country, has attempted to close that portion of the canal which passes through the city and to replace it by a roadway overlaying a sewer.

Happily this destructive scheme had not yet been carried out and a growing resistance to it which has been strengthened by an increasing awareness of the overall benefits of preserving the canal, may yet prevent this piece of economic vandalism.

It could be emphasized that the tree-lined canal, in its passage through the city, provides a scene of quiet beauty in stark contrast to the concrete jungle growing about it. It provides a haven, a resort and a place of rest for people of all ages and a playground for the young. Aesthetics, however, is a word almost unknown to the administrators of modern Dublin. Their obsession with concrete and with the hollow attractions of the new architecture is matched only by their lack of understanding of true architectural qualities and by their willingness to allow the indiscriminate destruction of buildings which made Dublin the beautiful city it once was.

In an age when, in other parts of Europe, the people of war-ravaged cites have painstakingly and at considerable expense restored their ancient buildings, stone by stone, the people of Dublin have rejected their own city and have actively contributed to its destruction. Modern Dublin displays a tasteless new gaudiness on the one hand and, on the other, a crumbling beauty both misunderstood and rejected by people whose values are strictly commercial. As a tourist attraction Dublin is fast turning into a concrete desert surmounted here and there by plaques to inform the visitor of the beauty that once was there.

If aesthetic ignorance and greed for gain have been successful in bringing about the continuing destruction of Dublin's beauty, the twin bogies of politics and sectarianism have been equally successful in inhibiting normal and proper tourist development in the Six Counties which constitute Northern Ireland. In this area, politically a part of the United Kingdom, the predominant political party has spent some forty years emphasizing the connection with Britain and endeavouring to establish its distinctiveness from the rest of Ireland. It has created a tourist organization, the Northern Ireland Tourist Board, but this body's functions have been distorted to serve political requirements. As a result both the organization and facilities provided for tourists lag sadly behind those of the Republic.

Before the onset of the motoring age Northern Ireland possessed a number of well-established tourist resorts which drew most of their visitors from Scotland and northern England. These resorts were in the eastern part of the territory and what tourist effort there was was largely concentrated upon them, to the neglect of the attractions of the lakeland area of County Fermanagh to the west. In Fermanagh the politico-sectarian pattern was that of the minority and its comparative neglect by the ruling majority was in accordance with customary procedure.

However, with the introduction of a car-ferry service between Larne and Stranraer in Scotland and a consequent large increase in the numbers of motoring tourists, Northern Ireland had to take a second look at the tourist scene. Two new factors compelled this. In the first place it became very evident that, despite the emphasis on things British and the attempt to hold the Republic at a distance, Ireland, in the tourist sense, was one. Then it also became obvious that the area of Northern Ireland was too small to hold the motoring visitor for more than a day or two. In fact, a very large percentage of the cars which crossed to Northern Ireland did so only in order to move on to the tourist areas of the Republic.

This being recognized, and despite the opposition of those who held everything republican in abhorrence, the practical decision was taken to co-operate with the Republic for tourist purposes. Ireland, as a tourist land, was to be sold abroad as a unit and exchanges of facilities and co-operation across the border were arranged. These arrangements were of more benefit to Northern Ireland than to the Republic and it

211

might have been expected that the North would have introduced the Republic's highly organized tourist services. However, the political pressures remained, with the result that, while Northern Ireland benefits from Bórd Fáilte Éireann's wide and well-organized publicity campaigns abroad, its internal organization lags behind. It has no organized system of Information Offices and Room Reservation services and instead utilizes, for this purpose, the services of local commercial tourist agents. These people, being engaged in a business enterprise, cannot and do not offer the same wide-ranging facilities as do the non-commercial Information Offices across the border. This system reaches the height of futility in the appointment, in certain towns, of two tourist agents, each representative of one or the other of the two political and sectarian groups.

In all fairness it should be emphasized that tourism is by no means the most important of Northern Ireland's industries. In fact, it lies well down on the list, but it could blossom if ancient prejudices were removed and monies and development applied solely in accordance with legitimate tourist requirements.

The land of Ireland, and the beauty of that land, does not change because of an artificial frontier and north-east Ulster possesses attractions equal to those in the rest of Ulster on the other side of the border. Despite antiquated licensing laws which make Sundays periods of minor deprivation for the modern tourist, and despite internal divisions, Northern Ireland shares with the rest of Ireland that beauty of land and kindliness of people which makes Ireland so attractive to the visitor and which emphasizes the essential unity of the island.

Ireland in now at a particularly critical point in its tourist development. The new regional organizations have established themselves; steady improvements in the provision of accommodation, in catering, in roadmaking and in the supply of services are being made and there is every likelihood that more and more motorists will come to the country as the car-ferry services expand. The overall picture is bright although one unfortunate development has been the rapid increase in charges of all sorts. This has been brought about mainly by an increase in the cost of labour and has resulted in Irish costs being equal to, and in some cases higher, than those in Britain. This situation has deterred some British visitors but the concurrent increase in the motoring public in Britain has produced sufficient new tourists to offset the loss.

The critical point hinges on the pattern of future tourist development. Tourism is not an unmixed blessing and, if not carefully watched and controlled, can become subject to the law of diminishing returns. Basically examined, tourism is an organized attempt to 'sell' the attractions of land and people to visitors so that the former can raise their standard of living. Luckily enough, in Ireland the most impoverished parts of the country are those which possess the finest scenic grandeur and so the tourists' money goes more or less directly to those who most need it. However, the very process of raising standards of living through tourist revenue has the effect of changing the habits of the people and so reducing their natural attraction. Added to this is the fact that increased income leads the people to reject their previous standards of life and accommodation and to replace them by others which, if superficially an improvement, only too often imply the loss of those attitudes and values which gave the people their colour, their dignity and their strength.

This effect has been most notable on the western seaboard where, for centuries, men and women endured a hardy existence while preserving their native mode of dress and speaking their own language. These people offered the visitor a unique view into another harsher but more colourful world. They themselves proved to be as attractive as the wild rugged land on which they lived but their reaction to the flow of tourist money was, if very human, unthinkingly destructive. Wishing to appear as others do, they shed their distinctive dress and aped the fashions of the urban world; wishing to communicate, they allowed the English-speaking tourist to intrude upon their native language; wishing to enjoy the concrete benefits of modern living, they shed the old and took the new without a full understanding of the values which gave to the new its proper substance.

There are phases, human phases, in tourist development. In Ireland the early stage is still with us. Other tourist countries, which have had a longer history of catering for visitors, have gone through the later phases in which, in order to attract people whose desire is to escape from the deadening uniformity of urban and industrial life, they have had deliberately to reintroduce forms of dress, regional customs and national usages in order to provide that contrast and variety now so eagerly sought. These are not artificial creations, merely the revival of real things once thoughtlessly shed in the rush to conformity.

We in Ireland have still to reach these later phases and if there is in the country what may almost be described as a national 'complex' about escape from a 'peasant' background we at least have the lessons of these other countries to guide us. A good deal of wisdom and much persuasion will be needed to lead people into a path of tourist development which can enrich them not only in monetary terms but also in terms of those cultural and national values which give them their strength, their identity and their pride. It is not the heritage of a 'peasant' background which can destroy a people; it is the uncritical rush into a faceless uniformity.

Architecture : Before 1850

Maurice Craig

The basic fact about architecture in Ireland since 1660 is that only in the middle of the seventeenth century was a condition of relative political stability, and hence of urban growth, achieved. The cost of that stability in humanitarian and cultural terms is not here our concern. To a large extent the situation then established and maintained for the next two centuries was a colonial situation. In other words, those who built towns and country houses were doing so *tabula rasa,* to almost the same degree as their contemporaries in Virginia or in the Sweden of Queen Christina or in the Russia of Peter the Great.

Only the oldest Irish towns contain, in their small-scale and usually insignificant nuclei, any vestige of their mediaeval configuration. Even the old coastal towns – Cork, Waterford, Limerick, Wexford, Galway, Carrickfergus or Carlingford – contain few visible mediaeval buildings; and nearly always the effective modern centre lies to one side, on a larger scale and often embellished with one or two public buildings of the eighteenth or early nineteenth century, which generally enjoy a situation equal to, and sometimes in excess of, their merits as buildings.

The same is even truer of the inland towns. In nearly every case they originated either as river-crossings, e.g. Athlone, Enniskillen, Clonmel or Carlow, or as purely colonial settlements, e.g. Portarlington, Mountmellick, Maryborough, Tullamore or Birr, and of course the regular towns founded by the London companies in the Plantation of Ulster, such as Coleraine, Limavady, Dungannon or Monaghan. In all cases, even if not founded for the purpose, these towns came soon to serve the traditional function which is Gaelic Ireland's principal contribution to the concept of the town – the holding of periodic fairs for the exchange of produce. Eighteenth-century directories list about 2,700 fairs a year, an average of about eight a day all over the country.

This aspect of the town's function is directly reflected in two of the most obvious characteristics of Irish towns – the breadth of their streets and squares, and the abundance of small shops, especially of those which are also public-houses. Irish towns, especially inland, often have a grandeur of layout which belies their small population.

Between these towns is a network of roads which likewise give the stranger the impression of being unexpectedly large in scale for a thinly populated country, even allowing for the fact that a century and a half ago Ireland had twice as many people as she has today. They have even been mistaken for Roman roads. They are in fact the Grand Jury roads made by the barony authorities, that is to say the landlords of the country, during the late eighteenth and early nineteenth centuries, and are thus a characteristically colonial undertaking.

Remarkably few of the important pre-Norman ecclesiastical centres are still important towns. Clonard has disappeared. Clonmacnoise is a graveyard, Clonfert a hamlet, Cashel hardly more than a largeish village. Armagh and Kilkenny are still considerable towns, perhaps the most attractive of their size in the country, but their histories since the end of the middle ages have diverged very significantly. Armagh was repeatedly burned during the wars of the sixteenth century, and by the opening of the eighteenth was derelict and largely deserted. It had lain outside the English pale, and though it kept its titular importance as the ecclesiastical capital, the archbishops lived elsewhere. Kilkenny, by contrast, was the seat of the great house of Butler who kept the kings' peace in their palatinate, and throughout the sixteenth and seventeenth centuries it remained a provincial centre of political and strategic importance. Both towns prospered in the eighteenth century. But whereas Armagh's prosperity dates only from the archbishopric of Robinson (1765 onwards), that of Kilkenny is a natural continuation of its existing importance. In consequence, while Armagh can show virtually no mediaeval buildings, it consists visibly of two parts: the ancient hill with its (much-restored) cathedral in the centre of a concentric system faithfully reflecting the shape of the ancient hill-fort, and, beside and below it, a more or less rectilinear eighteenth-century development on quite a large scale. Kilkenny, on the other hand, is basically a straight line, parallel to the river Nore, with the ancient hill and cathedral at one end, and the Castle of the Ormonde Butlers at the other. Half way between them is the town's principal eighteenth-century building, the Tholsel of 1761. A number of late mediaeval buildings survive, and where there was eighteenth-century development it took place mostly within the older framework.

Kilkenny excels even Dublin in its visible continuity of life, well exemplified by its possession of one of the earliest fully classical buildings in the country: the great Corinthian gateway to the Ormonde Castle, built in the 1660s.

Before the advent of true classicism such buildings as the large cubical semi-fortified house called Portumna Castle (1612) had shown the way. A quarter of a century later Strafford's unfinished Jigginstown Palace, near Naas, a large-windowed horizontally spread Jacobean building, exceptionally in brick, was something of a prodigy and a false start. By the 1660s compact wide-eaved houses in the Anglo-Dutch manner were being built: a survivor is Beaulieu near the mouth of the Boyne in

Co Louth, and the now ruined house of Eyrecourt in Co Galway was unusually rich in craftsmanship.

In the capital itself, the architectural first fruits of the Carolean settlement was the Royal Hospital at Kilmainham, by Sir William Robinson the Surveyor-General, strongly French-influenced, copied in function and in form (though reduced in scale) from the Invalides, and itself shortly to serve as a model for Chelsea Hospital.

At the same time the final shape of Dublin, with its open quays on both sides of the river Liffey, was initially fixed, though the seventeenth-century developments were still on a small scale. As Dublin developed it relied increasingly on imported as well as local brick except for public buildings which continued to be built of stone. Rubble stone, usually rendered with lime-plaster, was the usual material for building in the country and provinces, with tamped clay or turf for the humbler buildings except where, as in the west, loose stone was plentiful. If there were ever timber-framed buildings in Ireland, as no doubt there were, the unsettled state of the country and the systematic destruction of the forests in the sixteenth century have obliterated that tradition.

Two great buildings stand at the head of Irish eighteenth-century architecture: one a country house, the other a public building. Both are closely associated with one man: the immensely rich William Conolly who became Speaker of the Irish Parliament in 1715. His huge country house, Castletown, near Celbridge in Co Kildare, was begun in about 1720 and was externally complete by 1732. The probable architect of the central block was the Italian Alessandro Galilei, while part of the interior and probably the whole of the wings were designed by the young Irish Surveyor-General, Sir Edward Lovett Pearce. At the same time, from 1728 onwards, the new Parliament House in Dublin was built, designed and supervised till his death in 1733 by Pearce. As enlarged by Gandon and others later in the century, and adapted by Francis Johnston for the Bank of Ireland after the Union, it still stands, as does Castletown. Together they signalize the victory of Palladianism.

Another great Dublin building of this early epoch, the Library of Trinity College, by Pearce's predecessor Thomas Burgh, is more French than Palladian in inspiration. Nothing on such a large scale was to be attempted in Dublin again until the fresh burst of prosperity in the 1780s.

In the meantime country house building gathered volume. Pearce's practice initiated with Cashel Palace, Bellamont Forest, Co Cavan, and Drumcondra House, fell, at his early death in 1733, into the hands of his trusted German-born assistant Richard Castle, who built a long series of country houses among which Carton, Russborough, Summerhill (now destroyed) and Powerscourt may be mentioned. In Dublin itself Castle built Tyrone House, Leinster House (seat of the modern parliament) and the Rotunda Hospital.

It is noteworthy that Irish country houses, from the very smallest up to the largest, follow Palladio's practice in incorporating the working farm-buildings within the formal symmetrical layout of centre and wings, a practice which, though theoretically recommended, was rarely if ever carried out in England. External severity, and opulence of plaster decoration within, is generally characteristic of Irish houses, whether in country or town.

The middle of the eighteenth century saw the growth of the eastern quarters of Dublin, both north and south of the river, by the harmonious development of the three or four great estates, in a system of large squares and wide streets, fortified from 1757 onwards by the control of the Wide Streets Commissioners. Symmetrical terrace schemes are in general absent, unlike the practice in London, Edinburgh or Bath. The houses were generally built in groups of two or three, subject to an approximate uniformity overall.

Among the finest country houses of the early period is Mount Ievers, Co Clare, by the Limerick architect, John Rothery. Built in 1736, it has great scale and the uncompromising cubical emphasis found in Trinity Library and Castletown. Like Cashel Palace it has one front of stone contrasted with one of brick; and the neighbouring village of Sixmile-bridge has a neat layout of about the same date. Also in the Limerick area was John Aheron, who worked for Lord Inchiquin in the 1740s and wrote the first architectural book of Irish authorship, *A General Treatise of Architecture,* printed in Dublin in 1754. There have not been many since.

The Piedmontese architect and engineer Davis Ducart (Daviso de Arcort) all of whose work lies far from the capital, came to Ireland in about 1760 and was occupied partly in mining and canal-engineering, and partly in architecture. His finest house is Castletown (Cox) near Carrick-on-Suir, for Archbishop Cox of Cashel (about 1770): it has an elaborate and unusual layout, as has the sister house of Kilshannig, Co Cork, built for a Cork Alderman in 1766. Other works by Ducart include the Cork Mansion House and the Custom House at Limerick, and probably also the wings of Florencecourt, Co Fermanagh. His style was, for the time, somewhat on the archaic side. He died soon after 1780.

The amateur architect Nathaniel Clements (d. 1777) is of less distinction, and best known for his Phoenix Lodge (now in altered form the President's House), though if Colganstown, Co Dublin and New-berry, Co Kildare are indeed his also, and still more if he is rightly credited with Belview, Co Cavan, he exemplifies the Irish ability to combine the Palladian formula with traditional rubble-and-roughcast finishes for farmhouses of very modest size. The same is true in greater measure of Thomas Ivory from Cork, whose exemplary farm layout at Kilcarty, Co Meath, is balanced by his elaborately refined King's Hospital School in Dublin and his neo-classic Newcomen's Bank near

Dublin Castle. Ivory's earliest known work is the fine bridge over the Blackwater at Lismore (1759). Other fine bridges of the period are by G. Smith of Kilkenny and by members of the Semple family (Graiguenamanagh and the vanished Essex Bridge in Dublin). The Dublin architect John Smyth was an accomplished Palladian and built the Provost's House, Dublin (1759), two notable Dublin churches (St Catherine's, 1769, and St Thomas's, destroyed, 1758), as well as the Poolbeg Lighthouse in Dublin Bay (1762).

The same period saw the earliest surviving post-Reformation Catholic churches, St Finbarr's South in Cork (1763) and St Patrick's, Waterford (before 1764). Their architects are unknown, as is that of the elaborately splendid but little-known Wilson's Hospital School at Multyfarnham, Co Westmeath (about 1775). The Waterford architect John Roberts built both the Protestant and the Catholic Cathedrals in Waterford at about the same time, an indication of how far conditions had by then improved.

The arrival of the great English-born architect James Gandon in Dublin in 1781 marks the opening of the most brilliant phase in the embellishment of the capital. The tradition on to which his achievement was grafted was already in being: beside Pearce's Parliament House of 1728 stood the West Front of Trinity College (Keene and Sanderson, 1752–9). At the other end of Dame Street, close to the Castle, the Royal Exchange (now the City Hall) had been built by Thomas Cooley, the winner of an open architectural competition in 1769; and across the river the first office block in Dublin, Cooley's Public Offices on Inns Quay, were already rising. As remodelled by Gandon, they were to become the west wing of the majestic Four Courts which, like Gandon's other major masterpiece, the Custom House (1781–91), fronts directly on to the river and so dominates a great stretch of the Quays.

It was during Gandon's time that the Wide Streets Commissioners widened what is now Lower O'Connell Street to accord with the great width of Gardiner's Mall (Upper O'Connell Street) and to reach the river. The bridge, which in rebuilt form survives as the present O'Connell Bridge, was also designed by Gandon, and he was consultant architect to the Commissioners when, in the 1790s, they cleared away much mean and aimless small-scale development to make the 'v' of two great streets which converge on the bridge from the south. On the more important of these two, Westmoreland Street, Gandon built the eastward extensions to Pearce's Parliament House, and very soon afterwards similar extensions for the Commons were built on the west side. Gandon, who lived in or near Dublin for the rest of his life, rounded off his contribution to the city with the King's Inns (1795–1808).

This activity was largely conditioned by two factors: the increased prosperity of agriculture and industry (it was during these years that the foundations of the prosperity of Guinness's Brewery were laid), and

the increased concentration of social and political life in Dublin following on the achievement by the Irish Parliament under Henry Grattan of
a degree of independence. Few great country houses were built in this
period, but town houses, such as Powerscourt House in South William
Street, were. The landed proprietors did, however, set afoot elegant
schemes for the improvement or even creation of the country towns.
Sometimes, as at Westport, Co Mayo, Mitchelstown, Co Cork, Birr,
Co Offaly, they prospered: sometimes, as at Stratford-on-Slaney, Co
Wicklow, they were still-born and survive only as 'ghost towns': sometimes, as with that which might have been the finest of all, Gandon's
New Geneva in Co Waterford (1782–4), they were barely begun. One
of them, Belfast, laid out by the Marquess of Donegal in the 1780s as
a grid surrounding a handsome Linen Hall, developed in the next
century into Ireland's principal industrial city.

The Grand Canal, which linked Dublin to the Shannon in 1804
having been begun in 1756, left its architectural impress on towns which
still prosper, such as Tullamore and Monasterevan, as well as on
Shannon harbour which has long been derelict. Other towns such as
Clonmel and Newry, and of course Limerick and Cork, Galway and
Sligo, have fine old eighteenth-century warehouses reflecting the volume
of waterborne trade.

During the first thirty years of the nineteenth century many of the
country towns were adorned with handsome classical courthouses, by
such architects as Gandon, Francis Johnston, William Farrell, John
Bowden and, most notably, the Morrisons. Richard Morrison, the son
of a Cork architect, took his own son William Vitruvius into partnership, and their more notable courthouses include those at Carlow (perhaps the finest) Dundalk, Tralee and Galway. That at Armagh is by
Francis Johnston: that at Cork by George Richard Pain. Their function
was to house not only the Courts but also the Grand Juries, which were
the nearest approach to local government that Ireland possessed until
the Act of 1898. Minor municipal buildings, sometimes of considerable
charm and nearly always well-sited, are numerous in this period, often
in association with tree-planted 'malls' or squares.

Francis Johnston and Richard Morrison largely divided between them
the spoils of the renewed wave of country house building between the
Union of 1800 and the Great Famine of 1847. A few of these houses
were classical (Townley Hall by Johnston, Ballyfin by Morrison), but
most were in revived mediaeval styles (Charleville Castle, Tullamore by
Johnston, Kilruddery, near Bray by Morrison). The Irish castellated
houses of this period have a peculiar flavour to which the closest
parallels are in Scotland among the followers of Adam.

Also in the first third of the century come the fine classical Catholic
churches of Patrick Byrne (St Audoens, St Paul's etc.) and the remarkable Protestant 'gothic' churches of John Semple (the 'Black Church',

Monkstown, Rathmines) in Dublin and others in the provinces. Francis Johnston's contribution to Dublin included the GPO in O'Connell Street and St George's Church with its crescent and radiating streets. Johnston died in 1829; Morrison ten years later.

In the provinces new reputations were rising: Lanyon in Belfast, Deane and Woodward in Cork. Pugin and Ashlin and J. J. McCarthy were building Catholic churches as the fruits of Emancipation (1829) began to be manifest in the countryside. Dublin began to stagnate: though the Union did not immediately produce the expected fall in population and wealth, in time the Famine did. Before that, however, the coming of the railways had given Dublin her last notable monuments in the classical tradition: Kingsbridge Station by Sancton Wood (1845), Broadstone Station by J. S. Mulvany (1850) and Harcourt Street Station by George Wilkinson (1859). The tradition of two centuries had come to an end.

Racing

Niall Sheridan

In Ireland, what used to be called the sport of kings is the bond which cements a vast, colourful and heterogeneous democracy – the vivid world of owners, trainers, jockeys, punters, tipsters and the racing public. The breeding, training and racing of horses is an important industry, an endless topic of conversation, almost a national obsession. Among a race of fervent individualists, hippomania is a great unifying force cutting clean across all social, cultural and economic barriers. It may be significant that while thousands of punters regularly put a half-crown on a horse, Ireland is the only country in the world which, in designing its official currency, has put a horse on a half-crown.

I was reared in the great horse-breeding area of County Meath and the exploits of famous local horses were part of the folklore of my childhood. Steeplechasing was the main topic of the endless discussions which centred around pedigrees and bloodlines, riding tactics, training methods and recollections of memorable races, often relived stride by stride and fence by fence. Interest in the sport was, of course, practical as well as academic, and I well remember how I first experienced the impact of the racing world on our own household in a curious little domestic drama.

Three days before the Grand National of 1928, my mother and two lady visitors, over tea and seed-cake, took the notion of having a collective flutter and went into close consultation over their selection. Unencumbered by any expert knowledge of the subject, their minds were open to other helpful influences from outer space.

We had at that time, among our canine menage, a scruffy mongrel terrier, given to us by a Tipperary cousin. He had been christened 'Tim' – a studied insult to Tim Healy because of his betrayal of Parnell. This pointed firmly to Tipperary Tim as the probable winner. My aunt, a strong supporter of the temperance movement, approved of the initials 'TT'. And the matter was clinched when one of the visitors noted that the horse was to be ridden by a man called Dutton – this being the maiden name of her maternal grandmother.

In these circumstances, the selection of Tipperary Tim was logical – indeed, inevitable. The total investment of the syndicate (or consortium, as it might nowadays be called) was fifteen shillings, and it was decided that the placing of the commission should be entrusted to Bartley, the gardener and general handyman, a recognized expert on Turf matters.

He, in his turn, acted with a more rational logic. As a keen student of racing form, he could scarcely approve of a bunch of crazy women throwing money away on a rank outsider that seemed to have about as much of a chance as a snowball in hell. So he decided to hold the bet himself and let the matter drop.

There was great jubilation among the ladies when Tipperary Tim – the only horse left standing out of forty-two starters – won at 100 to 1, but everything turned to gloom when it was found that Bartley had disappeared. It was rumoured that he had found it necessary to make an urgent visit to a distant cousin and that he had taken to his bed with an unspecified ailment. At any rate, like a guilty bureaucrat pursued by the Press, he remained unavailable for comment. But all was forgiven in the end, though the name of Tipperary Tim had for long afterwards the power to inject a chilly pause into the liveliest discussion.

In that lush Meath countryside, which has bred so many famous jumpers, the Grand National was an inexhaustible topic. As the days grew shorter, friends and neighbours would drop in, and around the fire in the parlour there would be the tinkle of glasses and the gurgle of pouring whiskey. As the early dusk thickened over the sleeping fields outside, the talk would go back and back to the great Irish heroes of Aintree, men and horses.

How the Beasleys won it three times in the 'eighties, and how Jack Gourlay steered Drogheda to victory through a blinding snowstorm in '91 (or was it '92?), with the horse's hooves stuffed full of butter to prevent the snow from packing in them during the race. How the immortal Manifesto, trained only a few miles away, won it for the second time in '99 with twelve-stone-seven on his back, bringing off a great betting coup for his owner and enriching every punter in the county.

And what about the mighty Troytown, who once made such a leap at Becher's Brook that he put four feet of daylight between himself and that formidable fence? There were other magic names as the years rolled on – Easter Hero and Golden Miller, Reynoldstown, Workman, Royal Danieli. Would we ever see their like again?

Those fireside talkers, like their equine heroes, are dead and gone now, but if they could return they would find other names to conjure with – Ballymoss, Cottage Rake, Hatton's Grace and the incomparable Arkle, the greatest 'chaser in the whole history of racing. They would marvel at a trainer like Vincent O'Brien who could win three Cheltenham Gold Cups, three Cheltenham Hurdles and three Grand Nationals in successive years – apart from winning the Epsom Derby with Larkspur and the St Leger with Ballymoss. They would revel in the feats of Paddy Prendergast, Tom Dreaper and Pat Taaffe, who have become legends in their own lifetimes.

For Irish-bred and Irish-trained horses have, during the past twenty-five years, made a tremendous impact on the international racing scene. Indeed, the Irish racing and breeding industry has never been in a more flourishing state, because of several favourable factors. The administration of the sport is highly efficient, and funds available from the tote are wisely used to improve amenities and increase the value of stakes. The leading trainers can rely on the support of wealthy patrons (many of them American) who can afford to buy the best breeding and wait for results. An important landmark was the inauguration in 1962 of the sponsored Irish Sweeps Derby (with total prize-money of approximately £70,000), which has already established itself as one of the great classic races of Europe. And finally, there has been the emergence, during the post-War period, of two Irish trainers unsurpassed in skill and virtuosity –Vincent O'Brien in County Tipperary and Paddy ('Darkie') Prendergast at the Curragh in County Kildare. It is an astonishing fact that these two trainers, based in Ireland, have topped the table of winning trainers in Britain for the past four years – Prendergast taking the laurels in three successive years, with O'Brien repeating the feat in 1966.

The figures alone tell an impressive story. During 1965 (later statistics are not available) Irish-bred horses, racing in seventeen countries, won stakes valued more than £2,000,000. In the same year Irish exports of bloodstock were worth £3,723,000. In 1966 Irish-bred horses won four of the five classic races run in Britain; the winner of the remaining classic (the Oaks) was bred in France but trained in Ireland.

The figures indicate what an important part the breeding and racing industry plays in the Irish economy, but statistics cannot reflect the perpetual drama, excitement and expertise which lies in the background. The late-night study of the form book and the pre-dawn gallops, as a trainer brings his horse to peak fitness for a big coup. The slow-talking, long-sighted countrymen, who can pick out the jockeys' colours a mile away and store in a computer-like memory every vital move in a race.

The racecourse is a microcosm of life, a focus for triumph and disaster, glory or defeat, a setting for the endless duel with fate or chance or destiny, call it what you will. As starting-time approaches, there are swift dramatic changes in the betting-market when the 'inspired' money moves in. There is that tense hush just before the start, and the rising fervour of the crowd as the horses rise together to the final fences or the two-year-olds – a wavering spectrum of colour – come thundering down the five-furlong stretch.

Away from the course, the same drama is being played out for another section of the racing community – the stay-at-home punters who frequent the offices of the turf accountants. These are the licensed betting offices, which cater for the off-the-course gambler.

Inside, the setting is invariably simple, indeed Spartan – a counter with a brass grille, a few bare cubicles, and a generous supply of paper slips. Along the walls are pinned some racing-pages torn from the daily papers and a set of programme-sheets with the names of the horses engaged at the day's meetings. On these sheets a runner or 'marker', retained by the proprietor, enters the starters for each race, the result and the starting-prices of the first three horses, as the details are received over the 'phone.

Much of the business is done on English racing, the customers being convinced that the Irish variety is conducted with a degree of finesse which calls for personal supervision on the spot.

The clientèle of every betting office falls into two categories – the 'casuals' who leave after placing their bets, and the 'residents' who remain on duty for the afternoon. These casual punters can afford to make their bets – often sizeable ones – and be done with it. Most of them belong to the white (or off-white) collar class – businessmen, office-workers, solicitors and the like. But sometimes an anonymous yokel wanders in, makes a childish scrawl and departs with a great wad of notes, never to be seen again.

The resident punter, with his scantier resources, is engaged in a much more elaborate enterprise. He must cast his bread upon the waters. He must make a little go a long (and very roundabout) way. He must set a sprat to catch a whole school of whales. Perturbed by this remote contingency, most starting-price bookmakers set limits to the odds payable against certain cumulative betting combinations. Others refuse to accept specified types of wager.

Such obstacles merely sharpen the ingenuity of the punter. Within this restricted sphere of action his staking methods take on a complexity never achieved in Tattersall's or the Victoria Club. Given a lucky start, he can watch his money playing leap-frog with itself for the next three hours.

But the price of a safe landfall is constant vigilance. The horizon must be scanned and regular soundings taken. The captain must never leave the bridge. Even a temporary absence may invite disaster. Even a minor hitch may bring the elaborate mechanism to a standstill.

Among these resident punters there is an impersonal fellowship, and the tribe includes few bums or touchers. Some are even persons of substance. There is the sallow-faced pensioner in the bowler hat who bivouacs under the warning notice: LOITERING ON THESE PREMISES IS STRICTLY FORBIDDEN. BY ORDER.

'I have the first two favourites, up and down,' he confides, 'going on to Grasshopper, each way at Kempton; any to come, all on Piggott's mount in the last race.' This belief in Piggott's ability to win the last race is widespread among office punters; they argue that the champion jockey – an exemplary family man – likes to get home early and wouldn't accept a mount in the final event unless it were a virtual certainty.

Then there is the excitable little Latvian who won over eight hundred pounds on a £1 five-horse accumulator in 1949 and is still trying to repeat the miracle. But, for him, Piggott is a jinx: 'If I back him to vin, he gets pipped; if I back something else, he vill beat it; if I back him each way, he vill be fourth.'

Every punter takes a spell at the sheets; a group is always to be seen, staring intently at the scrawls and figures made by the marker. Sometimes he is respectfully questioned about one of his entries, and, if in a kindly mood, he may shuffle over to discuss the matter. Though normally shabbier than most of the clients, his position gives him a certain cachet; he is held slightly in awe and is even permitted an occasional gruffness of manner. His journeys to and fro between the counter and the sheets are the highlights of the afternoon. He is, after all, a messenger of destiny, a herald of victories on far-off fields, a Pheidippides with fallen arches.

So the afternoon wears on, its recurrent crises announced by the cool, heartless contralto of the telephonist: 'They're off at Doncaster . . . Kempton result coming now.' Often the taut nerves of the punters are stretched still further by telephonic delays, an objection to the winner, or the intervention of the camera. 'Kempton, four o'clock. A photo-finish between Grasshopper and Big Two.' As the strain increases conversation lags. Only the little Latvian is voluble. His first three horses have won, and the money is piling up.

'Vot did I tell you?' he says tapping the sheets with his finger. 'Now I have twenty quid going on to this one in the four-thirty.'

'I hope it keeps fine for you,' the pensioner growls. But his grim mask relaxes when the telephonist speaks again. In the dark-room, three hundred miles away, Grasshopper has just won by a short head. Now for Piggott in the last.

Minute by minute the atmosphere grows tenser, and denser. The proprietor, worried by that thriving accumulator, emerges from the inner office and glares through the murk of tobacco smoke and CO_2. Caught by a sudden yawn, he bites off a chunk of the ozone and staggers back into his den. The time has come for a sop to the more fastidious clients.

At a shout from his employer the marker seizes a hand-sprayer and, firing just over the heads of the mob, fills the room with a nauseous mist of disinfectant. The punters are a jumble of pallid faces swimming in the fog under the greenish glare of the neon tubes.

'Doncaster result now.'

Clutching his scrap of paper, the marker fights his way across the room, the crowd swirling in behind him as he reaches the sheets. A few highly-strung customers, with too much at stake, may slip quietly outside during this ceremony and expose themselves briefly in the garish sunlight.

It's another good result for the Latvian. His fourth horse has come home at five-to-two against.

'Vot did I tell you?' he shouts, wriggling through the crowd. 'Seventy quid going on to the last race. I vill do it again like in 1949.' He retells the story and finds several listeners; the possibility of a big coup broods over the assembly. The news has spread, and newcomers crowd through the narrow doorway.

'What are you sweating on in the last one?' one of them asks the Latvian.

'Rainbow,' he answers. 'Seventy quid going on to Rainbow.' A new surge of the crowd forces him against the wall.

'But don't you know that's Piggott's mount?' somebody shouts.

'Sure. Sure. I know.' Pinned in his corner, he smiles like a child caught stealing the jam. 'But there you are, I could not leave him out.'

Five minutes past five. Silence falls over the crowd, jammed shoulder to shoulder, a tense, solid, waiting mass.

At last comes the callous contralto: 'Kempton result now.'

There is an interminable delay before the proprietor comes out and hands a piece of paper through the grille. The marker plunges into the crowd, jostling and squeezing his way towards the sheets. But this time he doesn't make it. Nature abhors a vacuum. The pressure in the centre is too great. Securely wedged, he stands with head lolling and arms crushed to his flanks.

Rushing from his den, the bookmaker roars: 'Stand back! Stand back and give him air!' Neither expedient being feasible, the limp body is passed over the heads of the punters towards the door. A tall, goitrous gentleman snatches a scrap of paper from the victim's fingers and reads the result in a booming voice: 'First, PRINCE CHARLIE; second, RAINBOW; third, HAPPY HARRY.'

The crowd empties itself into the street, but the little Latvian stands gazing at the sheets with a wistful smile. Taking a pencil from his waistcoat, he slowly marks up the placings he has just heard.

'Vot did I tell you,' he says. 'It is alvays Piggott alvays the bogey.'

The pensioner, stowing his racing literature carefully away, takes a quick glance at the sheets. 'Let me down for a bundle, too,' he grunts, starting for the door. He's had a hectic afternoon – net loss two shillings. But tomorrow is another day.

The visitor to Ireland who is interested in horse racing will find himself very well catered for. There is racing every Saturday throughout the year and there are also a large number of mid-week meetings.

Dublin has no less than three race courses (Phoenix Park, Leopardstown and Baldoyle) within thirty minutes from the city centre, while the Curragh (Co Kildare), Headquarters of the Irish Turf, is only thirty miles away.

In Ireland the Flat Racing season opens on St Patrick's Day (March 17) and runs to the middle of November. The National Hunt season (steeplechasing and hurdle racing) officially runs from October to May, but, in fact, mixed meetings – featuring flat races and steeplechases – are held right through the year.

The following are some meetings which should not be missed, for their social elegance, convivial atmosphere, or the quality of the sport on offer:

FAIRYHOUSE (Co Meath). The two-day meeting which begins on Easter Monday is one of the highlights of the steeplechasing season. The Irish Grand National on the first day usually attracts a very large crowd and the meeting features a number of other important races.

PUNCHESTOWN (Co Kildare). The great Irish tradition of steeplechasing is vividly expressed in the three-day meeting which is usually held towards the end of April. Some of the finest horses and riders compete over a testing course noted for its natural features, and many a Punchestown winner has gone on to triumph in the Aintree Grand National.

CURRAGH (Co Kildare). This splendid course is the venue for all the Irish classic races, the outstanding event being the Irish Sweeps Derby (late June or early July), with a total prize money of more than £73,000, which attracts the leading three-year-olds and is recognized as one of the outstanding races in the European calendar.

PHOENIX PARK. Situated on the edge of the city, the course is very convenient for visitors to Dublin, and offers a number of evening meetings during the summer months. There are two meetings here during the Dublin Horse Show (first week of August) which attract a fashionable attendance of local and foreign racegoers.

The Gastronomic Irishman

Monica Sheridan

In Ireland the first thing you think about when giving a dinner party (and you only do this when your back is to the wall) is where you will find amusing and congenial guests. The food itself is a secondary consideration. By and large the Irish, and particularly Irish*men,* are not great gourmets. They are far too interested in conversation to give their full attention to the food. The *bon mot* is more important than the *bonne bouche.*

In my younger days, when I was an enthusiastic and rather ostentatious cook, I remember spending a whole afternoon struggling with an elaborate pudding known as a croquembouche which I copied line by line from *Larousse Gastronomique.* When the time came to serve it, I proudly planted this complicated confection right in the middle of the dining-room table expecting it to call forth squeaks of admiration from the assembled guests. Nobody even noticed it except my husband, who glowered at me, obviously furious at the intrusion. He was momentarily distracted in the middle of a very funny story he was telling about Brendan Behan, stark naked, in some hospital in Dublin. I had heard the story maybe a dozen times before and felt that my own labours deserved more attention.

It was a salutary lesson to me. Ever since then I have been content to serve the simplest of food and learned to savour and enjoy the good company around me rather than give half my attention to a temperamental soufflé rising in the oven.

Some months ago I was at a dinner given by an English tycoon who has been living in Dublin for some years and is by now well tarred with the Irish brush. The dinner had, as guests of honour, Mr Stanley Marcus, scion of the famous Neiman-Marcus store in Dallas, and his wife. The wily host made sure to have *his* wits about him. He had assembled together some of the best talkers in Dublin – Micheál Mac-Liammóir, the wittiest conversationalist since Oscar Wilde; Freddie Boland, of UN fame; Patrick Scott, who rivals Patrick Campbell as a cliff-hanging stutterer with the same line in self-deprecation, and a scattering of earls and their lieges. Irish earls, unlike most of their English counterparts, can be very entertaining. Generally they have been reared on the smell of an oil rag but, unfortunately for their articulation, have all been sent to English public schools. They tend to talk without opening their teeth. A pity, because too often their punch lines, which have a nice throwaway quality, never quite make the outer air. It was a very successful evening, with plenty of scandal and highly salacious stories and nobody listening when he was interrupted. I am quite sure the dinner was well-chosen and cost a packet, but I would lay odds that nobody remembered a bite we ate. I can remember many of the stories, though, but it would never do to have a book on Ireland banned by the Irish censor.

By the way, before I move on to food (and I am coming to it all in good time), I feel I should give a word of advice to nervous hostesses about choosing suitable guests. Mature bachelors can always be relied upon to put in a good performance. Because of the shortage of person-able escorts for rich widows, clever career women and divorcees, they are in constant demand at all the best houses. By the time they reach their fifties they have acquired a smooth patina of verbal sophistication. And their humour has a waspish quality which has already been beaten out of most married men. Besides, they are unhampered by wives who have an awkward habit of interrupting their husbands' best stories by quibbling over unimportant details. ('No, Sean, it was *not* the year we went to Majorca. It was when we were doing Killarney in the rain.') I might add that husbands have been known to do the same sort of thing. The only trouble with bachelors is that they will never ask you back. They don't need to. The demand for their services (conversational, naturally) far outweighs the supply of odd-men-out. But no successful dinner is complete without at least one.

Having chosen your guests you must turn your mind to the food. In Ireland there is no tradition of elaborate cooking and there are at least two very good reasons for this. Firstly, Irishmen are notoriously conservative about *what* they eat. They have all been spoiled by their mothers (all good plain cooks) and will treat with the greatest suspicion any dish that is not instantly recognizable. A black sole grilled on the bone is acceptable but a *sole bonne femme* will cause grave doubts about whether you are trying to palm them off with whiting, or trying to poison them and get your hands on their life insurance. A duck is a duck and must come to the table with the two fat thighs sticking out of it. A *canard à la presse* is, to most Irishmen, a piece of newspaper speculation or possibly an instrument of torture invented by the Spanish Inquisition. My young sister, fresh from her honeymoon, made an omelette for her new husband. He looked at her coldly across the table, turning the omelette over with a searching fork. 'If I must have eggs I'd rather have them boiled,' he said with finality. That clipped *her* culinary wings.

Apart from our pernickety men, another reason why our cooking is simple is that the raw materials are of such excellent quality. There is

229

no reason in the world why we should sauce them up in order to disguise what is already quite perfect. Because of our rich pasturelands Ireland is famous for the high quality of her beef cattle. We export pedigree strains all over the world. Oddly enough there is no tradition of veal cooking in Ireland – and there is a simple explanation for this. Since we have such an abundance of lush grass there is no economic necessity to kill off the young calves, as they do in the continent of Europe. Here, even when they are slaughtered for the table they are often big enough for their minds to turn to thoughts of love. Nearly all Irishmen look upon veal as 'ladies' food' and would far prefer a sirloin steak. Me too.

Despite the dreams of our economists Ireland is basically an agri-cultural country. This gives us not alone excellent beef but the other by-products of our doe-eyed cows – a plentiful supply of milk and high grade butter. We have delicious young lambs reared on the salty grass of the western seaboard, and we have our pigs which produce the sweet Irish rashers, wonderful sausages and our celebrated hams.

In order to stem the flight from the land to the cities, our farmers are cossetted by government grants and subsidies. City dwellers, harrassed by income tax on unhideable salaries, have been heard to remark that every cow has a vote.

Then we have the sea around us with all the fish of the northern waters there for the taking. And the rivers and lakes abounding in brown and white trout.

Even though we are an island country the Irish have never taken to fish as a diet. It smacks of Lenten days and black fasts. The Catholic Church, by imposing the Friday abstinence, has ruined our palate for this most delicate of foods. Except among sophisticates and Protestants (they are not synonomous) fish is rarely eaten in Ireland, except as a penitential collation on days dictated by the Church calendar. The fish trade has suffered greatly because of this – and so has the quality of the fish. Fishmongers, anticipating the rush of shoppers on Friday morning, fillet the fish on Thursday evening and leave them on trays in the cold room overnight. This blunts the flavour and leaves the fillets both tired and flabby. Throughout the rest of the week very little fish is sold. This creates a situation where the fishmonger must make all his profit for the week on *one* day thus causing fish to be far more expensive than seems reasonable in a country that is surrounded by the sea. Even if the Friday abstinence were removed, I suspect that it would take a whole generation (and a great reduction in the price of fish) before it was enjoyed with the same zest as it is in, say, Spain.

But there is one fish that transcends the penitential prejudice and that is salmon, which is plentiful and cheap in high summer. Three summers ago there was so much of it around that it was served in the fish-and-chip shops at 2s 6d a portion and plenty of chips on the side. But that was a freak year and it is unlikely that we will enjoy that particular good fortune again. Nowadays, the larger salmon of twelve pounds and upwards rarely find their way into the shops. They are all bought up by the fishmongers and smoked. One of the great Irish delicacies is our smoked salmon. Madly expensive, of course, but very, very good. Every summer a friend of mine who is an enthusiastic fisherman, sends me a giant salmon, neatly imprisoned in green rushes. I send it in to the fishmonger to have it smoked. Every morning for maybe a fortnight afterwards I have slivers of smoked salmon on thin brown bread and butter for breakfast. I must admit it makes me feel like some gartered beauty out of the gay nineties – very wicked and self-indulgent.

I have a poor opinion of frozen fish and particularly of frozen salmon. No matter how carefully you cook it the flesh is dry and woolly. A very poor substitute for the succulent flakes of a fresh salmon. By the way, in case I forget to mention it later, the traditional way to cook salmon in Ireland is to poach it either in sea-water or, failing that, in water that is very heavily salted. If I am poaching a salmon of six or seven pounds I will add three or four fistfuls of salt to the boiling water before lowering the fish into the fish kettle. Strange to relate the flesh does not take up the salt taste, but it does remain moist and oily.

Up to about ten years ago lobsters were plentiful and comparatively cheap in Ireland. I can remember buying them for as little as five shillings each from the fishermen on the western seaboard. But times have changed. Nowadays the bulk of the lobster catch is flown to the great restaurants of Europe. More's the pity!

The best lobster is the one that comes straight from the lobster pot that the fisherman harvests in the morning or evening. The flesh is firm, but never tough, and the waistcoat is full of the most delicious mousse which is the choicest part of the lobster. Crayfish are also relatively plentiful but the Irish have never taken to them with the same enthusiasm as have the French.

I have a friend who is a lighthouse-keeper off the north-west coast of Ireland. In this isolated habitation he and his mates live in modest luxury. They have a little garden on the leeward side where they grow fresh vegetables. They keep a dozen hens, a milch goat and, sometimes, a few geese. Twice a week they put a batch of lobster pots among the rocks. They never catch less than a dozen.

'And there's nothing you get so sick of as lobster. It can get very monotonous,' said my friend. 'It's hard to beat a dinner of bacon and cabbage.'

I was reared on a farm in the country, and it seems to me when I look back on it now that we surely lived off the fat of the land. We had six milch cows standing in the byre smelling of hot cows' breath and milk. These supplied all the milk and cream and butter for the household.

231

Mother made the most beautiful country butter in a barrel churn. It was many years since I had tasted country butter until last month, when a farmer's wife sent me a pound of her own making. The moment I tasted it, thickly spread on a slice of brown bread, I was right back in the kitchen of my childhood with the red coals glowing through the bars of the friendly black range, the flitches of bacon hanging from the ceiling, and those wonderous smells of apple tarts and currant buns and soda bread cooling on the kitchen table. Talk about Proust and his madeleine. Which reminds me that my young nephew, who is a doctor and a James Joyce enthusiast, once said of Proust: 'I don't dig that fellow at all. He dunks a bun in a cup of tea and comes up with a total recall. It's a damned good thing he didn't have a go at LSD, or the book might have been twice as long.'

But, to come back to life on an Irish farm. In common with all her neighbours, mother baked all the bread for a household of sixteen. There was white soda bread, brown bread, Indian meal bread, treacle bread, spiced bread and porter cake. At Hallowe'en there was barmbrack, a yeast cake well fortified with butter, eggs and dried fruit. Barm Breach (the speckled barm) is the Gaelic name for this delectable native cake, which is always sliced and generously spread with butter before eating. When Lady Gregory made her frequent journeys from Gort to the Abbey Theatre she always carried a huge barmbrack in her holdall. It was her custom to preside over tea in the Green Room surrounded by the many writers and actors who went on to make international reputations. The barmbrack came to be affectionately known as the Gort Cake.

But barmbrack is not the only representative of our native cuisine that has a literary flavour. During all the years that James Joyce was living in Paris no compatriot would have thought of going to visit him without smuggling a couple of pounds of Irish sausages. Many years after he died, when Sylvia Beach (the publisher of *Ulysses*) came to Ireland the first thing she asked for was a plate of sausages.'We always had a party at the Joyces when the sausages arrived. And they were so delicious. Nobody can make sausages like the Irish.'

And what about Dean Swift, sitting up in the Deanery at Christ Church with his quill pen dipped in gall? What was his favourite nosh? Dublin Coddle, a savoury stew made from sausages, rashers and onions. Brendan Behan was another devotee and so was Sean O'Casey. It is a favourite dish with all true Dubliners, who have lived in the city for generations and look upon the place as their local village. It is eaten especially on Saturday night when the men come in from the pubs. I must admit I could live without Dublin Coddle, but if I thought it would make me write like Swift or Behan or O'Casey I would be quite prepared to lump it and like it. Outside of Dublin it is completely unknown and a stranger is unlikely to come across it.

What do the Irish drink? I mentioned earlier that they are conservative about what they eat; well, the same applies to their drinking. The two most popular tipples in the country are Irish whiskey and stout. Light beers have a modest vogue during the summer and gin is popular among women, who still look upon whiskey as the drink of whores and grandmothers. But stout, and particularly draught stout, is the gargle for the working man, the student and the intellectual. Whiskey is the drink for prosperous middle age when the bank manager is affable and it is no longer necessary to post-date cheques or charge up drinks on the publican's slate until the next month's pay arrives.

If I appear to give the impression that there are no gourmets (both of the eating and drinking variety) in Ireland, this would be quite wrong. Our better restaurants are crowded by bon vivants – mostly expense-account eaters – who are living it up on *homard thermidor* and the most expensive of French wines. But, alas, there is nothing duller, if you are looking for a stimulating evening, than the talk of selfconscious gourmets, out-boring each other, on the subtleties of a sauce or the bouquet of a wine. Unlike sharp wit, a little goes a long way. Perhaps the greatest offenders in this field are the wine snobs who have evolved a language of their own to extol the merits of their cult.

Some years ago a celebrated Irish cleric, a man of giant intellect, distinguished as a poet, a mathematician, and a linguist, was reluctantly brought along to a wine tasting in a famous Dublin cellar. His own favourite brew was a glass of Irish whiskey.

There were five or six wine experts at the tasting, all very knowledgeable men. Bottle after bottle was opened and ceremoniously poured into the appropriate glasses. The wine was swirled in the glasses, smelt for the bouquet, held to the light to examine the colour, sipped, rattled in the mouth, swallowed and the lips smacked before judgement was passed: 'What body!' 'What authority!' and so on and so on.

The cleric stood in a corner, bored stiff. 'What do you think of it, Canon?' asked the host. 'Does it meet with your approval?'

'It's lovely,' said the cleric, 'Truly lovely. It would remind you of an Archangel pissing on your tongue.'

Before I finish, let me remind you of the specialities to look out for.

If you are rich, or eating on an expense account, you cannot do better than Galway oysters, smoked salmon, trout, steaks, pheasant and grouse. Irish coffee is another thing you should not miss. Black velvet is good for a hangover. It is a mixture of stout and champagne. If you are poor you can still get by on Irish sausages, Irish stew, bacon and eggs, ham and cabbage, pork steak, chicken, fresh eggs, beautiful bread.

And don't neglect to visit an Irish pub. Here the life and vitality of the Irish are everywhere around you.

Deep Sea Fishing

Garry Culhane

Capricious is the word I would use if asked to sum up my impressions of Ireland in one word. The moments of incredible beauty, twilight in May, the scent of blackthorn on summer mornings, the golden blaze of gorse on a hillside in March, the throbbing call of the spring cuckoo, the raucous scratch of the corncrake on a June evening. Moments of magic, and overall the shifting play of light from a slanted sun. Moments as unforgettable as they are unpredictable.

Knowledgeable men have explained to me that these moments of poignant beauty are merely the whimsical playings of the ancient gods the Celts brought with them when they settled here in remote times. These ancient ones, I am told, rest here in lake and stream, sea and mountain, waiting the call to return to their primaeval haunts. Meanwhile they relieve their boredom by occasional exhibitions of their powers, to dazzle men and remind them of presences unseen but powerful.

However this may be I must admit that it goes a long way towards explaining the capers of the particular deity in charge of the seas. Long since I have come to know this fellow as a bum, first class, the most irresponsible of the lot. Let me put it to you.

My trouble is that I can never look on a body of water without feeling profoundly moved. The sight of it seems to arouse some sleeping atavist in me. The urge to get a craft out on that surface or more likely still, simply to count the ripples spreading over the placid depths from a bit of line to which I have attached hook and sinker, cannot be denied. I am a 'water queer', and my tale is addressed to all other 'water queers'.

Long ago I stopped wondering about this fascination with water which governs my life and the lives of many others. I have read carefully all the headshaking analyses advanced by the psychologists, and no doubt they are right, they say it's all sex, and wonder and mystery, and female symbols and suppressed urges, and aggression, and primitive instinctual drives and such like wonderful things. Well they're damn right too. I am guilty as hell on all counts. The rest of you can speak for yourselves.

So, I love the water and all it evokes in me. Particularly I love the sea and the challenge of its boundless mystery, its endless moods, its

234

colours and fragrances, its movement and symmetry, its terrifying power and the sheer abundance of its infinitely variable life forms. I love too the frontier ambience of the towns, villages and harbours to be found along any coast line. There is much of the sea's mystery ashore along this border where land and sea meet, eternally wedded, yielding, resisting, assaulting, quarrelling, penetrating, assuaging, and so often filling the horizon with promise of bliss.

Water lovers court the favours of their mistress in many different ways but I am concerned only with those who like myself search out the richness of the seas' bounty with rod and line. Is it really fish we are after? Or do we seek endlessly for the truly fabulous? I think the latter, and it is in this quality, the fabulous, that Irish fishing whether on lake, river or sea, abounds.

Ireland is a strange and ancient land. You are not long here without feeling stirrings in the depths of your being whether water-lover or not. But for us water-lovers Ireland is a real mother land. Here lake and river combine with mountain and plain and all roll sweepingly down to the sea. In the south west long fingers of land reach out to the edges of the Continental Shelf where the warm waters of the North Atlantic Drift flow southwards to a rendezvous in the Bay of Biscay. The secret of the abundant fish life in Irish seas lies in this combination of warm Gulf Stream waters and rocky serrated coast line and sea bottom. Conditions are ideal for the oceanic life cycle, fish spawn in these waters and grow to impressive sizes protected over large areas from the worst ravages of rampant trawlers by the rugged nature of the bottom.

Wherever you go in Ireland with your rod you will find kindred spirits who will put you on the track of the most memorable day's sport you have ever had. The Tourist Board is well informed and equipped to help you select a centre to your choice, and should it prove a dud you are never far from alternatives. You need never go away disappointed.

Let me get back to my story, let me tell you about the God of the Seas and his antic touch. Come with me now on a deep sea fishing trip, one of many I have enjoyed out of Kinsale, south west Cork.

Here on the estuary of the Bandon river is a magnificent combination of ideal conditions for the enjoyment of sea fishing. An excellent natural harbour, quick and easy access in all weathers and conditions of tide to deep sea marks, first class estuarial fishing for bass and sea trout, a headland that reaches out some eight miles to provide reasonable shelter in most winds over an incomparable sea bottom.

We board a fast diesel cruiser, specially designed and built for this job, she boasts a fighting chair and is equipped to handle the big sharks and monster rays which are plentiful in these waters. We are four anglers aboard, and we have each brought two rods, one light and one heavy. We have planned to get in some light fishing, in the shelter of the headland before going out some thirty miles or so to the true oceanic waters beyond the fifty fathom line.

'Jero' the skipper is a taciturn fellow, a traditional deep sea fisherman he 'knows his bottoms' as the language goes. At sea he is not very communicative but at night ashore in his favourite pub where he holds court he is a fund of sea lore, superstition, and mystery tales of huge congers, sharks too big to boat, and skate that 'med away wit t' hanchor n 'awser'. Kinsale was in its heyday an Elizabethan port of considerable importance and was a 'settlement town'. English sailors were settled here and the town walled up against the Irishry. Much of the old Elizabethan speech has survived in the town and it takes some getting used to. Jero and his neighbours who live at 'World's End' will speak of 'the holdes 'ouse in t'willage'.

But back aboard the *Rapparee* – a name which evokes a memory of the native Irishry who were dispossessed of their lands at the time of Elizabeth's conquest and who escaping the Queen's soldiers took to a Robin Hood-like existence harrying the Queen's Equerries from mountain fastnesses. The ancient town is full of reminders of those days and as we leave the harbour and put to sea we pass the huge fort built as a harbour defence against the Spaniards in 1640 where a garrison was maintained until 1922. Like many of man's military efforts this one too is a picturesque monument to futility. No shots were ever fired, no invader ever came, neither Spaniard nor Frenchman. For nearly three hundred years the fort guarded a harbour which had lost its military importance. There it stands sombre, Mediterranean, in appearance, behind it rises a peaceful pastoral scene of hill and farm, cottage and little Normanesque Church. Cattle graze, trees etch the sky, children swim off the beach below the fort, its empty embrasures looming impotently above them, staring vacantly out to sea watching for an enemy that never comes.

Aboard the *Rapparee* we speed out to sea. The roar of the diesel has imposed a silence on us all. Each man surveys the scene before him, locked in his own thoughts. It is a beautiful day, all is colour, vaulting blue, green-blue seas flecked with lacy white, blue-grey cliffs dip gracefully to the water's edge there to show a fringe of lacy-white petticoat. Behind us the rolling landscape shows greens and yellows and deep brown, marking man's efforts in crop and pasture. On the ridge of a hill, trees offer a blessing on land and sky.

We speed on, Jero's practised eyes scan the horizon for signs of sea birds. Suddenly one sees his back stiffen, the restless turnings of the head, the peerings, the twistings, have all stopped, he has fixed a point on the horizon and is steering steadily and tautly.

Soon we are there, come to share the spoils with myriads of sea birds. Here surely we have found at last that millennial frontier whose call has stirred us so deeply. Green and burgeoning seas thrust lavish breasts against a teeming sky. Gulls and gannets, shearwaters, kittywake and skua wheel and dive, and dive and wheel and dive again, down, down, into the fish laden depths, up, up, into the blue, screaming with lust, maddened by plenitude, a crazed scar upon the sky. A skua, great black winged pirate, hovers aloft choosing a gorged and sotted gull so freighted with spoil, as to be unable to leave the surface, down he swoops, the hapless victim, to escape must unload, the work of hours floats upon the sea, the disconsolate gull flies off filling the air with grievance and complaint, the skua takes his ease and his easy meal in comfort while all around life and death mingle and merge.

The tension and excitement of shoaling fish and gorging bird has now taken hold of the party on board the boat. Strings of feathered lures are tied to the lines, mackerel are all around us by the thousand. Down go the lines, we want a meal too and we want bait.

The rod tips bend before the furious onslaught of the attacking mackerel, up come the lines, in a few minutes the boxes are full. We have enough fish for tea and enough for bait.

Now the skilled amongst us are changing their gear. Various types of traces come to light. Most are individual inventions of the angler. Jero is shifting the boat, and we become aware of the silence we had enjoyed when the motors were shut off. We are going on now to a 'mark' famous for its yield of turbot and skate.

Jero has found his 'marks', he has lined up the headland to the north over the creek on the inland side. He has opened the lighthouse clear of the western headland, and now he has gone up tide to let down the hook. We drift back on the hawser waiting for the hook to take hold and then the thing is done. We will have only an hour's fishing here on the slack of the tide. Each man has baited up for turbot, surely the best able fish of the lot, we are in twelve fathoms of water and about five miles off shore. There is a bank here which consistently yields turbot of more than 20 lbs weight and frequently a monster skate. Jero has shut down the motors and the silence of the ocean closes in on us. Now we cannot stop talking, we are all suddenly small boys yielding to the excitement and the mystery of it all. We are full of wonder. The air is intoxicating, we tell one another about the extraordinary fishing we have just enjoyed amongst the mackerel, Frank announces that this is the last day of his holiday, that so far he has landed eighteen different species of fish during his stay and that today when he has landed his turbot he is going to get himself a skate. He is competent and confident. 'I feel lucky today' he says.

John doesn't give a damn, he is so happy to be out here 'away from it all' that he will settle for anything which will take his hook, or for nothing at all if that is to be his luck.

Arthur, a timid and sickly looking man of sixty or more years, confesses that this is the first time in his life he has ever fished. He is a

Londoner, never been out of London before he says. Usually took a bus tour for a holiday. Had a bad heart attack last year and the doctor had told him to take things easy.

We all exchange uneasy glances at this news. Deep sea fishing is not really the best way to take things easy after all.

However we are all so full of our own optimism that we give only a passing thought to Arthur. Even when we hear him instruct Jero to bait him up for skate. 'Never caught a fish before,' says Arthur, 'Matter of fact never did anything much in my life, don't expect I'll do much now, but if I'm going to fish I might as well fish for a big one.' I catch Jero's eye and see there a flicker of apprehension. I know what it means and yet I disregard it. Words have been spoken over the sea, has she heard? Has she heard?

We all exchange indulgent glances and yet from long experience of the caprices of the god of the seas we know that sure as hell if a fish is to be caught it is on Arthur's hook it will be found. Time passes, however, and not Arthur, but Frank, the most experienced man on board, has landed a smacking turbot of about 22 lbs. John has boated a cod of about 27 lbs and I have filled my box with whiting, codling and bream. I have changed my gear to fish the middle waters while the rest are fishing bottom. We have all forgotten Arthur until we hear his heavy sea reel begin to roar against the ratchet and then at once we all know that the god of the seas has been at it again. We know it unerringly, we look for the proofs we know will be there, the heavy rod is bending ferociously and without let up, the line is being taken off the reel at a steady and irresistible pace. The taut line knifes the water with an ominous hum, Arthur numb with terror and apprehension, all bent over like a dog screwing a football, flutters helpless hands at the reel while the rod pulls him down towards the gunn'l by reason of the strong shoulder harness which Jero has provided.

As I say we knew already in our heart of hearts what was to be expected. We had all of us met the god before and knew his ways. Now each man reacts according to his estimate of the situation. Arthur is whining in fright, 'I'm a sick man, some of you take the rod, it'll kill me.' Frank yells at Jero 'cut him loose', John goes towards Arthur and reaches for the rod. I look towards Jero and from the defensive glare in his eyes I know we are in the grip of the ancient deities. I should intervene but I know I won't. I am not surprised to see Jero strike down John's reaching hand, Jero stands at bay, the handle of a heavy gaff held strongly in his hands. I know he will knock down any man who interferes in the situation now.

For Jero is a seafaring man. He wrests his living from the seas as did his ancestors down through the centuries. His life, like theirs, is dominated by the terms of their bargain with the sea. Talking their living from her they are all her debtors, and when she sees fit 'to claim her own' no man may interfere, lest worse befall.

Jero puts it to us: 'Get the hell back ower dat. He come out 'ere to fish, said he wanted a big 'un didn' he. He's intill it now ha? Got t' land i' hisself. Ye dasn' cut him loose, 'twould come agin me.'

There it was. Words had been spoken. And the sea had heard, picked up man's wish and gave him what he asked, it was up to him now but the gift must not be spurned. Ominous forces were at work, nothing now could stop the chain of events – would the terrible mistress collect her debt?

Jero is bent over Arthur, for him it is deadly serious. Come what may the challenge must be taken up, No quarter may dare be asked and none must be given. 'Mister,' he says, 'you're into t' biggest fookin' fish ever I seen, let go dat ratchet, dere like dat. Put some drag on t' line, like dis see, turn dat wheel dere dats de drag, turn it de oder way to ease him off. You're gone a land dis fish yerself Mister, ye jist got t'.'

'Lend a hand 'ere all of ye,' he goes on. 'Get dis man intill de fightn' chair.' We all grab the limp heap which is Arthur and heave and shove him into position in the fighting chair. Jero straps him in and rams the rod into the gimbal rest. 'Sit up straight', he says. 'Let him fight t' rod and de drag. Let him take lots of line. Jist 'ole hon.'

Meanwhile the line keeps reeling off, we can all feel the inexorable power of a truly big fish. We scream advice to Arthur and he is too insensible to hear or heed. We scream at Jero: 'He's a dying man cut him loose.' 'Wanted a big one didn' he? Well what's he got? Biggest damn fish this season.'

Frank says (wistfully, I thought), 'If it was my fish, I'd stay with it too, I'd cut the throat of anyone who'd cut my line. We all have to go sometime, and that's as good a way as any. Poor old blighter he's got what he wanted and it will kill him for sure.'

Now the fish showed signs of tiring, the line had stopped paying out and was slanting slowly up through the water towards the surface; excitement gathered as the end drew near, nobody could think of Arthur, all thoughts centred on the fish.

'Watch it now, he's going to break water and then sound for the bottom.' 'Keep your rod up man, keep it up for God's sake.' 'Wind up that slack.' 'Jesus man get that slack in.' 'Jesus Christ there he is,' 'My God, what a brute!' 'Pump that rod, man, pump it.' 'Pump it, don't let him sound.' Our straining knew no bounds, we fought the air, we screamed and yelled, only the catch mattered. Jero was huddled down over Arthur, directing, coaxing, demanding, showing him how. The monster fish churned the waters to froth with its massive wings, the line strained and hummed, we feared it would snap. Tension mounted, and then the creature was alongside.

We heard Jero scream, 'Yerra man don' die on me now, I'm going for me gaff.' The urgency galvanized us all, we rushed for gaffs, we

239

grabbed the wire trace, we flailed away and pulled and hauled and finally dragged the skate aboard. Two men on the gaffs, two more on the trace, and with a heave the thing was done and the fish lay there filling the whole space of the well-deck.

Seven feet of wing spread we reckoned and over six feet long from snout to tail tip, about 200 lbs we said and mopped our brows and smiled and laughed. And then we thought of Arthur, we turned to look at him. 'What way is he at all?' said Jero. 'Is it dead or alive he is?' Indeed we couldn't tell at first, limp and blue-pallid, he slumped in the fighting chair, he gazed through glazed eyes at the monster in the bottom of the boat, through cracked lips he croaked, 'Is that my fish? Did I land that?' He was no more incredulous than we. 'You sure did'; we tell him and we ask how he feels now, after such an incredible feat. We pat him on the shoulder and try to conceal the envy as we congratulate him. He just sits there staring, fighting for comprehension, lost in his own complex thoughts.

We all return now to our own rods. There is an unabashed haste as we change to heavy bottom gear and wire traces fit for skate; we have seen what's to be found in the area. Arthur is forgotten once again, as each of us weighs his own chance of getting such a prize.

Frank, says ruefully, 'It's my last day.' I know what he means. The sea has given all its going to give and we all know it. Jero stands by his wheel, he is looking only at the sea, I catch his eye and I see that the apprehension is gone, the game has been played according to the rules and the sea is reckoned content.

I turn to look at Arthur. He has straightened up and is fingering his wire trace. Jero has freed it out from the jaws of the skate. Suddenly Arthur makes up his mind. 'Skipper,' he says quietly holding out the trace, 'bait up my hook and let's do some fishing.'

'Greedy little bastard,' says Frank.